BEST
FOOD
WRITING
2007

Also edited by Holly Hughes

Best Food Writing 2006
Best Food Writing 2005
Best Food Writing 2004
Best Food Writing 2003
Best Food Writing 2002
Best Food Writing 2001
Best Food Writing 2000

Also by Holly Hughes

Frommer's New York City with Kids
Frommer's 500 Places to Take the Kids Before They Grow Up

BEST
FOOD
WRITING
2007

Edited by
HOLLY HUGHES

Marlowe & Company
New York

Best Food Writing 2007

Published by
Marlowe & Company
An Imprint of Avalon Publishing Group, Incorporated
11 Cambridge Center
Cambridge, MA 02142

AVALON
publishing group incorporated

Library of Congress Cataloging-in-Publication Data is available.

ISBN-10: 1-60094-039-0
ISBN-13: 978-1-60094-039-2

9 8 7 6 5 4 3 2 1

Designed by Michael Walters and Susan Canavan
Printed in the United States of America

Personal Tastes

Why I Cook

Introduction

by Holly Hughes

It was the roast chicken that did it.

Throughout this past year, choosing what to cook for dinner every night had gotten to be Just No Fun Anymore. I was overloaded with weight-watching and nutrition-monitoring and balancing my three kids' colliding preferences (my daughter has now declared herself a "flexitarian," which apparently means a vegetarian who still eats chicken—and ONLY chicken). I saw myself in a war against junk food, and I wasn't winning. Pressed for time, exhausted by work, I resorted to takeout more and more often . . . and my husband showed no resistance, either, a sure sign that my cooking had gone downhill. And then a friend of ours suffered an unexpected stroke. Helpless to do more, we offered to bring over a meal or two for his family. Determined to produce the utmost in comfort food, I decided on roast chicken—even though I'd never roasted a chicken before. (I grew up in Indiana, where chicken generally comes country fried; I'd served my family roast chicken many times, but only the ones in the grocery rotisserie case.) But I'd offered to *cook* this meal for our friends; buying a rotisserie chicken would be . . . well, cheating. Besides, how hard could it be?

Ha.

Leafing through my cookbooks, I found an astounding number of competing theories on chicken roasting—brining, trussing, stuffing, etc. Flummoxed, I resorted to the simplest recipe I could find, in Nigel Slater's *Appetite*. It's dead easy: rub the skin with butter, salt, and pepper and stick the bird in a 425-degree oven for twenty minutes per pound. I nervously slid a roasting pan into the oven with two chickens side-by-side (might as well feed my family at the same time). To my astonishment, they came out moist and tender, their skins a lovely shiny amber . . . like *magic*. I bundled one up in tinfoil and rushed it across town. My car smelled so good on that crosstown jaunt that I couldn't wait to get back to the sister chicken waiting for me at home.

Cooking this meal took very little time, no exotic ingredients, and no culinary techniques I hadn't learned in eighth grade home ec. Yet what came out was so delicious that my family actually raved. (And you know how hard it is to get teenagers to rave about anything.) It's entirely possible that the chicken tasted better because I cooked it for a noble purpose—but all I know is that, for the first time in months, I enjoyed cooking again.

It's so easy these days to let the essentials slip through our fingers. Things in the food world have become incredibly complicated, as Michael Pollan laid out in a long journalistic investigation in the *New York Times Magazine* this year. The diet directive in his lead paragraph sounds almost shocking: "Eat food. Not too much. Mostly plants." (He adds, in explanation, "Once, food was all you could eat, but today there are lots of other edible foodlike substances in the supermarket"—and proceeds to go on for pages to explain how those non-food foods got there in the first place.)

It isn't only in the supermarket. Go to an upscale restaurant and you'll feel the repercussions of another sort of food war. Ever since Spain's Ferran Adrià won worldwide acclaim for his high-tech innovations (Francis Lam in his article on page 39 dubs it "molecular gastronomy," but most folks just call it "foam"), his American disciples like Wylie Dufresne and Grant Achatz have been alternately praised and mocked by the foodie establishment. In my reading this year I ran across a surprising number of pieces blasting away at highly-composed (and high-priced) cuisine in general—

just check out Frank Bruni's "You May Kiss the Chef's Napkin Ring," p. 33, and Violaine Charest-Sigouin's "French Revolution," p. 26. The divide between high and low cuisine just keeps growing wider; even the travel pieces in this year's collection (see the section "The World's Kitchen") seem hyperconscious of it. Maybe it's just a coincidence, but I can't tell you how many pieces I read this year about that most basic ethnic food, tacos—I've included just three, by the estimable Jonathan Gold (p. 191), Robb Walsh (p. 193), and Bill Addison (p. 182), but believe me there were plenty more. The reaction has set in.

Perhaps the ongoing discussion in my own household makes me more conscious of it, but the battle lines between carnivores and vegetarians seem more sharply drawn than ever, too. The meat defenses that came across my desk were so numerous, I had to give them their own section this year (see "The Meat of the Matter"). I read more than a couple articles about buying an entire side of beef—hard to believe that that's a coincidence, either.

I was also surprised by the number of pieces I read that questioned the orthodoxies of the organic/Slow Food movement. (Check out Sara Deseran's "Feast of Burden," p. 43, Michael A. Stusser's "Organicize Me," p. 50, and Barry Estabrook's "Local Heroes," p. 10.) True, now that big agribusiness is muscling into the arena, the word "organic" on a label is no longer the imprimatur it once was, but there are many other related issues that are still important—buying meat and poultry that was humanely raised, favoring local produce over shipped-in out-of-season produce, supporting the small independent farmer. We can't throw the baby out with the bathwater. I suspect it isn't so much the basic goals of the movement that are being questioned, but the zealotries it has spawned in certain holier-than-thou circles. Amid the clash of ideologies, no wonder we question everything we put in our mouths these days.

When I began this annual anthology back in 2000, magazines, newspapers, and books were all I had to cover—that and a few foodie newsletters. That was before both TV food shows and internet foodsites went into exponential-growth mode. This year, no fewer than four of our selections were published on the internet (see David Leite, p. 64, Steven Shaw, p. 304, James Sturz, p. 254, and

Ivy Knight, p. 152). I could easily get addicted to the many blogs and discussion boards out on the web. And when it comes to recipe-hunting, I read recently that more people get their recipes from the internet these days than from either cookbooks or magazines. Just Google macaroni-and-cheese and see what turns up.

Food TV? I must admit I'm baffled by it. Does America really think that Rachel Ray is a legitimate cooking authority, or that every restaurant kitchen is run by a foul-mouthed tyrant like Gordon Ramsay? It's just ENTERTAINMENT, folks. The only "cooking show" I've found even marginally credible is Bravo's *Top Chef.*

We live in confusing times, that's for sure—why should the food world be exempt from it? The gap between haves and have-nots, the dumbing-down of our culture, the increasingly partisan behavior of even well-intentioned people, all have their corollaries in the culinary universe. So it's no surprise that I lost my bearings for a while this year—I'm just glad the roast chicken came along to set me straight again.

Food Fights

Waiting for Asparagus

by Barbara Kingsolver

from *Animal, Vegetable, Miracle*

Anyone who's read Barbara Kingsolver's novels *(The Bean Trees, The Poisonwood Bible)* won't be surprised at the luminous quality of this nonfiction chronicle of her family's year of getting back to the land on their new Virginia homestead.

On a Sunday in early April we sat at the kitchen table putting together our grocery list for the coming week. The mood was uncharacteristically grave. Normally we all just penciled our necessities onto a notepad stuck onto the fridge. Before shopping, we'd consolidate our foraging plan. The problem now was that we wanted to be a different kind of animal—one that doesn't jump the fence for every little thing. We kept postponing our start date until the garden looked more hospitable, but if we meant to do this for a whole year, we would have to eat in April sooner or later. We had harvested and eaten asparagus now, twice. That was our starting gun: ready, set . . . ready?

Like so many big ideas, this one was easier to present to the board of directors than the stockholders. Our family now convened around the oak table in our kitchen; the milk-glass farmhouse light above us cast a dramatic glow. The grandfather clock ticked audibly in the next room. We'd fixed up our old house in the architectural style known as recycling: we'd gleaned old light fixtures, hardware, even sinks and a bathtub from torn-down buildings; our refrigerator is a spruced-up little 1932 Kelvinator. It all gives our kitchen a comfortable lived-in charm, but at the moment it felt to me like a set where I was auditioning for a part in either *Little House on the Prairie* or *Mommie Dearest*.

They all sat facing me. Steven: my faithful helpmeet, now quite happy to let me play the heavy. And whose idea this whole thing was in the first place, I'm pretty sure. Camille: our redheaded teenager, who in defiance of all stereotypes has the most even temperament in our family. From birth, this child has calmly studied and solved every problem in her path, never asking for special help from the Universe or her parents. At eighteen she now functioned in our household as a full adult, cooking and planning meals often, and was also a dancer who fueled her calorie-intensive passions with devotedly healthy rations. If this project was going to impose a burden, she would feel it. And finally, Lily: earnest, dark-pigtailed persuader and politician of our family who could, as my grandfather would say, charm the socks off a snake. I had a hunch she didn't really know what was coming. Otherwise she'd already be lobbying the loopholes.

Six eyes, all beloved to me, stared unblinking as I crossed the exotics off our shopping list, one by one. All other pastures suddenly looked a whole lot greener than ours. All snack foods come from the land of Oz, it seems, even the healthy ones. Cucumbers, in April? Nope. Those would need passports to reach us right now, or at least a California license. Ditto for those make-believe baby carrots that are actually adult carrots whittled down with a lathe. And all prewashed salad greens emanate from California. Even salad dressing was problematic because of all the ingredients—over a dozen different foods logging their own mileage to get to a salad dressing factory, and then to us. As fuel economy goes, I suppose the refrigerated tropicals like bananas and pineapples are the Humvees of the food world, but multi-ingredient concoctions are sneaky sports cars. I drew a pencil line through one item after another. "Salad dressing is easy to make," I said. The vinegar and oil in our pantry were not local, of course, but with a small effort, thirty seconds spent shaking things together in a jar, we could improve the gas mileage of our vinaigrette. In the herb garden we already had garlic chives and oregano, the hardiest of the spicy Mediterranean perennials, braving the frosts of late winter.

We were getting plenty of local eggs too, so in a reckless burst of confidence I promised to make mayonnaise. It's supposed to be pretty easy. I had a recipe I'd been saving since my high school French class, waiting for the right time to try it, because of one irresistible step that translates as follows: "Whip heartily for two minutes while holding only pleasant thoughts in mind."

Back to the grocery list, trying for that positive mindset: a few more items fell without significant protest. Then I came to block letters in Camille's hand, underlined: FRESH FRUIT, PLEASE???

We were about to cross the Rubicon.

I shifted tactics. Instead of listing what we can't have, I said, we should outline what we knew we *could* get locally. Vegetables and meat—which constitute the bulk of our family's diet—would be available in some form throughout the coming year. We had met or knew of farmers in our county who sold pasture-fed chickens, turkeys, beef, lamb, and pork. Many more were producing vegetables. Like so many other towns, large and small, ours holds a farmers' market where local growers set up booths twice a week from mid-April to October. Soon our garden would also be feeding us. Our starting point would be this: we would take a loyalty oath to our own county's meat and produce, forsaking all others, however sexy the veggies and flesh of California might be.

What else does a family need? Honey would do instead of sugar, in a county where beekeepers are as thick as thieves. Eggs, too, were an easy local catch. Highly processed convenience foods we try to avoid, so those would not be a problem categorically. The other food groups we use in quantity are grains, dairy, and olive oil. We knew of some good dairies in our state, but olives don't grow in this climate. No reasonable substitute exists, and no other oil is produced here. Likewise, we knew of a local mill that ground corn, wheat, and other flours, but its wheat was outsourced from other states. If we purchased only these two foods from partly or wholly nonlocal sources—grains and olive oil—we would be making a sea change in our household economy, keeping an overwhelming majority of our food transactions local. We would try to buy our grains in the least processed, easiest-to-transport form available (bulk flour and some North American rice) so those food dollars would go mostly to farmers.

I put down the list, tried not to chew my pencil, and consciously shut out the image of my children going hungry . . . Lily begging leftovers from somebody's lunchbox at school.

Let me be clear about one thing: I have no interest in playing poor. I've logged some years in frugal material circumstances, first because I was born into a fairly modest rural social order, and later due to years of lousy paychecks. I understand Spam as a reasonable protein source. Both Steven and I have done our time on student stipends, government cheese, and the young-professional years of beans and rice. A huge turning point for me was a day in my mid-thirties when I walked into the supermarket and realized I could buy any ten things there I wanted. Not the lobsters in the aquarium, okay, but not just dented cans in the bargain bin, either. I appreciate the privilege of food choices.

So why give them back voluntarily? It is both extraordinary and unsympathetic in our culture to refrain from having everything one can afford. Yet people do, mostly because they are allergic, or religious. We looked around the table at one another, knowing we had our reasons too. Strange, though, how much it felt like stepping into a spaceship and slamming shut the hatch.

"It won't be that bad," I said. "We're coming into spring."

It wasn't spring yet, however. We were in for some lean months before the midsummer bounty started flooding us with the real rewards of local flavor and color. But April is a forward-looking time on the farm, full of work and promise. It seemed best to jump in now. Sink or swim.

Hedging, we decided to allow ourselves one luxury item each in limited quantities, on the condition we'd learn how to purchase it through a channel most beneficial to the grower and the land where it grows. Steven's choice was a no-brainer: coffee. If he had to choose between coffee and our family, it might be a tough call. Camille's indulgence of choice was dried fruit; Lily's was hot chocolate. We could get all those from fair trade organizations that work with growers in Africa, Asia, and South America. I would rely on the same sources for spices that don't grow locally; a person can live without turmeric, cinnamon, and cloves, I've heard, but I am not convinced. Furthermore, dry goods like these, used by most households in relatively tiny quantities, don't register for much on the world's gas-guzzling meter.

With that, our hopeful agreement in place with its bylaws and backstops, we went back one last time to our grocery list. Almost everything left fell into the grains category: bread flour and rolled oats are big-ticket items, since Steven makes most of our bread, and oatmeal is our cool-weather breakfast of choice. We usually buy almonds and raisins to put in our oatmeal, but I crossed those off, hoping to find local substitutes. Then we came back around to the sticky one. FRESH FRUIT, PLEASE???

At the moment, fruits were only getting ripe in places where people were wearing bikinis. Correlation does not imply causation: putting on our swimsuits would not make it happen here. "Strawberries will be coming in soon," I said, recognizing this as possibly the first in a long line of pep talks to come.

The question remained, What about now?

"Look," I said, "the farmers' market opens this Saturday. We'll go see what's there." Around the table went the *Oh sure, Mom* face that mothers everywhere know and do not love.

Saturday dawned dark, windy, and fiercely cold. The day's forecast was for *snow.* Spring had been slapped down by what they call around here "dogwood winter," a hard freeze that catches the dogwoods in bloom—and *you* thinking you were about to throw your sweaters into the cedar chest. April fool.

The cold snap was worrisome for our local orchards, since apple and peach trees had broken dormancy and blossomed out during the last two sunny weeks. They could lose the year's productivity to this one cold spell. If anybody was going to be selling fruit down at the farmers' market today, in the middle of blasted dogwood winter, I'd be a monkey's uncle. Nevertheless, we bundled up and headed on down. We have friends who sell at the market, some of whom we hadn't seen in a while. On a day like this they'd need our moral support.

It was a grim sight that met us in the parking lot. Some of the vendors huddled under awnings that snapped and flapped like the sails of sinking ships in a storm. Others had folded up their tents and stood over their boxes with arms crossed and their backs to the mean wind. Only eight vendors had turned out today, surely the bravest agricultural souls in the county, and not another customer in sight. What would they have this early, anyway—the last of last year's shriveled potatoes?

Hounded by the dogs of *Oh sure, Mom,* I made up my mind to buy something from everyone here, just to encourage them to come back next week. My farm advocacy work for the day.

We got out of the car, pulled our hoods over our ears, and started our tour of duty. Every vendor had something better than shriveled potatoes. Charlie, a wiry old man who is the self-appointed comedian of our market, was short on cheer under the circumstances but did have green onions. We'd run out of our storage onions from last year's garden, and missed them. At least half our family's favorite dishes begin with a drizzle of oil in the skillet, a handful of chopped onions and garlic tossed in. We bought six fat bundles of Charlie's onions. This early in the season their white bulbs were only the size of my thumb, but when chopped with their green tops they would make spicy soups and salads.

From Mike and Paul, at the next two booths, we bought turkey sausage and lamb. At the next, the piles of baby lettuce looked to me like money in the bank, and I bagged them. Fruitless though our lives might be, we would have great salads this week, with chunks of sausage, hard-boiled eggs, and experimental vinaigrettes. Next down the line we found black walnuts, painstakingly shelled out by hand. Walnut is a common wild tree here, but almost nobody goes to the trouble to shell them—nowhere but at the farmers' market would you find local nuts like these. The vendor offered us a sample, and we were surprised by the resinous sweetness. They would be good in our oatmeal and a spectacular addition to Steven's whole-grain bread.

Each of our purchases so far was in the one- to three-dollar range except the nuts, which were seven a pound—but a pound goes a long way. I frankly felt guilty getting so much good fresh stuff for so little money, from people who obviously took pains to bring it here. I pushed on to the end, where Lula sold assorted jams and honey. We were well fixed for these already, given to us by friends or made ourselves last fall. Lula's three children shivered on the ground, bundled in blankets. I scanned the table harder, unwilling to walk away from those kids without plunking down some bucks.

That's where I spotted the rhubarb. Big crimson bundles of it, all full of itself there on the table, loaded with vitamin C and tarty sweetness and just about screaming, "Hey, look at me, I'm fruit!" I bought all she had, three bundles at three dollars apiece: my splurge of the day.

Rhubarb isn't technically fruit, it's an overgrown leaf petiole, but it's a fine April stand-in. Later at home when we looked in Alice Waters's *Chez Panisse Fruit* for some good recipes, we found Alice agreed with us on this point. "Rhubarb," she writes, "is the vegetable bridge between the tree fruits of winter and summer." That poetic injunction sent us diving into the chest freezer, retrieving the last package of our frozen Yellow Transparent apple slices from last summer. For dinner guests we threw together an apple-rhubarb cobbler to ring out the old year and ring in the new. Rhubarb, the April fruit. I'm a monkey's uncle.

If not for our family's local-food pledge to roust us out of our routine, I'm sure we would not have bothered going down to the market on that miserable morning. Most of us are creatures so comforted by habit, it can take something on the order of religion to invoke new, more conscious behaviors—however glad we may be afterward that we went to the trouble. Tradition, vows, something *like* religion was working for us now, in our search for a new way to eat. It had felt arbitrary when we sat around the table with our shopping list, making our rules. It felt almost silly to us, in fact, as it may now seem to you. Why impose restrictions on ourselves? Who cares?

The fact is, though, millions of families have food pledges hanging over their kitchens—subtle rules about going to extra trouble, cutting the pasta by hand, rolling the sushi, making with care instead of buying on the cheap. Though they also may be busy with jobs and modern life, people the world over still take time to follow foodways that bring their families happiness and health. My family happens to live in a country where the main foodway has a yellow line painted down the middle. If we needed rules we'd have to make our own, going on faith that it might bring us something worthwhile.

On Saturday morning at the market as we ducked into the wind and started back toward our car, I clutched my bags with a heady sense of accomplishment. We'd found a lot more than we'd hoped for. We chatted a little more with our farmer friends who were closing up shop behind us, ready to head home too. Back to warm kitchens, keeping our fingers crossed in dogwood winter for the fruits of the coming year.

Local Heroes?

by Barry Estabrook

from *Gourmet*

As a contributing editor to *Gourmet*, Estabrook often plays devil's advocate, focusing on the food world's hot-button issues in his regular feature Politics of the Plate. His healthy skepticism about buzzwords and bandwagons helps to put trends into context.

I'm beginning to get grumpy. The problem dates back to a slice of Australian grass-fed beef I was served recently at a restaurant in my home state of Vermont. Before allowing us to order, our waiter launched into an impassioned sermon praising "Chef's" abiding respect for local, seasonal ingredients. He made this assertion without a trace of irony, even though one of the four entrées on the menu we were perusing once grazed in another hemisphere—this in a state where, until recently, folk wisdom maintained that there were more cows than people. Indeed, driving along the rural road leading to that restaurant, I had spotted several plump, perfectly yummy-looking steers.

Air-freighted tenderloin was just the first of several insults to local sensibilities. The chef's bread had been shipped in frozen from the La Brea Bakery in Southern California. The cheese selection was heavily French, as if our state were not itself the home of dozens of top-notch artisanal cheesemakers. All of which would have been fine with me (even though the beef did taste like stale, freezer-burned hamburger meat) had the guy not been cashing in so blatantly on the local-and-seasonal platitude. Even more frustrating, it seemed like no one was calling his bluff. On the contrary, *The Boston Globe* had run a glowing review of the restaurant, praising the chef for using "meat from local animals." A nationally renowned food commentator had written about the chef's ability to keep any flavors from detracting from "beautiful local ingredients he procures from surrounding farms."

"Chef" is far from alone. The same hypocrisy seems to pop up every time I sit down in a restaurant or deal with a produce vendor. Vacationing in southern Massachusetts, a hotbed of all things local and seasonal, I stopped at a farm stand. "Native Fruits and Vegetables" proclaimed the roadside sign. Yet the neatly displayed tomatoes bore stickers declaring that their country of origin was Canada. I'm not sure what astonished me more: that the native tomatoes came from Canada, or that the stand's owner managed to attract any customers at all, given that every patio pot, garden, and vegetable patch within 100 miles was awash with bright red orbs.

A restaurateur in Manhattan who sits on the board of the Chefs Collaborative, a national group that advocates local sourcing, recently listed dessert selections that included kumquat, coconut, blood orange, and Meyer lemon. Nor is the problem limited to the winter-bound north. One legendary restaurant in the San Francisco Bay area—known internationally for pioneering the cult of fresh and local in America—boasts on its website of dealing with "nearby" producers. But a single day's menu offers lobster from Maine and shrimp from North Carolina. Surely you don't have to go that far from the Golden Gate to procure good seafood.

To get a sense of the definition of "local" in the restaurant trade, I turned to Jennifer M. Hall, executive director of the 1,200-member Chefs Collaborative. I had always assumed that any business that belonged to the organization was required to meet certain minimum standards. But here, too, it seems that cooks and purveyors may be preying on consumers' feel-good emotions. According to Hall, any restaurant or vendor that pays the $250 annual dues can join, no questions asked. "Our real purpose is to educate chefs and people in the food system," she said. "I want to celebrate any and every step people can take, and if right now that means they can only source local greens, that's great, because that's so much better than nothing."

But not a lot of help for the consumer wanting assurances that local actually means local.

Maybe what's needed is a food cop. One late afternoon last March, I wandered into New York's Union Square Greenmarket. The pickings were reassuringly slim: apples, onions, potatoes and other produce that keeps; hothouse greens and tomatoes; cheeses; milk; meat products; cider; preserves; eggs; fresh fish; baked goods. Except for some of the ingredients in the pies and muffins, every-thing did seem to be from the area.

This is no accident. Greenmarket, which operates in 40 loca-tions throughout the five New York boroughs, has strict standards concerning who is allowed to sell there. Vendors must make, catch, raise, or grow everything they sell. Cheaters can be kicked out. The operation is policed by Rachel Faber Machacha, Greenmarket's farm inspection coordinator. The first time I tried to call her, the produce detective was unavailable because she was visiting a farm halfway out on Long Island. I took this as a hopeful sign. Machacha, who trained in Iowa as a soil scientist ("I'm into dirt," she said) and somewhere along the line picked up a wry wit and a stand-up comic's delivery, conducts regular inspections of the 172 producers who attend Greenmarket. "Local, seasonal, fresh . . . you hear those words so often they've almost become a mantra," she said. "You feel like you should chant them." Machacha makes sure vendors are paying more than lip service to that credo. "If a pineapple showed up in a farmers' market, I would go out and say, 'Goodness, you don't have a pineapple field.' " Greenmarket also clearly delineates the geographic boundary within which foods must be grown: a slightly off-center circle radiating outward from New York City for about 200 miles.

In the absence of an organization like Greenmarket, local is pretty much in the eye of the beholder. Unlike *organic, local* has no legal definition attached to it. And there is a considerable disconnect between what consumers and food purveyors consider local. I don't expect most sellers to be as strict as the guy who runs the stand up the road from my house. When I asked if some early sweet corn was local, he glanced nervously at his work boots and confessed, "Nope. My cousin grew it over in Monkton." That's a village that borders ours. According to a survey conducted by Richard Pirog of The Leopold Center for Sustainable Agriculture, in Ames, Iowa, the greatest number of consumers set the limit at 25 miles. Most of those who stood to make a buck from it, on the other hand, said that anything from within the state counted. Pirog agrees that the term *local* is being widely abused. "There is confusion," he said. "And we are at an important point, where large food companies are beginning to see the power that local has in the marketplace. I worry that we've moved so far away from the farm in our culture, we might not know the difference between what is truly local and what is not."

Until we can agree on formal standards, I have a warning for the next Vermont waiter who tries to serve me a Maine crab cake topped with Key lime coconut sauce. I'm willing to give you some leeway. "Chef" need not limit himself to root-cellar potatoes and mushy turnips in the winter, and I understand perfectly that there may not be a swaying coconut palm behind your restaurant. Just do me a favor: Hold the heaping side order of pontification.

Rare Tuna

by Todd Kliman

from *The Washingtonian*

When Todd Kliman reviews a restaurant for *The Washingtonian* he goes beyond mere what-I-ate narrative to meditate on the soul of the place. Sometimes as in this investigative piece, his curiosity takes him even farther afield.

I remember the moment it began, the night that launched me on a yearlong quest to solve the mystery of what happened to tuna.

Two slabs of tuna sat on the plate, ruby red and shining with moisture. I was sitting with my wife at the bar in one of the city's best sushi restaurants, and my mouth began watering in memory of what so many previous meals had told me was coming. The next bite would bring the sweet, saltwatery succulence I'd waited an entire meal for. We dug in with our chopsticks.

My wife would often close her eyes when eating tuna, the better to savor it. But now she turned to me in astonishment. This fish was an impostor. It looked the part, but it was mealy, soft, flavorless.

Maybe, I said to my wife, it was a bad piece of fish. I brought up this possibility with the chef, who gladly sliced us off a couple more pieces from a ruby-red loin. But these were no better.

We chalked it up to a bad night, although it was a little hard to accept that line of reasoning, since every other piece of fish we ate that night—yellowtail, mackerel, salmon—had been as wonderful as before.

A month later we returned. We ordered the same meal as before and got the same results. The usual sushi chef was not there, so I asked his assistant about the tuna. Were they going somewhere else for their fish? A different supplier, a different variety? "Nope," he told me. "Same tuna we always get." He seemed more perplexed than I did.

Was it possible they were doing something different in the kitchen? "We do," he said, "what we always do."

As I made my rounds about town as a restaurant critic and traveled to other cities to keep abreast of trends, I decided to see whether I'd had a bad run of tuna or whether tuna itself was having a bad run. I ordered tuna everywhere I saw it. In all, I consumed some seven dozen different preparations. I was struck, first of all, by the consistency of what I ate. It did not matter whether I was in Northern Virginia, Maryland, or DC—or in New York, Philadelphia, or Charleston. It did not matter whether it was served raw—in any number of iterations of sushi or sashimi or carpaccio or tartare—or seared in a pan and offered up as a fish-like version of steak. The tuna was as mealy and soft and tasteless as what I'd eaten at the sushi bar in DC.

Only two tuna dishes I ate all year reminded me of what I used to crave. One was an appetizer, called Fire and Ice, at the Inn at Little Washington, a Band-Aid-size portion paired with a cucumber sorbet. It costs $138 or $168—the prices of the inn's prix fixe four-course menu—to get it. The other was at Bar Masa in New York, the "cheaper" alternative to Masa, where dinner goes for $600 a person. The fish was good. Very good. It also cost a small fortune.

Most preparations of tuna I tried didn't even approach "good." At some point during one of these tuna-eating excursions, my wife turned and said, "I know you're obligated to keep ordering it. But you know? I don't care if I never eat it again."

A generation ago, most Washingtonians thought tuna was something that came out of a can. Tuna was tuna fish—firm, taupe-colored flakes that were blended with jarred mayo to make a nice spread for sandwiches.

Then sushi arrived, and suddenly the notion of tuna not from a can—of tuna you paid good money for—was not so far-fetched. Tuna, with salmon and yellowtail, formed the holy trinity for sushi eaters. We judged a place by the quality of those three fishes—how succulent, how firm, how cool. Toro, or fatty tuna, the belly of the fish, became an obsession, the single piece sushi eaters lived for. I had come to believe that a great piece of toro was akin to a great steak and in some ways superior to it. When it was good, toro virtually melted on the tongue.

Chefs who were not sushi chefs discovered that tuna, because it was firm and meaty, could be turned into a substitute for steak. With some customers spooked by mad-cow disease and fearful of a high-beef diet, seared tuna became a piscatorial savior for many chefs. It was the new swordfish, only more popular than swordfish ever had been. By 2000, even chains such as Friday's and Applebee's were featuring seared tuna

Once a luxury, tuna had been democratized to the point of ubiquity. Somewhere along the way, it became something else: a food that is only good when prepared at the highest level.

Who is to blame? According to the more than 30 chefs I talked with, there is no shortage of culprits. The explosion of sushi in the West has resulted in overfishing in the Mediterranean and the Atlantic, which has depleted the supply of bluefin tuna, the backbone of the sushi industry. Many chefs believe that the bluefin, with its high fat content and rich, marbled flesh, is the world's best tuna; the bidding wars that break out in the auction houses of Japan for these hulking specimens bear this out. These days, the bluefin is approaching extinction.

According to the World Wildlife Fund, bluefin catches have dwindled to less than a sixth of what they were ten years ago. Sergi Tudela, the head of fisheries at the fund's Mediterranean program, has issued a warning: "We are near collapse of the bluefin tuna species in the Mediterranean and the east Atlantic."

Equally uncertain is the fate of the bigeye tuna, which is found in and around the Pacific and is nearly as good as bluefin. (The leaner yellowfin tuna is much less prized; it often turns up on many midlevel and chain-restaurant menus under its marketing name, ahi.)

It's not just demand outstripping supply. If this is the age of the global-minded chef, when buying ingredients from around the world is as simple as clicking and pointing, it's also the age of the global-minded fisherman. A number of chefs in Washington depend on independent buyers to deliver them fresh, line-caught fish, whether from the cold waters of New England or the warmer waters of the Mid-Atlantic and the Gulf. In recent years, fishermen have gotten wise and begun overnighting their catches to Japan for double and triple the prices they can get domestically.

Russell Gravatt, one of the owners of Sushi-Ko, has watched the tuna market explode since he and his partner, Daisu Utagawa, opened DC's first sushi restaurant in 1976. "It used to be pretty straightforward," says Gravatt. "You could get what you wanted, no problem. Now all those big mondo fish are going to Japan. I got a guy in Chatham, Massachusetts. FedEx has changed his life. He sends to Japan all the time. He can get twice what he can here."

According to the National Marine Fisheries Service, only 5 percent of all bluefin tuna caught in the North Atlantic ends up in the hands of American chefs; the rest finds its way to the auction block in Japan.

Japanese buyers will pay as much as $100,000 for a good-size, fatty bluefin tuna. "It shouldn't come as any surprise why most of it winds up in Japan," says Bob Kinkead, executive chef and owner of Kinkead's, the popular downtown DC seafood emporium. "The difference now is that they have their fishing boats all over the world."

The Japanese boats are helped by strict US quotas that curtail the ability of American fishermen to compete. American commercial waters stretch 200 miles into the Atlantic. But beyond that, waters are open to international competitors who do not have to abide by the same regulations as American fishermen.

Robert Wiedmaier, the chef and proprietor of Marcel's in downtown DC, says the relationship between the Japanese and tuna is about more than economics: "You're talking about a culture that understands and recognizes tuna for what it is. In America, you have the steak. In Japan, you have tuna. The Japanese will pay top dollar for good tuna."

The result is that it's becoming harder and harder for American chefs to get the good stuff.

Yet the public's appetite for tuna—despite the mealiness of so much of the fish out there and increasing reports of high levels of mercury that have been tainting tuna and making news since last summer—shows no signs of flagging. Which means more and more of the not-so-good stuff finds its way into the marketplace. It also means that more and more dubious practices are becoming commonplace.

"I can't even fathom how tuna still exists," says Wiedmaier. "The fish industry is probably the most corrupt industry in the food chain, because there are no controls."

As the tuna industry has become as global as the diamond trade—and as frenzied and competitive—illegal fishing is rampant, and freezing fish at the docks has become common.

Cheaper sushi bars often use what is called saku, or wood-gassed tuna, suspending the fish in a cloud of below-freezing air to fix its color and stall its deterioration. Saku is also what shows up in the sushi assortments in the refrigerated cases of some grocery stores. "You'll know it if you see it," says Gravatt. "It's beautiful to look at. It doesn't taste like anything, but it's as red as a bottle of ketchup." Because this tuna is cold-smoked, freezing doesn't affect its texture too much. And if texture is not everything with tuna, it is most things.

Tuna and salmon are easier to freeze than other fish. That and tuna's popularity account for the ubiquity of subthermal freezers. The function of these freeezers is to extend the shelf life of a fresh-caught tuna—preserving its texture and color—so it can stay out of the water longer without suffering the effects of exposure. Because of subthermal freezers, a piece of fish can arrive at a restaurant in Washington weeks after it was caught and still be put to use.

"You take it out, put it in 98.6-degree water for a few minutes with a couple of tablespoons of salt, and it's pretty good," says Gravatt.

Will it taste as fresh as when it was just taken from the deep? No. But neither will it be spoiled.

Kaz Okochi, of DC's Kaz Sushi Bistro, told me that among the varieties of tuna he buys is one that is caught off the western coast of Florida. It takes an average of three days from the time the fish is caught to reach his supplier and another day to reach his restaurant. Without subthermal freezing, the fish would have spoiled before it arrived in DC.

If four days sounds like too long out of water for a piece of raw fish—the antithesis of the credo of freshness that many sushi restaurants trade on—consider this: Kaz Sushi Bistro is among the most reputable sushi restaurants in the area. Okochi considers himself a purist.

Yu Sheon, manager of Café Asia, with locations in Arlington and DC, says that a skilled chef can do much to prolong the shelf life of fish: changing its wrapper frequently ("several times a day, at least"), maintaining a strict temperature, continually washing his hands. "If you can really preserve it well and nicely," Sheon says, "you can keep a piece of fish around for a while."

James Tan, the manager of Dupont Circle's Uni, notes that once a fish has thawed, it can be kept around "a maximum of three days." Which means that even at a popular, well-regarded restaurant you might be eating a piece of tuna that was caught a week earlier and kept frozen until dinner.

The nation's poorly developed distribution system is partly to blame—in Japan, a four-day wait is unheard of. But also to blame are new technologies that have arisen to mask the problem.

Besides freezing to prolong the shelf life, there is the growing practice of injecting fish with red dye to make it more eye-catching. Some stores, such as Whole Foods, have taken it upon themselves to alert consumers to this practice. But I've never seen any such notice on a restaurant menu.

Some diners are victims of their own expanded knowledge. Early in our sushi educations, we were taught to prize tuna that was a deep, dark red—the redder the better. According to Sheon, this is a misconception: "Brilliant red does not necessarily mean fresher." Sometimes sushi chefs can tell a doctored piece, he says, and sometimes they can't. And if a chef can't tell the difference between the two, woe be to the diner.

All the chefs I talked to deplored the state of tuna today. Yet all were quick to tell me that they have been able to procure the good stuff for their restaurants.

Their dishes betray them: Many have contrived ways to get around the tuna problem. At less-premium sushi bars, paper-thin lemon slices are appearing on platters of sashimi as colorful dividers separating the varieties of fish. But they're there for more than mere aesthetics. A hit of citrus can perk up a slice of otherwise ordinary tuna.

Good sushi bars are not beyond employing some tricks. At Joss in Annapolis, the kitchen has been featuring "a trio of toros," a dish that allows the restaurant to fly the flag of innovation while obscuring the fact that its tuna isn't superlative. In each iteration, the tuna is duded up with other ingredients—capped with a mashed paste of mountain yam, spiked with sesame and chili oils, grilled and anointed with a dab of grated radish and spicy ponzu sauce. As Joss shows, masking, if done right, can taste good.

Non-sushi chefs are slicing their tuna into a waferlike thinness for carpaccio or chopping it up into cubes and mixing it with oils and spices for tartare—anything but serving it as a whole, thick steak, where the quality of the fish would come under scrutiny.

At Mendocino Grille, chef Barry Koslow has been serving a dish called "tuna carpaccio." Shorn into sheer bands, then spritzed with the juice of yuzu, a tart Asian fruit, the tuna is served in a thick, mossy tangle of seaweed. The dish is less about the fish than about the seaweed, the tuna intended mostly to provide a textural counterpoint—not to mention the cachet of its name. But it would be hard to imagine the fish any more stripped of its once-kingly status than this—first cut thin, then bathed in citrus, and finally mixed with another, stronger-tasting ingredient.

Morou Ouattara, the chef at Farrah Olivia, goes to similar extremes for something he calls "shocked tuna." The shock refers to the blanching technique of dipping an uncooked loin into boiling water, then submerging it in a bucket of chilled soy sauce and red wine. Shocking changes the texture of the fish, masking the mealiness that characterizes so much tuna these days. Meanwhile, the soy sauce accentuates the meatiness of the fish. Ouattara plays up this fact, embroidering the plate with a tiny mound of powder made from dehydrated Burgundy.

"Shock" is the appropriate word for what Ouattara has done because only such a bizarre tactic could turn a fish that is often tasteless into something tasty.

• • •

Much as I admired the ingenuity of those coping strategies, it only reinforced for me how far tuna had slipped, from something that chefs once promised to get out of the way of to something that needed to be managed.

The more tuna I ate in Washington and beyond, the more I kept coming back to the tuna at the Inn at Little Washington. Why was the tuna at the inn so much better than the tuna I ate everywhere else?

I had thought the difference in taste had mostly to do with price. Mostly it does. But that doesn't begin to explain the complex set of decisions that occurs before either of chef Patrick O'Connell's two tuna preparations—the aforementioned Fire and Ice and Tuna Pretending to Be Filet Mignon, in which a thick slab of seared foie gras is set atop an even thicker slab of seared tuna—comes within sight of the inn's hand-painted, 24-karat-gold dishes.

It starts with O'Connell's personal buyer, the man responsible for getting him the best tuna possible. The buyer, whose name the chef won't disclose, also procures tuna for Charlie Trotter's, Le Bernardin, and Per Se—three of the country's best restaurants.

The buyer works only in Hawaii, where O'Connell believes the best tuna—bigeye tuna—comes from. Even so, the chef claims, only "one out of 300" tunas this buyer finds for him is good enough to make the 5,000-mile journey to Virginia. O'Connell buys only one tuna at a time. And he purchases only one grade: 1++.

"If I can't get 1++," he told me, "I don't put it on the menu that night. I think most restaurants don't even know that grade exists."

Grading is done at the docks, where the tuna is evaluated for color and fat content. This last analysis is accomplished by sticking a sashimo, a long, needlelike probe, into a sample steak cut from the tail. The greasier the probe, the higher the grade. Not content to rely entirely on an official grade, O'Connell has his buyer squeeze the tuna to check its oil content.

Grading has nothing to do with the freshness of a fish, although you might never know it to read a restaurant menu or buy tuna at a high-end supermarket. Diners and buyers alike are wooed with the prospect of "sushi-grade" fish.

O'Connell says he was like a lot of us in believing that that label was a guarantee of quality: "I used to think, 15 years ago or so, that it meant impeccably fresh."

He's learned better.

"You can have a fish that's just been pulled from the water that's a 3," says O'Connell. The way he says it, he makes Grade 3 tuna sound like something you'd find at a truck-stop diner.

After O'Connell's choice, Grade 1++, comes Grade 1+, followed by Grade 1, Grade 2+, Grade 2, and Grade 3. That's three levels of separation between the inn and most good restaurants. And five levels of separation between the inn and most cheap sushi bars.

The process by which the tuna is transferred from the buyer's hands to O'Connell's custom-designed kitchen unspools with the precision of a spy operation. O'Connell's order is in by 8 A.M. Hawaii time. It arrives at the inn by UPS between 10:30 pm and 1:30 A.M. The fish is delivered to the kitchen in a permeable airbag filled with ice, with a quarter of the fish exposed to the air. This lets O'Connell get a look at the fish in a natural state. A plug, or sample, of the tuna is cut from the tail and laid atop the fish so O'Connell and his staff can sample the flesh and make a quick call as to whether they want to keep it. They eat the plug while the deliveryman waits, his car idling.

O'Connell assesses each piece according to five criteria: firmness, texture, clarity, color, and oil. This last is critical to achieving what food critics and gastronomes call "mouthfeel"—the quality of luxuriousness in the mouth.

O'Connell says he pays anywhere from $16.95 to $25 a pound for his tuna, but he appreciates the fact that most restaurants can't play that game and suggests that he wouldn't pay it either if he weren't working at the level of the famed inn.

"It's like antiques," he says. "There's just not enough of the good stuff . . . to go around. And who wants to pay upward of $20 per pound? And if the public doesn't know the difference, then is it money well spent?"

I put the question to Wiedmaier. Marcel's is among the city's most expensive restaurants. Its tasting menu—at $98 per person—is about half of the price of the inn's. Wiedmaier is committed to finding the freshest, most exquisite ingredients he can find, but when it comes to tuna, he told me, he draws a line.

Wiedmaier says he is currently serving Grade 1 tuna. Why doesn't he make the leap up to Grade 1++?

"Because then I'd have to charge about $46 for tuna. The Japanese, they'll pay that kind of money because they love fish and they understand it. But not here. No way. I'd be hanging from Pennsylvania Avenue if I put that on my menu."

Some chefs, faced with the prospect of pricing themselves out of the market or doctoring the tuna, have bailed out. Johnny Monis is one. The chef and proprietor of Komi, a Greek-accented restaurant a few blocks from Dupont Circle, Monis no longer serves tuna. You might think it would be a natural for his menu, as it's such a common sight in and around the Mediterranean, the region Monis's parents are from and from which he draws his inspiration.

Years ago he served a carpaccio of tuna with olive oil and shaved fennel, but it long ago left the repertory. "People don't want to sit down to a $17 first course," he says.

Five or six years ago, he says, he was able to get good-quality fish at a price that a small cafe could afford to splurge on. No more: "I can't find tuna that's worth the price I was paying for it."

And Monis isn't talking about Grade 1++ or even 1+. He's talking about Grade 1, two levels below what Patrick O'Connell brings in six nights a week at the inn.

For a while, Monis devised a clever solution to the tuna problem. Early on he realized that running an ambitious restaurant on a limited budget would require him to cut back on the size of his portions; to compensate, he ratcheted up the richness of each dish. Out of the same necessity he began serving what he called "white tuna."

In fact, it wasn't tuna—it was a loin of Hawaiian waloo. What it had that a lot of red tuna does not is "a good amount of fat." It also had a "lot more flavor."

One of the quirks of waloo is that it absorbs whatever it's cooked with, says Monis, so the chef wrapped it in speck, a cured and cold-smoked bacon from Italy. The speck amplified the richness of the fish and provided a kind of skin for the loin, which kept the flesh moist during roasting. Monis no longer serves the speck-wrapped white tuna, but not for lack of popularity: The dish flew out of the kitchen.

So why call it tuna if it's not tuna?

"Because people already know what tuna is. They have an expectation. And the waloo approximates that same taste and oiliness."

Monis hasn't been alone in looking for tuna replacements, and waloo isn't the only one. Escolar, a tropical fish, has also been rechristened "white tuna" and has been popping up at restaurants and sushi bars.

Bob Kinkead argues that the practice is nothing new, that white tuna belongs to a long tradition of tinkering with names when it comes to fish. "Nobody wanted to eat Patagonian toothfish," he says. "You call it Chilean sea bass, and suddenly everybody's eating it."

The comparison is especially apt, says Kinkead, when it comes to escolar. "You can cook that thing to death, and it'll still be juicy, just like the Chilean sea bass." He says this with the disdain of a kitchen veteran for whom fetching a pan of fish out of the oven at precisely the right moment separates the real cooks from the wannabes. He also refers to escolar as a "bottom feeder."

So-called white tuna—whether waloo or escolar—has become a draw at many sushi restaurants, largely on the strength of the very quality that Kinkead sneers at. It's almost never dry, its sheen of surface oil making it a close textural cousin to red tuna at its best. It's a top seller at Kotobuki in DC's Palisades, at Joss in Annapolis, and at Matuba in Bethesda.

At Sushi-Ko, the cooks sear the escolar and serve it with onion, ponzu, a garlic chip, and a garlic sauce or stuff it into a roll with jalapeño and mint. "Americans like it," says Gravatt. "It doesn't really taste like fish, and the texture's good. It's about what you do with it more than any flavor it has on its own."

Some chefs are even less kind in talking about it. One night I watched the chef at Sushi Kappo Kawasaki deliver an assortment of sashimi to the table. Several white fishes were included, and I asked whether one of them was white tuna. His grave face softened. He seemed to be laughing. In Japan, he explained, white tuna is considered cat food.

• • •

I haven't given up on tuna, even if I have given up my yearlong quest. Let's just say I'm a wiser, more questioning consumer.

One question in particular kept nagging at me as I brought my research to a close: Many chefs are no longer working with tuna. Was it safe to assume they were no longer eating it?

Most dodged the question, which was an answer in itself. But Monis was candid when asked if he would order tuna in a restaurant. He paused, then said: "I wouldn't order a tartare, and I wouldn't order a tuna steak, unless it's of the highest quality and the person preparing it is really conscientious."

I told him he was making tuna sound like fugu, the poisonous Japanese blowfish that requires special training on the part of the sushi chef to handle.

He realized the severity of his tone and backed off. Tuna, he said, isn't dangerous, just costly, and often not worth the investment. "If I were in a restaurant I didn't know well, I would want to know where it's from, when the fish was caught, and how long it was out of the water."

Good luck, I said.

"You asked," he replied.

French Revolution

by Violaine Charest-Sigouin

translated by Jennifer Edwards

from *En Route*

Writing for this bilingual Canadian magazine, Charest-Sigouin turns her eye to Paris, where the reaction against fussy haute cuisine gives rise to a weekend of decidedly quirky culinary events, *et voilà*—Le Fooding.

No way," I say as I take my first step out of the taxi. The rain hasn't let up, and even though it's only 7:15 P.M. (they *did* tell me to be here at 7), a huge crowd has gathered at the entrance of Village Saint-Paul in the trendy Marais district. For better or worse, I begin to weave my way through the crowd with my umbrella, discovering a new extreme sport. Finally, I burst through to the courtyard.

It's the Semaine du Fooding, and Village Saint-Paul has been transformed into a kind of open-air gourmet central. Each night, a chef from one of Paris's venerable palatial hotels descends to the street to offer his version of popular favourites like hot dogs or crepes—with an haute cuisine twist. This evening, Jean-François Piège, the star chef of the Hôtel de Crillon, is filling the orders at a makeshift restaurant. It's like an upscale street fair, with all the vendors hawking food and drink to "bobos" (bourgeois bohemians) and families.

Started six years ago by food critics Alexandre Gammas and Emmanuel Rubin, Le Fooding set out to create a mini-revolution in French cuisine. The English-sounding word that is oh-so-French in its coinage is explained on page 4 of the dictionary *Fooding, le dico:* "The word literally connects food with feeling. It's the art of eating and cooking, at your home or at a restaurant, with an open spirit, one that appreciates novelty and quality, that shuns boredom and that takes the time to savour simple foods."

As I sample a tiny crepe with caramelized apple, Rubin explains how the movement was born out of a general disenchantment with French food, which had become stifled under the weight of tradition. "What has really been missing from French cuisine for far too many years is a sense of humour," he says. With spontaneous and playful events like the Semaine du Fooding, he and his partner attempted to popularize haute cuisine and bring back food's primary function: to please.

So how do you put on a Fooding event? First you cover the floor of the Palais de Tokyo with Astroturf and set down gingham tablecloths and wicker baskets. Then you ask the cream of young Parisian society to sit on the ground and sample the creations, placed inside tiny fridges, of top chefs. You'll soon have a smashing success on your hands, and people won't be able to get enough. Although Le Fooding had some early naysayers, the most renowned chefs now want a taste of the action. "Six years ago, we were ignored and written off as just a group of snobby Parisians," explains Rubin. "They gave us six days, then six weeks, then six months. Now we've been going for six years!"

But democratizing French food is not necessarily about getting rid of tradition, says Rubin. "For plants to grow, they have to have roots." Piège agrees: "France is a country rich in culinary tradition. But we aren't living in that past anymore; we are living in the now. What has become tradition was once the now. It's a typical French flaw, but I think that we're getting better at recognizing it."

Thirty minutes after my arrival, an announcement confirms our worst fears. "There will not be enough for everyone," says the grill cook as I stand in line (with the rain still beating down), hoping to nibble on a little kebab. As soon as I reconcile myself to the awful truth—even the tiniest of hot dogs has been gobbled up—a charitable soul slips me the address of a clandestine Le Fooding event. Without hesitating, I jump into another taxi with the precious piece of paper clenched in my hand. It's scribbled with code words: "I like beans."

As the taxi pushes through the glistening streets of the City of Lights, I think about Le Fooding and all its contradictions. The events may be open to all, but as soon as the public's desire burns bright, it's doused with the news that there's only enough for the first arrivals. It has the lofty mission of democratizing French food, and yet only a select group of Parisians knows about these secretive nighttime affairs. French chefs step down from their thrones to prepare the commonest of foods, and while these noble representatives deem their French cuisine pasé, the great palatial hotel is chosen as a theme. Le Fooding reminds me of the Surrealist movement and its penchant for turning everything on its head, only with the sincerest of intentions. For example, in a conscious nose-thumbing of the Michelin stars, those attending the Fooding 2005 awards event could only access the luxurious Lutetia by the back door, where they had to sample the sauce in the kitchen before reaching the ornate ballroom where the maître d' announced all the dishes with the help of a loudspeaker.

After having sworn my love for beans to the doorman, I find myself in a swarm of cool people, sampling sesame cognac and delicious croque monsieurs whipped up by the inspired Inaki Aizpitarte. When I run into Alexandre Cammas, I share my impressions: "Le Fooding will never become an international movement like Slow Food because only French cuisine is elitist enough to need reforming." He considers this for a few seconds before responding that as far as he is concerned, Le Fooding is a state of being that exists everywhere: "If my grandmother lovingly makes chicken with sauce, it's Le Fooding. And when Jean-François Piège reinvents the hot dog in an affectionate way, that's also Le Fooding." Satisfied with his answer, I reach for another croque monsieur, telling myself that while Le Fooding may be all about sentimentality, it captures something larger about the sentiment of our lives.

Do Recipes Make You a Better Cook?

by Daniel Patterson
from *Food & Wine*

One of the fallacies of chef-written cookbooks is a dirty little secret—that chefs rely on instinct even more than written directions when executing their dishes. Patterson, chef-owner of Coi in San Francisco and a cookbook author himself, confronts this paradox.

I've never been much for technology, so when I bought a car recently that came with GPS, I imagined that the device would go largely unused. But a few months later, on my way to visit friends at their new home in Oakland, California, I decided to give it a try. A patient yet firm woman's voice guided me easily to the exact location, and much to my surprise, I fell in love with the feature. Then one night, as I drove to see my friends for the fourth or fifth time, I realized that I had no idea how to get there. I'd been blindly following instructions from a disembodied voice without paying attention to where I was going.

This troubled me to no end. I liked to think I wouldn't automatically take the path of least resistance, yet here I was, in full capitulation mode. As I drove along, I considered the possibility that our national obsession with convenience was adversely affecting other areas of our lives as well. Like how we cook.

I have always thought of recipes as culinary road maps, demarcating a route from a list of ingredients to a finished dish—not so much hard-and-fast rules but a set of guidelines to lead the way. Not everything is accounted for in a recipe. The ingredients, the pans, the ovens, even things like humidity all play a role in the final outcome. Just as driving directions don't include tips like "Stop at red lights" and "Don't drive into oncoming traffic," recipes assume a certain baseline knowledge. But from perusing the kinds of recipes being published these days, it's clear that the baseline has fallen dangerously low. It seems that people have started to use recipes the way they use GPS—something to follow unthinkingly as a way to get from one place to another, without noticing the route.

Good cooks rely on recipes—to a point. In a professional kitchen, recipes are essential to creating consistent food, so that everyone takes the same path to the same place. But cooks who rely only on strictly codified formulas miss out on what is really important. Are the carrots more or less sweet, more or less tender? Is the ginger very strong, so that less should be used, or too weak for the amount specified? Or the thorniest problem: How long does it take something to cook, in a specific oven, on a specific day, with a certain set of ingredients?

When I wrote my cookbook, the how-long-should-it-cook-for question reared its head early and often. My publisher seemed to assume that the recipes would be followed by people who were inattentive and easily confused. I did my best to be accurate, but telling someone to cook a piece of fish for exactly five minutes is like saying, "Drive for exactly five minutes and then turn right." Sometimes you'd hit the road, other times the side of a building.

It wasn't until I spent the past year out of restaurant kitchens and cooking at home with friends that I started to get a sense of what was happening. People who are comfortable cooks—often with quasi-training (a year of catering or some such) or who learned to cook from a family member—start with the ingredients on hand, and then weave them together into cohesive dishes. The more literal ones stumble when the conditions don't precisely match that of the recipe creator's kitchen, often with alarming results. They would then tell me either, "The recipe doesn't work," or more frequently, "I'm just not a good cook," to which I would answer, "Nonsense." Anyone who can raise kids, pay bills and otherwise participate as a functioning member of society can learn how to make good food. It's all in the approach.

Take kale, for example. When I brought some over to my friends' house in Oakland as my contribution to dinner one night, I was met with grimaces. I don't remember the exact exchange, but the words *tough* and *chewy* figured prominently. So I showed them a simple, foolproof way to prepare braising greens: Cook sliced onion in olive oil with a little salt in a covered pot, over low heat, until tender. Add kale that has been washed and cut into two-inch pieces, a little water and more salt. Cover and cook over moderate heat, stirring every once in a while, until it's tender. Not tender yet? Keep going. Water evaporates? Add more. Before serving you can season it with olive oil, lemon, chili flakes, really any flavoring you like. I refused to answer their repeated queries about how long it takes to cook, saying only, keep tasting: When it tastes good, then it's done. This was a revelation to them, and cooked greens became a staple of their meals, perfectly cooked every time and easy, because they understood the why behind the how.

Baking, everyone says, is different; it's all about the precision of the recipes and how closely they are followed. But that's not entirely true. Last year in Park City, Utah, I made what were supposed to be moist, delightful, baked-to-order chocolate cupcakes for a party. I followed the recipe precisely, forgetting that I was in ski country. As I discovered the hard way, altitude affects moisture content, which resulted in dry, not in the least bit delightful baked goods.

When I got home to San Francisco I decided to remedy my baking shortcomings. I started by re-creating recipes from Rose Levy Beranbaum's *The Cake Bible,* and then used those basics as a jumping-off point to create new ones. There were some notable disasters, like my first attempts at a cornmeal butter cake. I used the book's yellow cake recipe as a starting point, then made a guess as to what to add or subtract to adjust for the new ingredient. On the first try, the ratio of cornmeal to flour was too high, and the cornmeal grabbed more than its fair share of liquid, resulting in a yellow bricklike affair that went directly into the garbage. But I kept trying, adjusting the measurements each time, and in the process learned things like how sugar affects moistness and how salt changes structure. The recipe improved with each subsequent attempt, until I finally arrived at a delicious result. I conducted similar experiments with other recipes, and now when something I'm baking goes awry, I can usually fix it.

Part of the problem with recipes today is that they seem to be predicated on the idea that a good recipe should eliminate the possibility of mistakes. But here's a secret: Good cooks make mistakes all the time. They take wrong turns and end up in strange places. Their attention sharpens as they try to figure out where they are and how they got there. Eventually they either reach their original destination, or discover that wherever they stumbled into is really the best place to be. Sometimes it's important to get lost.

I know, I know. Who has time for getting lost? Two-income families, kids, commutes—nothing about the pace of life today allows for the same luxury of time we had a few generations ago. As someone who eats way too many PowerBars, I am acutely aware of this phenomenon. Yet oddly, even though we are cooking less, we are reading more cookbooks. Cooking has become entertainment, something to watch on TV while sitting on the couch with a Hungry-Man dinner. As our interest in cooking has become more voyeuristic than pragmatic, the recipes that we do follow have become automated in their simplicity, largely a way to get as quickly and mindlessly as possible from one place to another. In our single-minded pursuit of the destination, we've lost our love of the journey.

But the journey is what a recipe is all about. Cookbooks should teach us how to cook, not just follow instructions. By paying attention, a cook should be able to internalize the process, rendering the written recipes obsolete. The point of a recipe should be to help us find our own way.

When I visited my friends a few weeks ago, I decided to turn off the GPS. At first everything seemed oddly unfamiliar, and I was uncertain about exactly where to turn or to merge. I got lost, of course, but only a little. I started to recognize a street here, a house there. When I finally arrived they had dinner ready. Roast chicken. And kale.

You May Kiss the Chef's Napkin Ring

by Frank Bruni

from *The New York Times*

As chief dining critic for the *New York Times*, Frank Bruni has no fear of stirring up controversy in Manhattan's hyper-charged restaurant community. This opinionated essay tackles a touchy question: Do celebrity chefs tyrannize the dining public?

The person taking your reservation is the first to put you in your place.

It's not just the unsavory dinner times—"We'd be *delighted* to seat you at 4:45 or 11:30!"—that the voice on the other end of the line trills. It's the rules laid out, the threats:

Call to confirm your reservation precisely 36 hours in advance, or else. Call if you're running more than 12 minutes 45 seconds late, or else.

The blessed night at last arrives, and so do you, and you're immediately made to feel you should kneel in gratitude and supplication. Just inside the restaurant's door, displayed like a religious icon, is the chef's book, bearing the chef's visage. It lets you know you're in the presence of holiness. It lets you know you can spend another $34.95 on your way out.

You spend plenty before then. Servers muscle you toward a 47-course tasting menu, replete with shochu and grappa pairings, telling you it's the only way to appreciate fully what "Chef" (no pesky, plebeian "the" needed) can do.

It's crucial that you appreciate fully, so each dish comes with a disquisition on its origin and proper consumption.

Chef got the eggs from an old lady with cataracts upstate. Chef foraged for the mushrooms in a thicket near the Tappan Zee. Chef counsels a bite from the ramekin on the left, then a sip from the shot glass on the right, then a palate-clearing curtsy.

I exaggerate, of course, but only about the details. Not about the climate around too many upscale restaurants these days. Not about an unmistakable, unsettling shift in the balance of power between self-regarding restaurants and self-effacing diners.

Once they were lucky to have us. Now we're lucky to have them. They don't meet us on our terms. We meet them on theirs.

Gordon Ramsay swaggered into town late last year and, instead of unfurling a welcome mat, laid down a gauntlet. Callers were told that the tables they reserved in his shimmering dining room at the London NYC hotel were good for only two hours, after which diners would be shooed to a peripheral lounge for any coffee or after-dinner drinks they might desire.

When this proviso was reported, Mr. Ramsay backtracked, saying that reservation agents had misspoken or misunderstood, and that the time limit applied only to tables in the London Bar, a more casual area just outside the inner sanctum.

But he made no apologies for setting up a ticking clock there, even though diners in the London Bar are on the hook for as much as $85 each in food alone if they listen to servers' ordering advice.

Thomas Keller just changed the rules of engagement at Per Se. When the restaurant opened in 2004, diners didn't have to sign on for the nine-course, $150 tasting menu it showcased most prominently. They could elect a less time-consuming menu of five courses for $125. They could eat at Per Se without surrendering three hours or more.

As of this month, though, the nine-course menu is the shortest, and it now costs $250. That price includes a 20 percent tip and free bottled water, coffee and tea, while the old price didn't.

Mr. Keller said by phone recently that a vast majority of visitors to his restaurant ordered the nine courses anyway, so a simpler, speedier route seemed unnecessary.

But he also made clear that nine courses were what he deemed best for diners visiting Per Se or its sister restaurant in the Napa Valley, the French Laundry.

"I'd like them to experience the entire experience, the entire Thomas Keller, the entire French Laundry," he said. People who stop at five courses, he said, are doing the equivalent of leaving a Broadway play at intermission or walking through only half of a special exhibition at the Metropolitan Museum of Art.

"Has the exhibit given them the full impact of what it was supposed to by whoever designed the exhibit?" he asked. "Probably not."

Chefs at the pinnacle of their profession have long considered themselves artists, with ample reason. But it's no longer just the top chefs—it's no longer just chefs, period—who hoist themselves onto pedestals, inviting reverence.

At Porter House New York, a lesser restaurant that, like Per Se, is on the fourth floor of the Time Warner Center, a line on the menu tells you that autographed copies of a cookbook by the executive chef, Michael Lomonaco, are "available for purchase." Never mind a doggie bag. Take home some instructive reading material.

After the restaurateur Danny Meyer's "Setting the Table" was published last fall, he propped up copies right inside the front doors of Gramercy Tavern, Eleven Madison Park and Tabla, where the book was also displayed above the bar, just to be safe.

Mr. Meyer isn't a chef. He's essentially a host, renowned for his humility and hospitality, for rounding out your meal with a prettily wrapped coffeecake for breakfast the next morning.

And yet he set things up so that when you walked into one of his restaurants, your first encounter wasn't necessarily with a host or a hostess saying hello or taking your coat. It was with a photograph of him on a self-flattering book ("America's most innovative restaurateur," trumpets the cover) about how he always puts you, the customer, first.

The lucrative publishing contracts that restaurateurs and chefs receive, the cable television shows on which they appear—all of this has encouraged a showboating that travels into restaurants, where the open kitchens sometimes seem less like peepholes for us than pulpits for them.

When the chef Laurent Tourondel opted for an open kitchen in the main, third-floor dining area of BLT Fish, he had to sacrifice a restroom. Diners must go to the first floor to find one. But look at what Mr. Tourondel got: a broad, beautifully framed stage for his ministrations—provided, of course, that he's not at BLT Steak, BLT Prime, BLT Burger or BLT Market (coming soon).

The chef Gray Kunz can indeed be found regularly at Café Gray, where he strides through a seemingly blocklong open kitchen positioned between the main dining room and a wall of windows onto Columbus Circle. He and the kitchen staff get the city views; diners get a view of him and the kitchen staff.

It's partly our fault. It's largely our doing. Chefs and restaurants wouldn't behave the way they do if we penalized them for it, instead of readily demonstrating our fealty. We take the 9:45 P.M. reservations (no exaggeration there). We agree to call a second time to confirm.

We buy the books and watch the television programs, granting our culinary heroes the celebrity that they then lord over us. Those of us who love restaurants—of course including critics, of course including me—talk and write about chefs the way movie lovers wrote and talked about directors in the 1970s, ascribing outsize authority to them, treating them as mystically endowed auteurs rather than what they really are: key—but by no means solitary— figures in an ultimately collaborative process.

And they gladly play the parts of creative demigods, roles they've helped fashion for themselves.

I visit L'Atelier de Joël Robuchon, in the Four Seasons Hotel, during its first week. The restaurant is supposed to start serving lunch at 11:30 A.M., but by 11:40 it hasn't opened, and by noon only 8 of the 20 or so people angling for a seat have been escorted inside. Most of the others stare poignantly at the hostess. And wait. And don't complain.

After my friends and I get a table and place our order, one of our servers volunteers, in a jubilant voice, that Mr. Robuchon thinks we've made excellent decisions. I survey the path between my table and the door. Is it long and broad enough for cartwheels?

I visit the restaurant Ureña, owned by the chef Alex Ureña, whom our server ceaselessly invokes. "Chef has sent out these amuse-bouches," the server says toward the start of dinner. "Chef was so pleased you liked your desserts," he says toward the end. Chef is apparently above such things as names. And we're apparently expected to know who he is—and to be primed for his genius—before we sit down.

Of course L'Atelier and Ureña have tasting menus. It won't be long before Hooters has a tasting menu. Tasting menus are all the rage, reflecting more than the desire of many diners to sample little bits of lots of things.

In places where these menus are pushed aggressively—Gordon Ramsay labels his own six-course option the Prestige menu—they also represent ways to transfer control from diners to restaurants.

"I personally love to have tasting menus," Floyd Cardoz, the executive chef at Tabla, said in a telephone interview last month. He was referring to the five- and seven-course menus he puts together there, and his word choice made me wonder.

Are such menus about coddling diners or flattering chefs? Are a diner's whims being trumped by a chef's wisdom?

And are the wine pairings really necessary? Some restaurants insist so, effectively shaming diners into submission and creating an evening of relentless verbiage, the soliloquies by the sommelier filling any gaps in the soliloquies by the servers.

Not that there are many gaps. Even in restaurants well below the top end, servers describe dish after dish, from an amuse-bouche hardly bigger than a semicolon to a scoop of vanilla ice cream, in exhaustive detail and priestly voices. They interrupt diners if they have to. They press on even if the gazes at the table are averted, the jaws clenched. The ceremony and the sweetbreads must come first.

The restaurant must have its say and way. At several casual restaurants over the past year—restaurants, mind you, that seem to exist in part for snacking and for cobbled-together meals—companions and I were told that we couldn't order a few appetizers to sate our hunger while we sipped drinks and perused menus. We had to place our entire dinner order at once.

The reason, surely, had to do with the understandable challenges of a small kitchen's trying to pace a large number of orders during a busy dinner service. But it was stated in terms of how the chef preferred to operate, as if that should be our concern, or about our own best interests, as if the restaurant were the final authority on those.

At Freemans, a self-consciously scruffy redoubt on the Lower East Side, the server who denied us our cheese toasts and hot artichoke dip explained, "You'll have a more pleasant experience that way." Such altruism. Moved us to tears.

And now, confessions: I gave moderately or hugely positive reviews to Ureña, BLT Fish, L'Atelier, Eleven Madison Park and Per Se, all of which had virtues that, to varying degrees, outweigh their vanities. Besides, those vanities are too pervasive to hang on any one restaurant, or to hang any one restaurant with.

I raved about Babbo, where the seductiveness of the food transcends a bullying rock soundtrack that puts the cult of its chef before the comfort of diners. When you're at Babbo, you listen to what Mario Batali wants you to, at the volume he elects, no matter how unlikely you are to enjoy it. It's his house, not yours.

That's the subtle or unsubtle message at too many restaurants. And while it hasn't killed the joy of eating out, it has at times certainly sullied that pleasure.

The inconveniences mount, the orgy of enforced adulation intensifies, and bit by bit, dining in New York's most prized restaurants becomes cause for exhaustion instead of elation, an act of obeisance rather than indulgence. Something's got to give.

At Del Posto, Mr. Batali's newest Manhattan restaurant, he and one of his business partners, the restaurateur Joséph Bastianich, send you out the door with crumbs. Literally. Instead of a Meyer-style coffeecake, the parting gift is a bag of bread crumbs.

It may not be suitable for breakfast. It may not be glamorous. But for Mr. Batali, it's an opportunity for synergy. The bag includes instructions for using bread crumbs, sourced to Page 39 of "Molto Italiano," one of Molto Mario's cookbooks.

It's a gesture that's as much a come-on as a thank-you, pointing you toward another way to show Mr. Batali some lucre and love. Reminding you of his glory. Affirming your good fortune in being privy and witness to it.

Discovering New Worlds

by Francis Lam

from *The Financial Times*

A CIA-trained chef with as much passion for words as for food, Lam is ideally suited to explain to us mere mortals what's up with all this space-age techno-cuisine. He is a regular food writer for the *Financial Times* and blogger on epicurious.com.

I knew everything when I graduated from cooking school. Texture, flavour, colour—whatever you had, I could tell you how you got it. This was the gift of my training at the Culinary Institute of America: a logic of food, a knowledge of action and reaction, of cause and effect. In learning technique, I learned ways of constructing and deconstructing dishes, in the way that learning grammar lets you take a sentence apart and know how it works. But beyond learning the rules of grammar, it was more like learning a whole language, and I drew the basic rules of food in close like instinct.

Then I ate bread at Wylie Dufresne's restaurant, wd-50.

It was shatteringly crisp, fragrant of wheat and the sesame seeds sprinkled on it. I knew, because of my training, that salt amplified these flavours. But I did not know how this bread had come to be paper thin, translucent.

I picked it up, stared at it and stared through it. It was—there is no other way to describe it—a sheet of bread. And really, then, this thing was not bread, but a thing that gave a distilled experience of the first impression of bread, just the crisp and crackle of crust. I didn't know quite what it was, or how it had come to be. And it was only the first thing I ate that night.

Recently, I dug up the menu from that dinner. Rereading it and the excited notes I scribbled all over it, I remember the thrill of seeing, for the first time, perfect cubes of hot, fried, solid mayonnaise or a piece of smoked fish whose skin was, in fact, pork. I remember the pasta course, a tangle of linguini cooked perfectly al dente, served on a brushstroke of smoked yoghurt. It tasted incredibly, deeply, of shrimp.

At the time, I reasoned my way through it—fresh pasta is made of three things: flour, water, eggs. A little salt for flavour and a touch of oil for tenderness, but that's basically it. Those are the variables you have to work with. So, to flavour a pasta, you can add things to the dough as long as you don't interfere too much with the basic ratio of those elements. Spinach pasta, for instance, works when you remember that the juice of finely chopped spinach will replace some of the water. This dish was making sense to me now. What Dufresne must have done was replace the water in this dough with a concentrated shrimp broth. Inventive and brilliant, a play perhaps on a Cantonese noodle that adds tiny savoury shrimp eggs to the dough.

I was eating with friends; one was a great cook and a friend of mine from culinary school. We traded ideas and he liked my reasoning. To verify, we asked. "Oh, the noodles," our server said. "There's no flour in them at all. They're made entirely of shrimp."

Since that dinner, since I ran home and wrote in my journal feverish entries that apologised for using the phrase "paradigm shift," I've been fascinated with this kind of cooking. In the years since, I've eaten there a dozen times or more, talked to the chef, attended seminars on this new style of cooking. I can read that menu and talk about how that food was made. I can use words like methylcellulose and transglutamase and talk about techniques that employ machines developed for medical use. I don't practise this kind of cooking, but I can talk about it and think about it. Slowly, haltingly, I'm starting to draw in these new rules, and they are seeming a little less like magic.

But then again, the magicians keep coming up with new tricks. At a conference featuring Spanish chefs last year at New York's

International Culinary Center, I tasted an oyster by the chef Quique Dacosta. Barely cooked but warm, the oyster was coated in a smooth juniper jelly that exaggerated its bulges and curves, made shiny by edible titanium and dubbed "Oysters Guggenheim Bilbao." Seeing and tasting it evoked in me the same thrill as when I first saw images of that museum. That would have taken the prize for the most startling dish of the day, had I not had a nibble of Paco Roncero's cheese, which he had made out of olive oil. Just for good measure, he carbonated it, so that it tingled when I put it on my tongue, mimicking the spicy bite of a great Parmegiano. I would have asked him to explain, but in the moment, all I could think was: "I'm eating delicious cheese made out of olive oil that tingles when I put it on my tongue." What more was there to say, really? Sometimes it seems churlish to peek behind the curtain.

I've also eaten some of this food that frankly isn't very good. Since the innovators openly share their techniques, there is a tendency to copycat, or to present dishes that rely heavily on the shock of "I wonder how they did that." In such cases, we might say that this food is nothing more than novel or pretentious.

But the best of it presents its flavours, textures and look with a kind of aesthetic logic, a conceptual thoughtfulness coupled with a consideration of pleasure. I haven't loved every single dish I've ever had at wd-50, but most of them have been delicious and all of them made me think about what I'm eating, both in wonderment of the technique and the relationship between the flavours and textures.

People have been looking for names for this kind of cooking. It doesn't help that most of its innovators and practitioners take the "you-can't-label-me" attitude of your favourite artists. A name that seems to have stuck, much to the horror of the field's leading lights, is "molecular gastronomy."

I think the term is a bit overwrought, a little too in love with its own sound, trying too hard to affect the gravity of science. It's true that these chefs are interested in the science of food, but so is anyone who knows that 135°F is the temperature of medium-rare meat. "Molecular gastronomy" seems more like a theory than a practice. No one is breaking out the microscopes and cooking molecule by molecule.

A more typical term, "avant-garde," suggests these people are on the forefront of a field that will eventually become the norm. This food will in all likelihood not be the norm.

So I've just been calling it sci-fi cooking. I don't know why I called it that at first, it just kind of sounded fun. But writing this, a thought occurred to me: science fiction, at its heart, does not aim to show us what might be made possible by technology, but what we might make technologically possible by our values.

The truly exciting thing about this cuisine is not what the techniques and the technology can do. It's that it shows us what the mind can do, what new rules we can make, what new logic, what new possibilities.

Feast of Burden

by Sara Deseran

from *7 x 7*

Based in San Francisco—where she is senior editor for the magazine *7 x 7*—Sara Deseran covers one of the country's most fascinating, and passionate, food cultures. Which can sometimes present a problem . . .

It always starts out so innocently. There I am, doing my weekly shopping at Good Life Grocery, my neighborhood store in Bernal Heights. One of two Good Lifes in the city, it's locally owned and has a respectably crunchy name. It's the kind of place where the clerks grab a few non-transfat animal crackers from the bulk bins to give to my kids. I wave to a few friendly neighbors, get a cart, throw some sesame bagels in a bag, wheel around to the meat-and-fish counter—and immediately, my happy-go-lucky soundtrack comes to a record-scratching stop.

There it is: the lox. While other parts of the country are dominated by the biggies such as Wal-Mart, Kroger, Albertson's and Safeway, San Franciscans are fortunate to have stores, even beyond Whole Foods, that offer eco-conscious choices. In the case of Good Life and its smoked fish, my two-year-old's favorite food, I'm faced with three different brands of wild salmon—including one that sparkles with a seductive gold star that says "line caught" and another from the "pure waters of Alaska" with a stamp of approval from the Marine Stewardship Council, which sounds official enough. And then there's a pack of Ducktrap that clearly reads "Atlantic," which, since there's no commercial salmon fishing in the Atlantic anymore, means it's farmed.

I don't need to consult my "Seafood Watch" cheat sheet from the Monterey Bay Aquarium. I don't need to ask, What would Alice do? I know. Go wild.

Still, I can't help but note their price—they all cost twice as much as the farmed. I can hear the most-quoted voice on food politics, UC Berkeley professor and journalist Michael Pollan, whispering in my ear like Obi-Wan Kenobi: "Pay the price, Sara." Then I picture my son, a half-finished bagel in front of him, salmon bits littering my floor—probably a dollar per bit. I also know I've tried every brand of wild salmon here, and it's all been too salty, too mushy. The Ducktrap is simply better.

But my son's brain development is at stake. And what's a little mush compared with the dose of omega-3 fatty acids wild salmon has that farmed does not? I also can't shake my semi-founded vision of fish farms: miles of overcrowded, polluting pens swarming with silver automatons gobbling up pellets of antibiotics. Not to mention the dye used to enhance the color of their flesh, which their wild, well-adjusted cousins get naturally from eating krill.

By now, I'm thinking crazy thoughts—like maybe I should just wait until king salmon season rolls around in the summer, go deep-sea fishing for a salmon, cold-smoke it myself, make stock with the bones, fry up the skin as an hors d'oeuvre and serve the cheeks for dinner. (Head-to-tail salmon. British chef and proponent of whole-beast-consumption Fergus Henderson would be so proud.)

Ten minutes into my sustainable spiral, the woman behind the counter asks, with obvious concern, if I need some help.

Living in San Francisco, where the label "organic" is for wimps, is a mixed blessing. There's no excuse for not doing the right thing here. There's a farmers' market every day of the week, and the produce is bountiful year-round. While much of the rest of the country is just getting in line with the idea of eating organic—albeit based largely on watered-down government regulations—farmers here are reacting by labeling themselves "beyond" it and growing things biodynamically, by the light of the moon. Should you want to immerse yourself in the sustainable dialogue, endless resources lie at the ready, whether you're looking to go camping for a back-to-the-land kind of weekend workshop called "Solidarity with Mother Nature & Sustainable Health," put on by the SF-based group Indigenous Permaculture, or an Outstanding in the Field gourmet sit-down dinner cooked by a well-known chef and served on a farm, steps from where your vegetables were just plucked from the earth.

But as in any righteous movement, should you do the wrong thing, there's often a price to pay—even if it just means an awkward social moment. In this case, everyone seems to have their own salmon story. Roberta Klugman, the publicist for Campton Place restaurant and Berkeley's Pasta Shop, once relayed hers to me: "Right when there was a lot of talk about farm-raised fish versus wild fish, a friend of mine, an advocate for sustainable food, was visiting. I had set up a lunch for her to meet Sibella Kraus, the founder and president of SAGE [Sustainable Agricultural Education], as well as Molly Fraker, then the executive director of the Chez Panisse Foundation, and we ended up at a lovely Thai restaurant in Rockridge called Soi Four. I really love their salmon in green curry, and I said, 'Oh this is so good! This is what I'm going to get.' But it stated 'Atlantic salmon' right there on the menu. I should have known better. Everyone looked at me in horror. It was as if I had put a piece of shit in their lap." The curry was not ordered.

If ignorance is bliss, I'm having an increasingly difficult time feeling blissed out—for all the above reasons and more. I've read *Fast Food Nation*. I subscribe to the biweekly *Ladybug Letter* written by Andy Griffin, the political farmer-cum-scribe from Mariquita Farm, and *Edible San Francisco*, a non-glossy magazine about local "culinary heritage." I've visited farms, from an organic one in the picturesque setting of Winters, CA, where purple asparagus tips were just beginning to peek through the earth, small plots out in Fresno thriving with daikon radishes and gai lan grown by Hmong farmers who often don't have the means to pay for organic certification. And OK, I haven't killed an animal—à la the current face-your-inner-meat-eater trend started by Pollan when he shot a wild boar (documented in his latest book, *The Omnivore's Dilemma*)—but, for the record, I have witnessed a chicken's head being chopped off at Slide Ranch, a nonprofit teaching farm in the Marin Headlands. And I didn't faint.

Still, relatively speaking—relative to a lot of people from the Bay Area—I'm an armchair activist at best. Slow Food, of which I'm not a part, has more members here than in any other city in the US; I didn't participate in the first large-scale "locavore" experiment, the 2005 Eat Local Challenge started here by Jessica Prentice, daring people to eat things grown within our 100-mile-radius "foodshed."

The fledgling knowledge I do possess still makes me halt my cart in confusion at every turn, though. Cut to internal monologue: *Horizon cream cheese: The outrage! Commercial "big organic" ventures like this have defused the original grassroots movement's intent and are exactly why the "beyond organic" movement started in the first place. (But how can I have smoked salmon and no cream cheese?) Grass-fed beef from Argentina? Tempting, but the jet fuel! Red grapes from Chile? It's winter, and I've been living off apples for what feels like months. Plus, by the time I've reached the produce section, I'm beaten down, so what the hell.*

There used to be a little sentence typed up at the bottom of Delfina's menu: "Don't be afraid of your food." Well, I am—just not for the unadventurous, chicken-breast-centric reasons I imagine chef Craig Stoll was talking about.

I decide to seek sage advice. I have lunch with Patricia Unterman, the food writer and co-owner of Hayes Street Grill—the pre-theater institution known for its support of small farms and hook-and-line fishing. She admits to me that she agonizes over what to put on her menu: "It's a constant battle: what I can serve, what I can't serve. [Food] is our local religion, which means that everything becomes an issue of moral decision." At a dinner the next week, I'm seated next to Alice Waters. I run the salmon dilemma by her, and when I get to the part about smoking my own fish—the funny part?—she nods deeply, as if she's completely with me on this one.

I invite Dexter Carmichael, director of operations for the Ferry Plaza Farmers Market; Heidi Swanson, author of *Super Natural Cooking* and the website Mightyfoods.com; and Bruce

Cole, publisher and editor of *Edible San Francisco,* to a lunch of sufficiently organic *pizza* at the cute new Piccino, in Dogpatch. In a
moment of wanting to bond over being eco-conscious yet flawed,
I ask each one what they had had for breakfast, assuming at least
one will sheepishly admit to having eaten a Toaster Strudel or a
conventional banana from Ecuador. I'm wrong. Swanson had
instant organic oatmeal with goji berries; Carmichael had Wallaby
organic mango yogurt from Australia. Cole trumps everyone with
local *and* organic fare of Grace Baking pugliese with a soft-cooked
Marin Sun Farms egg and Blue Bottle espresso. "Ugh! You're putting us to shame," Carmichael moans.

But Cole, who has shopped at the Ferry Plaza Farmers Market
every Saturday for 15 years, isn't completely perfect. "I was eating
my Fra'mani salami sandwich on my Artisan Bakers baguette and
munching on Doritos the other day," he recalls. "And my wife says
to me, 'You're such a hypocrite! Doesn't that, like, cancel out
everything you stand for by eating those Doritos?' " Cole shrugs.
"Well, you know, you can only eat so much of the other brands
before you get burnt out. I've eaten all the organic tortilla-chip
brands, all the organic potato-chip brands—it gets boring."

My next question to the group is, Why do you buy local and
organic? Surveys often say that people buy organic primarily for
health reasons, but these three admit that taste is their number-one
priority—not saving the earth, although that would certainly be a
nice outcome. "I don't look at it as supporting the farm," says
Cole. "I look at it as, 'I'm going to have to buy grocery-store eggs,
which suck.' I'm going to have to go to Andronico's or Mollie
Stone's, and while they offer organic produce, it's about five days
older than what I get at the [farmers'] market." Selecting food primarily due to its taste makes things a lot less complicated. Maybe
I should take note.

Earlier, Unterman had warned me, "If you're buying food to be
politically correct, it's going to drive you crazy!" Like a lot of
people, she'd read the article published in last December's issue of
the British newsweekly the *Economist* debating whether or not
consumers can make a difference by shopping for organic, fair-
trade and even local foods—and more to the point, whether these
things are actually the best choice. The article—a tennis match of

food politics with Pollan endlessly quoted as the good cop—stirred up a lot of controversy. Among other things, it stated that organic food is not necessarily better for the environment; fair trade might encourage overproduction of crops such as coffee, provide less incentive for improving quality and be "an inefficient way to get money to poor producers"; and that local food isn't necessarily fresher than something picked the previous day and flown halfway around the world. It concluded that although the idea of saving the world by shopping is appealing, "conventional political policy activity may not be as enjoyable as shopping, but it is far more likely to make a difference."

Whether or not I agreed with the *Economist*'s big bummer (and let me tell you, there was a lot of howling in protest), it was a good reminder that the issue of sustainability is never going to be cut-and-dried. Not even Carmichael, Swanson and Cole—all of whom I would have deemed golden because they shop for almost everything they eat at the Ferry Plaza Farmers Market, a place that has a waiting list of virtuous purveyors vying for its coveted stalls—are not necessarily doing the right thing. I'm not sure there really is one right thing.

But ultimately, even considering the *Economist*'s points, I'd have to disagree, namely because shopping at any farmers' market allows you to have a human interaction with people, often the ones growing your food. Just as shopping at a local market gives you the chance to make yourself immediately heard. I can't expect any one person at one of the US's 193 behemoth Whole Foods (plus the new Wild Oats stores the company acquired in February) to listen and respond to my neurotic concerns. Which puts me right back at Good Life, having a face-off with the lox.

A Bernal Heights father I know, dressed in his usual Crocs, finds me there, crouched down and scribbling the names of smoked salmon for this article. I explain what I'm doing, and after suggesting I seek mental help, he informs me of the Community Supported Agriculture (CSA) program his family belongs to: For $20 per week, a well-respected organic farm delivers them all the healthy, farmer-to-consumer produce they can manage. They even spent a night at the farm once. I should definitely sign up.

Then the usual inferiority complex sets in. "But let me tell you," he warns, shaking a finger. "Even that stuff can't be totally organic. I mean, it's surrounded by a bunch of other commercial farms, and I saw them spraying. There's no way the pesticides from those farms don't land on our vegetables." He also admits that while his wife has reservations about Whole Foods, he has no problem shopping at a national chain. "I mean, the cheese selection!" he exclaims, a look of lust washing over his face. "I just want to rub my face in it."

I start to point out that Rainbow Grocery has a great cheese department, but I refrain. From Cole's Doritos to Unterman's struggles, everyone has their moment. But we're all trying, which is what matters. (Re-cue the happy-go-lucky soundtrack.) Call it an *I'm OK, You're OK* moment, or put it as Carmichael does: "In the big picture, we have no power. But if you look at the term *sustainability,* and then break it down into little parts, you can say I agree with this part, I like that part. Then it becomes yours in some way."

I decide then and there to declare my dedication to my local grocery store one of my little parts and be content with that. After all, the wild smoked salmon is stocked here because the neighborhood is full of people conscientious enough to demand it. And if I want to ask Good Life to carry something else, there's an owner that I can actually talk to and get an answer from—and maybe even some better-tasting lox. Which, in this day and age of the big-box economy, is pretty powerful. As I look up again at the woman behind the butcher counter, it dawns on me that she can help me—a lot more than she thinks.

Organicize Me

by Michael A. Stusser

from *Seattle Weekly*

A contributing writer for this Seattle alt weekly, Stusser—who's also a game inventor, playwright, and environmental activist—trains a questioning mind on the food orthodoxies of the day. Oh, and a healthy sense of humor, too.

I've made more failed New Year's resolutions than Charlie Sheen and Courtney Love combined. Lose a dozen pounds, quit smoking, slow down, speed up, get organized, drink less, exercise more—all abandoned within hours of the drunken promise. But this year, my editors at *Seattle Weekly* came to me with an offer I couldn't refuse: Go the opposite of *Super Size Me* and eat only organic food 24/7 for the month of January—and be paid handsomely for it. No Doritos, Big Macs, Starburnt coffee, brewskies, Red Bull, or Frankenfoods of any kind. And, if by going organic, I help save the planet, all the better.

Clearly, the first stop on this assignment would have to be the notorious PCC.

Since 1953, Puget Consumers Co-op Natural Markets have served as the state's Birkenstock capital; and, with 40,000 members, it's the largest natural food co-op in the nation. Once inside, there's more information alongside items than you'll get in *Mother Jones,* a bulk food section that looks like a grain refinery, teaching labs that clearly involve mung beans and re-education, and even an in-store nutritionist.

Perusing the deli case at the West Seattle branch, I begin to fathom the difficulty of my journey: Though soy burgers ($3.99), teriyaki drumettes ($8.99), and Brussels sprouts look nominally appetizing, the majority of the items contain nonorganic ingredients, and thus don't meet my newfound standards. (To qualify for the USDA Organic seal, at least 95 percent of the ingredients must be organic.)

"If you don't cook—even something simple—you're in trouble," warns PCC's director of public affairs, Trudy Bialic. Looks like trouble. "Prepared foods are going to have too many ingredients to keep track of, and are also more costly. You're also going to want to eat in season."

I have no idea what she's talking about. Adjusting for her audience, Bialic tries another tack: "Listen, transitional foods are important for people making big changes. You want to enjoy your food, and it's OK to have a can of Amy's lentil soup once in a while, or a frozen organic pizza, or even some popcorn. It's a slow process: None of us can change overnight."

Really? Where were you two days ago when I decided to change—overnight?

Within 72 hours, I've become aware of changes in my body. These results, of course, aren't scientific: The sight of blood—especially my own—makes me faint; and without health insurance, I can hardly afford to piss in a cup, much less order lab tests. Still, I feel cleaner somehow, less toxic.

While my mind is sharp, my energy level is more sluggish than normal—perhaps due to the loss of artificial colors and preservatives in my diet, which are linked to hyperactivity (in school-children, anyway). Luckily, I've got the organic antidote: regular doses of caffeine. Purely by accident, I've been drinking organic coffee for years at my favorite espresso shops, Java Bean and Caffe Ladro. I may starve to death this month, but at least I'll be jacked up.

One other medical note: My appetite has increased. Specifically, I'm hungry for a Dick's burger.

After a decade of debate over what would constitute "organic" food, the U.S. Department of Agriculture laid down its national standards for certification in 2002. (It should be noted that the first set of guidelines was heavily influenced by agribusiness and was significantly more toxic than current standards, until over 325,000 citizens raised hell and had the regulations toughened up.)

For organic food to wear the USDA Organic badge of honor, it must be produced without conventional pesticides, sewage sludge, genetic engineering, fertilizers made from synthetic ingredients, or ionizing radiation. "Natural" foods, on the other hand, while without artificial flavoring or chemical preservatives, may contain ingredients that were grown with pesticides or genetically modified.

Organic meat, eggs, poultry, and other milk products can't contain antibiotics or growth hormones. Regulations also deal with the introduction of new animals to the herd and even the handling of manure, ensuring runoff doesn't pollute waterways.

In addition to eliminating nasty toxins from the food chain, certified organic farmers are also required to emphasize renewable resources on the homestead, minimize erosion, and conserve soil and water in their processes. Even the packaging is scrutinized, making it doubtful those eggs will be encased in bubble wrap anytime soon.

Yet certified organic is clearly not a politically correct cure-all. Though the organic industry prides itself on a kinder, gentler process in regard to the environment, the entire system is still not fully regulated. While César Chávez and company may have successfully banned the short-handled hoe in the 1970s, for example, the organic label doesn't assure consumers that laborers receive health benefits for harvest-related injuries or have rights to organize. In fact, organic farm owners formed the most vocal opposition to a ban on hand weeding—the backbreaking alternative to applying pesticides—presented to the California Occupational Safety and Health Administration in 2004. Hence, a "sweat-free food" campaign is currently making the rounds among grassroots activists and the Organic Consumers Association, adding yet another potential label to your USDA Organic, homegrown, Certified Humane, Fair Trade, sustainable cherries.

Some organic growers are less than thrilled with the current USDA standards, and have created their own seals of approval. Hard-core cultivators use terms like "biodynamic farming," which prepares homeopathic recipes to enrich the soil, and terroir—French for "the essence of the place"—which tosses a spiritual and cosmic element into the mix. And pioneers such as Eden Foods won't use the USDA seal even though they're certified, believing that their practices of small-scale, sustainable, cooperative farming go "beyond organic."

David Lively of the Organically Grown Company, a Eugene, Ore.–based wholesaler, isn't so keen on the term. "[The] problem with 'beyond organic' is that it gives away the organic part, which was a hard-fought battle. I like 'organic and beyond,' because we can do even more. The current standards allow us to talk to the feds about the Farm Bill and try to increase research dollars. It doesn't go far enough in terms of sustainability and labor, but it's a great start."

PCC's Bialic puts the organic labeling in perspective. "Let's let the baby grow up a little before we throw him out," she says. "The organic standards are only four years old; they're evolving. They may not be perfect, but they're the best thing we've had happen in food since bologna and Wonder Bread."

Nationwide, organic food is booming. Last year, over two-thirds of Americans purchased an organic product. According to the Organic Trade Association, organics accounted for 2.5 percent of all food and beverage sales nationwide, with 2006 sales increasing to over $15 billion (from less than $4 billion a decade earlier). While the organic market has soared over 15 percent per year since 1990, nonorganic food companies have gained less than 5 percent over the same time period.

"The problem now is really supply versus demand," notes Barbara Haumann of the Organic Trade Association. With demand increasing, organic farmers (usually with 100 acres or less) have had a hard time keeping up, leading to periodic dairy shortages and producers unable to feed larger stores such as Costco and QFC. "In a recent study of organic food producers," Haumann adds, "52 percent said that the lack of organic raw materials is limiting what can be made. There's just not enough organic acreage right now."

While more than a million acres of certified organic farmland were added over the last four years, bringing the total to 2.5 million acres, that's chump change when compared to total farmland. Organic is still less than one-half of 1 percent of all cropland. One reason may be that small farms are dropping like flies. In the last decade, over 650,000 family farms have bit the dust.

But here in Washington state, organic agriculture has boomed bigger than ugly condos in Belltown. According to Miles McEnvoy, organic program director at the Washington Department of Agriculture, the organic industry has grown over a hundredfold since 1988. Today, there are 1,000 certified organic operators in the state, 630 farms, and organic sales of $438 million.

Andrew Stout's Full Circle Farm sits on 260 acres in Carnation. Though he can't use a crop duster, he sees huge advantages to being organic. "We farm about 75 different fruits, vegetables, and herbs," says Stout. "With all the [crop] rotation we do, we aren't putting all our eggs in one basket."

Still, wouldn't it be easier to spray the fields with chemicals? "Oh, definitely," Stout adds. "Herbicides and pesticides are like an insurance program for conventional folks. Thing is, if you abuse the land, you'll eventually run out of property. It's Manifest Destiny; it's why people kept having to move West."

Going organic is not as easy as putting a bug sprayer away in the barn, though. The transition from conventional fields to organic takes a minimum of three years, allowing soil to be free from pesticides and synthetic fertilizers, and farmers time to learn the trade. Worms eventually come back, too.

Jay Gordon's family has been dairy farming in the Chehalis Valley for 134 years. He brought home his first organic herd on Sept. 1, 2006. The hardest part of Gordon's transition wasn't eliminating the chemicals from his soil, or filling out the copious paperwork for USDA certification, but that he missed seeing his original group of heifers every day.

"Luckily, my older cows are just across the river," he says. "So I get to go visit them at my neighbors'."

According to Gordon, who is also executive director of the Washington State Dairy Federation, Seattle has the highest percentage (11 percent) of citizens who purchase organic dairy products in the country. But there's still room for growth: Two years ago, Washington state had three organic dairies; today there are 52. By the end of 2007, 5 percent of all dairy farms will be organic. (Realizing that planting crunchy granola crops is the fastest-growing field in agriculture, Washington State University has created the nation's first organic farming degree program.)

Gordon says part of the reason for this growth is the terrain:

"We've used chicken and cow manure since the early '80s and always grazed our cows. But it's just easier to do here than in Kansas or South Dakota. It just fits my farm. If we had to milk 1,000 cows, you'd have to haul in organic feed from somewhere and it may not work."

Gordon has something else he wants to say about my (albeit temporary) all-organic diet: "I know you have to pay a little more for organic milk, and farmers get a little of that back and we appreciate it. So thank you for switching over."

"Is this all organic?" I ask my lovely wife, as we sit over a fine-looking meal of pasta puttanesca. "Pretty much," she replies. "The pasta's organic whole wheat from Trader Joe's, the olive oil is definitely organic, along with the basil and olives. But I'm not sure about the red-pepper flakes. I know it's all natural, but I'm not so sure it's organic."

Not *sure*? We're not *sure* if we have sewage sludge or traces of mercury in our meal? Not *sure* if the children are ingesting endosulfan, a relative of DDT? Not *sure* if our nervous systems are being compromised? Not *sure*? "Well, *be* sure from now on," I say, pushing my plate to the side and focusing on the organic salad before me. "You know," I add, "67 million birds are killed each year from pesticides that are sprayed on the fields. I hope you're OK with that."

If looks could kill.

Visiting other people's houses is going to be a problem, too. I've always hated nebbishes with "food issues": lactose-intolerant, vegan, alcoholic, shellfish-sensitive, peanut-allergic pains in the ass. "Is there cheese in that? I can't do dairy; it gives me gas." Now I'd be one of them. "Uh, Cheri, I know you slaved for hours over this fantastic jambalaya, but I'm gonna need to see the receipts for all the ingredients. I'm on a bit of a health binge, and I don't think you care as much about what goes into your body as I do. It's not you, Cheri. It's me. Go ahead and enjoy your pesticide-laden feast. I'll just sit over here with my chickpea yogurt."

Just call me Organic Superman: While my entire family has been down for the count with some disgusting phlegmy cough, I am healthy as an ox. Could this be a result of organic produce having more antioxidants than conventional fruits and veggies? (This has to do with the plant's own defense system having to fight off critters, rather than letting pesticides take care of it.) In addition, thanks to pre-ripened picking, longer storage, and more processing, conventional crops typically have far fewer nutrients. So long as there's no organic kryptonite, it looks like I'm good to go!

Yet quandaries abound. Like a deer in the headlights, I'm frozen in the fresh produce section of Whole Foods (aka Whole Paycheck), with too many choices. In one hand, an organic apple from Brewster, Wash.; in the other, an organic orange from California.

"Buying close to home is always cool," enthuses David Lively. "Local is happenstance. Organic requires motivation. If you can get it both ways, do it."

If I were a "locavore" (i.e., health food nuts living on fare grown in "foodsheds" within 100 miles of where they live), this would be a no-brainer. "The issue is, really, 'What do you know about the food you're eating?'" explains Goldie Caughlan, PCC's nutrition education manager. "Support the organic label, and know who grows it."

But shouldn't I always buy from local farmers? "For the first 10 years of my life, we only ate what we grew or hunted," replies Caughlan. "But sometimes you're in the mood for some citrus."

Finding organic lunch options has also proven to be problematic. Ninety-five percent of my midday meals prior to the new year involved teriyaki or Taco Time. Now it's "make your own at home," which is difficult enough without having to read every damn label.

To compound matters, whereas my bologna that has a first name (it's O-S-C-A-R) can last in the fridge for several months without turning green or smelling of old tennis shoes, the organic sandwich meat I bought last week has turned rancid—the cost of not being filled with nitrates and preservatives. This part of the organic experiment does not please me or my wallet.

As the weeks wear on, I find myself shoving anything with the word "organic" stamped on it into my mouth. The most convenient choices, unfortunately, are all sweets: Morning Peanut Butter Bars ($3 from the Flying Apron Organic Bakery), Fabe's Mini-Macaroons ($4.89), Nature's Path Vanilla Animal Cookies ($3.29), Country Choice Double-Fudge Brownies ($3.69), and Coconut Curry Bars from 3400 Phinney ($3.29). A guy can get plenty fat on an unbalanced organic diet, and I've got the new belly to prove it (at this point, I've put on 5 pounds). I wonder if an organic fat cell looks any different during liposuction from a nonorganic fat cell?

"We're not talking about an organic apple that can cure cancer. Instead, it's about trying to maximize chances that you're healthy and will remain healthy," says Dr. Charles Benbrook, chief scientist of the Organic Center. "Americans have the most diverse diet in the world, with the most choices, but two-thirds of our population is dying from food-related diseases or health problems. There was a report by the USDA last year that said it all: We're overfed and under-nourished. People like you, seeking out organic, will get unexpected benefits: a nutrient-dense diet—more bang for their calories."

Still, even Mormons need a vice to get by: cigars, string cheese, porn—something. Luckily, I discovered an organic vodka called Square One. The production's as simple as a moonshine-makin' home distillery: Take pure spring water from the Snake River, add organic North Dakota rye, and distill using natural fermentation techniques. Shake and pour. (Result: hammered. Verrry nice!) Plus, the bottle's groovy, and can be reused as a vase.

In the U.S., regular produce travels an average of 1,500 miles between the farm and your grocery store. Food miles, they're called. The farther products travel, the more energy and gas are used to get the stuff to you. Buying local can cut a thousand miles off, but I still had to constantly schlepp to PCC for organic chow, eating up valuable time and precious gas in my Volvo. That's where companies like New Roots Organics come in.

"Basically, I'm doing organic shopping for 400 people," explains owner Carolyn Boyle. For $35 every other week, New Roots delivers a bin of 12–15 organic fruits and vegetables to your door. "The majority of my clients are super busy, but want to eat well and don't always know what to buy," adds Boyle. "Our service gives them a big variety, and makes sure there's always quality fruit around."

To be honest, when the New Roots tub arrives at my house, I have absolutely no idea what to do with a majority of the goods: Parsnips? Gold beets? Yukon potatoes? Celery root? For the cuisine-challenged among us, Boyle tosses suggested recipes into each bin. This week: kale, squash, and pancetta pie; risotto with spinach and herbs; and blue cheese with those odd-looking beets.

There are pros and cons to having the O-Bin delivered. Pro:

Fruits and vegetables are good for you; the more they're around, the more chance you'll shove an Anjou pear slice into your face instead of a Cheeto. Con: Who the hell can eat a giant container of baby turnips, cauliflower, and countless apples every other week? In our case, leftovers are going to our guinea pig, and gee his coat looks terrific!

Generally speaking, buying organic no longer means getting your produce from a grassroots co-op in Duvall. Mirroring conventional agribusiness, half of all organic sales come from the largest 2 percent of farms. And even though organic represents only 2.5 percent of all food and drink purchases, the U.S. organic industry will do over $16 billion this year in consumer sales, and everyone—even Wal-Mart—is grabbing a piece of the action.

Today, 13 of the top 20 multinational food manufacturers own an organic brand. General Mills bought Cascadian Farm, Hershey's snatched up Dagoba chocolate, Dean Foods purchased milk-maker Horizon, Coca-Cola took over Odwalla, and even M&M Mars owns Seeds of Change. (For a great chart illustrating how the big fish are buying the little organic ones, go to www.msu.edu/~howardp.)

"It's possible to gain something from the conventional guys," notes David Lively. "If they bring their labs and expertise in nutrition or quality control, that's a good thing. But if they say, 'OK, hippie, get out of the way,' it's a problem. It's important these megacorporations don't knock out the visionaries in the company. They need to do more than just follow the law; they need to move the agenda forward. It's still buyer beware. Consumers can't let up just because there's a seal."

With huge volumes come lower standards, factory farms, and suppliers from anyone but your local grower. According to the Organic Consumer Association, Wal-Mart is currently filling its shelves with organic foods and ingredients from as far away as China and Brazil. Though all imported organic products must still be certified, questions about being able to grow anything "healthy" in areas with horrific air quality and acid rain remain. (Wal-Mart may be jumping too fast into the fray, as it is being sued by the Cornucopia Institute for passing nonorganic food off as organic.)

Lively, who sells to natural markets along the I-5 corridor, is plenty concerned about corporate farms and Wal-Mart's treatment of growers, but claims it's all relative. Says Lively: "I had just finished some speech at a convention that bashed Wal-Mart's practices when this lady came up and said, "You know, it's easy for you to pop off and play elitist in the West. It's the natural food mecca. If you live in Kansas City, like I do, you go to Wal-Mart for organic food. It's all you've got.""

For plenty of families, buying organic produce is less of a priority than simply putting fresh food on the table. For those who must pick and choose, the Environmental Working Group (EWG) has established a "dirty dozen": produce that, due to high pesticide residue, absolutely should be purchased organic. Apples and nectarines top the list, followed by cherries, peaches, pears, raspberries, imported grapes, strawberries, bell peppers, celery, potatoes, and spinach. If you can't go 100 percent organic, certain fruits and vegetables—due to how they're grown and ease of cleaning—are less likely to be contaminated, including bananas, mangos, pineapples, corn, onions, avocados, peas, and cauliflower.

And don't think you can just peel a nonorganic apple and be done with it. "You may eliminate a majority of any chemicals," explains Dr. Benbrook. "But you'll also get rid of 60 percent of the nutrients that are in the skin and the layer just under it."

"This kale is so tasty!" exclaims Seattle Tilth director Karen Luetjen, pointing at a barren, winterized section of Tilth's Demonstration Garden in Wallingford. "If you'd like, you can make a little to-go salad right now, add some broccoli florets over there, that lettuce, and you're on your way."

The dirt diggers at Seattle Tilth have been promoting organic gardening since 1978. Today, Seattle Tilth runs over 300 programs that reach 15,000 citizens a year, including City Chickens 101 and a kids' class, *Don't Crush That Bug!"*

Living off the land, of course, is not the newest concept around. Seattle already has over 1,900 organic P-Patch plots, and while there may not be much sun, most of the patches are gardened year-round. If you want in, though, stand in line: There's a wait list for almost every patch in town.

Yao Fou Hin Chao works with over 600 members of the Iu Mien community in various P-Patches along Rainier Avenue and MLK Way, which are the primary sources of food for many

Laotian, Vietnamese, and Chinese immigrants. Says Yao: "Many come to me, say, 'I need food. I know how to garden, but I need plot.' My job is to teach them how to garden in this area. Laos climate is easy, like California. Here is different—all new crops, new time to plant, new method."

Yao also teaches his gardeners to grow mustard greens, beets, and bottle gourds, plus corn, tomatoes, and cucumbers that can be frozen and eaten all winter. "Some garden for therapy, for experiment, for fun, to meet others," explains Yao. "For me, to help my people eat, and eat healthy."

So does Yao ever *buy* organic food? "I don't eat organic from store. I know where it is, but can't afford. When I see PCC, I walk by window and don't feel bad. I have my own produce."

Mark Musick has been involved in the Tilth movement since 1974, and has worked with organizations ranging from farmers' markets to the Vashon CoHousing Community. "Food is a way to reconnect with the culture," Musick begins. "After all, the word culture comes from cultivate. Food is our most intimate link to the earth. It just makes sense that you'd want to know where your food comes from. And that's a great place to start."

One way people connect, he suggests, is by meeting growers at farmers' markets, where more than half the vendors nationally are organic. In the greater Seattle area, farmers' markets have expanded from 12 in 1996 to 86 in 2006. On any given weekend during the summer, 67,000 people will shop at a farmers' market.

Another direct connection is through CSAs (Community Supported Agriculture), where small farms market directly to consumers through regular drop-off locations around the state. There are 50 CSA farms in Western Washington, serving 4,000 families. At Carnation's Full Circle Farm, over 75 percent of the company's business comes from 2,500 CSA customers, including schools, Starbucks, Fred Hutchinson, Amgen, and various community centers.

Full Circle's Stout understands that what we really want is the ideal of the farm pastoral based on Old MacDonald: the red barn, the oak tree with a tire swing. "In recent surveys, the No. 1 thing customers say is important is where the food is grown," says Stout. "A sense of place; people you can trust. After that come quality, the price, and if it's organic."

In the end, Musick explains, the issues of organic vs. nonorganic aren't the most important. "The key is making local connections to the earth," he says. "If you ask PCC where their black beans come from, or a lot of their bulk items, they'll tell you it comes from China. What we need is Community Supported Agriculture. We're building a better constituency for a better type of agriculture, and now you've been enrolled."

I am exhibiting signs of the dreaded E. coli. And believe me, I know what the hell they are: In 1993, my pal Mike Schiller and I ate undercooked burgers at a fast-food restaurant and got the runs, massive stomach cramps, and nasty gas for weeks on end. Not to mention blood in the stool. (Sorry if you are eating while reading this.)

Good news: Turns out my E. coli scare was just too much dried organic fruit in one sitting. Doc says I basically ate the equivalent of 13 plums, six apples, and 11 apricots the other day. Oh, and the blood? Dried cherries.

With five days remaining in my monthlong experiment, I'm feeling vigorous and in a helluva lot better shape than that guy in *Super Size Me* was at this point. My pulse (64) and blood pressure (116/80) are slightly lower than before, I'm sleeping like a log (as usual), and like our guinea pig, my hair has a new, beautiful luster.

Fighting off my Mighty-O Donut addiction, I've finally figured out *how* to eat organic (a little endive salad here, a trip to the all-organic Sterling Cafe there), and my weight is back to normal. The constant produce from New Roots Organics has changed the color of my urine from the bright lemon-lime of Gatorade to a more foamy consistency and the color of a tangerine, indicating more beets, rhubarb, and vitamin C in my diet.

When I started talking to natural food junkies at the beginning of the month, they would rave about particular organic fruits or vegetables I *had* to try, as if I'd recently been dropped here from the barren Planet Zoron. David Lively was obsessed with a California orange that only came around once a year; Tilth's Karen Luetjen carried on about homegrown tomatoes at their annual tastings; and PCC's Goldie Caughlan had a food-gasm over Nash Hubor's carrots from Dungeness Valley. Thing is, it's true: At times, organic tastes better. Way better. And isn't flavor a huge part of the eating experience?

The final tally had me losing 3 pounds and more cash than I

was comfortable with. My family of four's food budget is usually around $800 per month; this month, thanks to several $6.99 pints of raspberries, $13 wedges of cheese, $21 steaks, and $7 grapefruits, our grand total was $1,372.51—a 58 percent increase.

All in all, organic food isn't always affordable, or even healthy. (Try living off Tostitos Organic Tortilla Chips and Natural American Spirit cigarettes.) And the more you think about the social issues surrounding the food on your plate, the more complicated things get. How many miles per gallon does the tractor on the organic farm get? Do you need apples from New Zealand, or is there a local alternative? What's the relationship between farmhand wages and farm owner profits? Are you cool that Kashi is really Kellogg's, or would you prefer getting your granola from Gary in Gold Bar? And if your corn is husked by some kid in Bangkok for 4 cents an hour, then shipped over on a nuclear submarine, is organic really the most important part of your purchase?

I had wanted my choices to be black and white: Organic equals good, everything else equals bad. But now the gray is all around me. The growers aren't necessarily families, friendly, or in the business for politically correct reasons. The products aren't always local, regional, or even national. The whole thing made me angry, confused, and jonesing for a Twix bar.

Still, some organizations are trying to address issues beyond land stewardship and ecology, paying attention to socially just food systems: the communal utopia that counterculture types established in the 1960s. These hippie homesteaders understood that eating right is as simple as knowing where your food comes from; and if that's an organic garden in your backyard, more power to you.

Next month, I've actually decided to kick my diet up a notch for an entirely different reason. Turns out, *cooking* food—organic or not—destroys much of its protein, vitamins, and minerals, making your immune system work overtime, aging you faster, and increasing the chance of deadly disease. Well, no thanks! I'm now eating truly old-school: 100 percent *raw*. Bring on the fresh seaweed, egg yolks, and celery juice. It's go time.

Home Cooking

Kitchen Existential

by David Leite

from *The Morning News*

It's no surprise that David Leite started out in advertising—he has an unfailing knack for the witty, succinct phrase, as well as a sharp visual eye that graces his award-winning website, leitesculinaria.com. Leite's also a regular contributor to *TMN* and is at work on a Portuguese-American cookbook.

I didn't think I had a problem, and I certainly didn't think I needed an intervention. To me, interventions were for the weak, the lost, the *Oprah*-obsessed. But if you scratched the surface, rooted deep enough, opened doors and pulled back tablecloths, it was true—I was powerless over my Pyrex, and my kitchen had indeed become unmanageable. If I was to make peace with my postage-stamp-size Manhattan kitchen, I had to turn my will and our Fiestaware over to the care of God as I understood Him. And in this case, God was dressed in a smart white-and-blue checked shirt, khakis, and a woven belt.

Justin Spring, author of *The Itty Bitty Kitchen Handbook,* a pocket-sized bible for city dwellers who, like me, love and loathe their tiny kitchens, agreed to visit my apartment for a once-over. For days, I had imagined he would cast a knowing glance at the contents of my cupboards, rearrange a few tumbled shelves of pots and pans with a sure hand, and calm would prevail. Instead, the poor man stood in the living room feverishly mopping his brow, for, of course, I'd chosen one of the hottest days of the summer to exorcize my kitchen demons.

Unfortunately, due to yet another aneurysm in the New York City postal system, I didn't receive my promised copy of his book (sent by his editor not 30 blocks away) in time for his visit, so I was unable to cram before Spring's miraculous laying-on of hands.

"I'm sorry," I said, "I don't have *Itty Bitty*."

He just looked beyond me, a beatific expression upon his face. "But you have a Wolf Kahn."

I turned to the painting of an orange barn hanging on the wall. Its name is, appropriately, "Overall Orange."

"Oh, that," I replied. The One Who Brings Me Love, Joy, and Happiness, and whom I share the apartment with, is a big art collector, and this was the latest acquisition.

"Well, I hope you have the book I wrote about him."

Damn! Second strike, and the man hadn't even made it to the kitchen.

"I know we have a book on him somewhere," I said. I riffled through the mess on the coffee table. Lying beneath a pile of cookbooks was an oversize art book, *Wolf Kahn,* with the byline "Justin Spring." He smiled upon me, and I was redeemed. He even signed the book for The One, a kind of belated gift with purchase.

I finally ushered him into my poor attempt at a Martha Stewart–green kitchen, and he was taken by the original '30s wooden cabinets and counter.

"Everyone says keep this, but it's all going," I said. Then added: "Shouldn't it?"

"When?"

"When we finish the renovation." Spring's brow cocked, registering something. Displeasure, perhaps? I tried to read it, but he remained silent, scanning the room. So what if we were a little late in finishing the renovation? When we bought the apartment seven years ago, The One insisted we do a gut renovation before moving in. But we left two things undone: the kitchen, because we wanted to live in it before we decided what to do with it, and, oddly, a bare hallway light bulb, which still hangs from its wires. Neither of us can remember why we didn't bother to put up a fixture, and neither of us now has the energy to fix it.

"You need to either renovate the kitchen," said Spring, "or do a stop-gap reorganization. But this," he swept his soothing hand across the kitchen, "isn't working as well as it could."

Ouch. Always competitive, I realized his comment meant there were other small kitchens out there that were better than mine, more organized. Looking back at the string of *cozinhas* I've cooked in, only my mother's was truly organized. And she did it with nothing more than shelf space and an under-the-counter lazy Susan. No overpriced Williams-Sonoma gadgets for her. It just was neat towers of nested bowls, stacks of graduated pots and pans, and a plastic silverware divider. Where did I go wrong?

Before I developed an interest in cooking, my kitchens were the picture of über-organization. They contained nothing more than a few bowls, plates, pieces of flatware, plus one frying pan and a pot. If the contents of my *batterie de cuisine* couldn't fit into a moving carton, it didn't make it into my cabinets. It was that simple. But then along came The One, and my one carton met a van full of boxes. All of it had to fit in our first kitchen, a much smaller galley space than this one, and I didn't see why I had to give up some of my stuff when The One had a lot more stuff to give up. But because Mamma One and Grandma One passed down so many of those dishes, glasses, and silverware (not to mention quilts, tchotchkes, and furniture— including a hulking organ), The One played the family card, and I, with nary a family tin cup to my name, had to back down, sometimes resentfully. Cabinets bulged, and as I studied cooking, I added even more to the throbbing mass behind those cupboard doors.

Perhaps seeing I was crestfallen, Spring was gentle in his assessment. "Look, your refrigerator opens the right way."

"Through no doing of ours. It came that way," I sulked.

"And, here," he said, pointing to a shelf two and a half feet above the worn butcher-block counter. "You moved canisters and books out of your way, clearing a workspace for yourself. Good."

Emboldened, I swung open two cabinets above the refrigerator. "This is the most clever thing we did," I said, acting like a bounding cocker spaniel pup trying to get approval from his master. Inside was the microwave. In an uncharacteristic moment of handyman prowess, I'd drilled a hole in the bottom of the cabinet and threaded through the cord. It kept the ugly appliance out of sight, but, of course, since it was at head level, I'd probably given myself brain cancer every time I heated up a Weight Watchers frozen dinner. Still, a small price to pay for a neat kitchen.

After a few more show-and-tells, Spring asked to go out to the living room where it was considerably cooler; his shirt was now sticking to him. I tried to keep us in the kitchen, tried to get a few helpful hints on how to fix the somewhat troubled room. Determined to extract from him just how it stacked up to other kitchens he's seen, I pressed him for a grade. He reluctantly gave it a B.

Sitting there, conversation drifted in another, unexpected direction. The kitchen, he explained, is where relational dramas unfold, where the gestalt of a family is dissected and laid bare. "Some people are uncomfortable in the kitchen because so many bad family events happened around the kitchen table." I thought on my childhood and of my raucous Portuguese family, who treated dinner as a time to guffaw, shout, pray, and debate. Not many troubling memories there. "It can also be a place where control and territory issues come up—especially for a couple." Suddenly, I began to sweat. Was he truly God-like? Had he divined our struggles from the jumble of Fiesta dishes? Did the cabinets whisper of shouting matches long forgotten?

Kitchen as Rorschach test. Kitchen as barometer of the emotional health of a couple. I was certainly in *Oprah* territory now, laying my psyche in Spring's hand, but it made sense to me. Appropriately, I was lounging on the couch while he sat upright in the nearby chair. As we talked, I confessed all our culinary intimacies. I mentioned the power struggles and one-upmanship. The One's heirlooms, and how I couldn't compete.

Spring then began telling me of his love of the art of the meal, and soon I was explaining that it was important for us, especially The One, to have different music for different parts of the evening: jazzier, upbeat music for hors d'oeuvres, classical music for dinner, and quieter music for post-prandial conversation. Location had to change, too. In the city we move from living room to dining room, back to living room. But in our new house in Connecticut, we'll move from family room (hors d'oeuvres), to dining room (dinner), to living room (drinks and dessert).

"So dinner as narrative is important to you," he said. Again, that beatific smile. I felt anointed, blessed. Maybe my B would be upped to an A-minus when entertaining was factored in, I thought. But dinner as narrative? It had never struck me that way. In fact, I never thought of it as a conscious decision to entertain like this. It's just something The One and I did. Sure, we type up lists of who does what for each course so that our guests are never left without at least one host. OK, we argue over who sits where, even having name cards made for large dinner parties so the class clown of our friends isn't seated next to the quiet one, making dinner uncomfortable for both. Granted, we scour the music collection to set the right mood (although The One has played the sound track to *The Prince of Tides* 100 times more than I would like). But *conscious* decisions? Never.

While chatting, I could see that I had appeased this Zeus of the kitchen. Even though my pots are scattered haphazardly throughout shelves and racks and I have grease to remove from the walls, pans to polish, spices to ditch, cabinets to clear out and restock using organizers from Crate & Barrel, I was essentially OK—and so was my relationship. Whatever lunacy rules in the kitchen we make up for in the dining room. I felt calm, the plumbing of my psyche purged, ready to tackle the enormous task of letting go of much of what we didn't need or use in the kitchen. I envisioned a tortuous process as we argued over whether the plastic Chinese takeout containers were dumped (according to Spring, yes), the kitchen painted (yes), the hanging pan rack trashed (no).

But let me warn you: This unmooring of yourself via kitchen clean-up, this thrilling freeing-up as you witness years of accumulated detritus being thrown out can be dangerous. Anticipating my liberation, I blithely invited Spring and his editor *(a freaking cookbook editor, for God's sake)* to dinner, post-organization. But faced with cooking for two such discerning palates, I suddenly needed all the stuff in those cabinets, overhead, underneath—to clutch on to, to soothe me. I'm a junkie who needs a fix. I can't do it cold turkey, man, I simply can't. I'll clean up, Justin, I promise. I will. Right after you come to dinner.

Cast Iron Skillet

by Andrea King Collier

from *Country Living*

In food writing, not enough attention gets paid to the hardware, those kitchen appurtenances that we use every day. When nonfiction writer Andrea King Collier looks at a pan, though, she sees more than a hunk of metal—she sees the cook's hands and the kitchen culture that have shaped it.

Over time, I started collecting cast-iron cookware, picking up the big, clunky Dutch ovens, deep skillets, shallow corn bread pans, wherever I found them. To me, they were an extension of the collection that I had inherited from my grandparents and used almost every day.

As with most collecting, what's one woman's junk is another's treasure. This is evidenced by a frying pan, almost too heavy to pick up, that I bought in Gambier, Ohio, for fifty cents at a church garage sale. Of course it cost me $30 to ship it back home, but to me it was every bit as valuable as the fine Irish crystal sherry glasses that I bought for $30 a piece.

Yet, when I brought the skillet home, I put it on the shelf with other cast-iron pieces that I had collected but had never put into service in my own kitchen. I'd look lovingly at them, dust them occasionally, and contemplate the day when I would have the nerve to use them.

I wondered for a long time as to why I never reached for them, but always used the old family pans instead. Then, I had a revelation. I would never cook with anybody else's cast-iron, because they weren't just the means to a perfectly fried chicken, but rather represented family food and its history and legacy. And everything I know about the perfect fried chicken came from the cast-iron skillets that were passed down for generations in my family. The real problems with my collection of other people's cast-iron is that they had other people's history.

If I was going to use the cast-iron to capture the history of my culture and keep the best of it safe and treasured and doing what it was designed to do over a hundred years ago, then it might as well be my own. Everything that truly mattered about the pans was because they had been passed down from my great grand-mother to my grandmother to me. My mother never used them, because she just felt like they were old garage sale junk. Then, again, my mother was never much of a cook.

I know that my grandmother Lucille never thought they were particularly magical or steeped in tradition. To her they were func-tional. They were just good, solid pots and pans. They had traveled from Commerce, Georgia, where she was born the granddaughter of a house slave, to Oklahoma, where she spent part of her youth on a Reservation, then passed on to her when, in the early 1920s, she set up her own home as a young bride at the age of 15. To my grandmother, they were like her and all the women in our family to that point—survivors that had earned respect. They even have names—the big one is Bertha, the stew pot with the handle and lid is Lizzy, there is one called Tiny Pot. "Go bring me Miss Tiny Pot," my grandmother would say. To me, those survivors are my legacy.

A good cast-iron skillet has a unique recipe of its own, a sort of DNA—its seasoning that it perfects over time. The seasoning is what makes it black and textured. The seasoning makes a cast-iron skillet impossibly ugly, and unexpectedly, startlingly inviting and beautiful to a real cook. The seasoning is the thing that you savor and don't want to lose. Almost all that is valuable in such a pot or pan is held in its seasoning.

As much as I love the other pans, I don't know enough about them. In Southern culture, we always want to know "Who your people?" And, so, it is with these pans who want to be old friends of the family. I want to know who were their people. I want to know how the pans got their shiny black patina. Was the pan layered with love of food and family and joy, or was the seasoning developed over the years from anger or disappointment or unbearable loss. I think that an angry pot makes angry gumbo. A skillet that has known great disappointment cannot do anything but make a sad little hot-water corn bread.

As I head toward my own shiny patina, at the seasoned age of 50, it is not unreasonable to think that the pot I make roux in has made this rich nutmeg-colored gravy for over a century, with more knowledge and hope and love passed down with each generation.

A few years ago, I went to France with a famous chef from North Carolina. He traveled with his knives and, believe it or not, the cast-iron skillet that he had gotten from his own grandmother when he finished culinary school. He unpacked it from a special cloth bag he had made for traveling and lay it out as carefully as he did his knives. He, too, had a healthy respect for this link to his past. "This pan know things, Baby Girl," he said to me, and I knew just what he meant.

My cast-irons, the ones that were passed down to me, seem to be intuitive. They always seem to guide me, knowing what to do, or what ingredient is needed to make ordinary into something so perfect that it makes you hum when you taste it. I can almost hear it whisper that it needs just a touch more of this or a pinch of that. I never have that kind of confidence in the collection that is lined up on the top cabinets in my kitchen. They may have their own mojo, but it is the mojo of a stranger, so they never make it into service here. They are better at being their own little culinary Smithsonian than they are at making fried corn, or smothered chicken.

A few weeks ago, I took a bold step and gave away the other pots and pans—a piece here, a couple there, keeping only the ones that I started with. Funny how life leads us back to family, if we let it. Even if it is through our cast-iron skillets.

Death by Lobster Pad Thai

by Steve Almond
from *Death by Pad Thai*

Steve Almond is blessed with a short-storyist's gift for homing in on the absurd side of human situations. The tale of a weekend's massive mass cooking project is perfect material for his witty, high-energy writing style.

I am frightened of many things: death, Mormons, Stilton cheese, scorpions, Dick Cheney, the freeways of Los Angeles. But I am perhaps most frightened by lobsters. The spiny antennae, the armor-plated cephalothorax, the serrated claws—they are, to my way of thinking, giant, aquatic cockroaches that can snap your finger off.

I mention this because for the past few years now I have been heading up to Maine to visit my pals Tom and Scott, and specifically to partake of the transcendent Lobster Pad Thai that they prepare together, lovingly, painstakingly, over the course of a long, drunken summer afternoon.

And because, this past summer, I played an unwitting (and unwilling) role in the preparation of the greatest single Lobster Pad Thai in the history of man. And of lobster.

It began with a simple request: would I be willing to stop by an establishment called Taylor Seafood to pick up some things:

Of course I would.

"We'll need a pound or two of shrimp," Tom said. "And some lobsters."

I swallowed.

"They're selling four-pound lobsters at a great price."

I now spent perhaps half a minute trying, and failing, to imagine myself picking up a four-pound lobster, with my actual hands.

"Hello?" Tom said. "Hello?"

"Yes," I said miserably.

"Did you get that?"

"Yeah. I got it. Four-pound lobsters."

"Four of them. We'll reimburse you when you get here."

You'll reimburse me, I thought, *if I live that long.*

I'm not sure how many of you out there have seen a four-pound lobster. (Most of what you see in the grocery stores or restaurants are less than half that.) Neither my girlfriend, Erin, nor I was quite prepared.

The creatures were—as Tom would later observe, unhelpfully —larger than many newborn infants. Their tails were Japanese fans. Their claws were baseball mitts. They squirmed unhappily as the guy working the counter packed them into flimsy plastic bags. The biggest one swung toward me before he was lowered down and I am here to tell you there was murder in those beady, stalked eyes.

Yes, of course the claws were bound with thick bands. The animals had been rendered sluggish by ice and air. They were in no condition to attack. And yet . . .

And yet the true phobia is marked not by the threat of actual harm, but by a fantasy in which the subject imagines harm into being. Thus, as Erin drove north, as the bags rustled about in the backseat, I felt certain the lobsters were merely *pretending* to be sluggish and out of sorts while, in fact, communicating with one another via their antennae, biding their time, preparing to launch a coordinated attack. How might this happen? I didn't know exactly. I envisioned them using their tails in a sort of ninja-pogo maneuver, bouncing from dashboard to emergency brake, while snapping at our fragile extremities.

Thus I kept close watch over the bags until such a time as we arrived at the home of Scott and his partner Liza, who is Tom's sister. Also on hand for our arrival were Tom's lovely wife, Karen, and their two darling children, Annabel (age: almost eight) and

Jacob (age: four), all of whom gathered in the kitchen as we lugged the four heavy bags inside.

Scott immediately opened a bag and hoisted one of our purchases out. He whistled admiringly while Jacob, perhaps the only other one of us who realized the danger we were in, took a step backward.

Some background is in order.

Fifteen years ago I flew down to Miami to interview for a job at the alternative weekly and, after two days of vapid schmoozing, decided not to take the job. Then two things happened: I ate my first bowl of black bean soup. And I met Tom, the managing editor, for a cup of coffee. I felt, almost immediately, that I had found a long-lost older brother, the kind of guy who might rescue me from my own glib excesses, both as a writer and as a human being.

There is plenty to explain this. We're both Jews, suburban depressives, painfully susceptible to the song of language. In the four years we spent together in Miami, Tom taught me most of what I know about writing. He also taught me how to eat.

I can remember practically every meal I've eaten with him over the years: not just the epic, five-course Am Ex–buster partaken at Kennebunkport's hallowed White Barn Inn, but the pillowy gnocchi in vodka sauce ordered from a tiny Miami trattoria called Oggi, as well as any number of grilled fryers, exquisitely prepared by Tom himself, using butter, rosemary, and sea salt.

The man has always been something of a foodnik. But in recent years, his culinary interests have bloomed. Part of this is due to Karen, whose abilities are of such a caliber that she routinely enters (and wins) national recipe contests. But it is Scott, his cheery brother-in-law, who has been his most concerted enabler.

Karen and Tom are deeply in love, and cooking has become the purest expression of their mutual devotion. For a number of years, they prepared crab cakes together. A few years ago, they decided to undertake lobster pad thai.

Tom's reasoning was based on the following factors:

1. He refuses, on principle, to eat lobster outside the state of Maine;

2. His central goal, therefore, when visiting Scott and
   Liza each summer is to eat lobster every single day;
3. The rest of his family, especially his children, do
   not care to eat lobster every single day;
4. The pad thai format is one way of sneaking lobster past these ungrateful philistines;
5. The recipe plays to Scott's strengths as a cook: an
   ability to organize and prep tremendous amounts
   of ingredients (what the French call, somewhat
   grandly, *mise en place*).

It is Liza's contention that her brother Tom employs one additional factor, namely that this recipe calls for the use of every single
utensil in her kitchen.

To return to the scene of my terror: Scott was holding one of the
lobsters in his hand, sort of waving it about, so that its claws
clacked like castanets. Jacob and I were not amused. Eventually, the
lobsters were shuttled down to the basement fridge. The people
rejoiced. (At least, I rejoiced.) Erin and I were fed many scones. A
miniature golf excursion was proposed, then a long discussion
concerning Liza's latest sandwich creation, a lobster roll Reuben,
which sounded obscene, delicious, and capable of clogging a major
coronary artery at fifty paces.

An hour or so after noon, Tom and Scott stood up and looked
at one another and announced (in the same way I imagine the lead
climbers announce an assault on the summit of Everest) that it was
time to get started.

I feared this would mean a reappearance of the lobsters, but
there was a good deal to be done before that. The chefs use a
recipe from Jasper White's noble volume, *Lobster at Home,* one
White attributes to Gerald Clare. As with most Asian recipes, it
calls for various esoteric ingredients (shrimp paste, fish sauce, Thai
basil, cilantro), all of which must be precisely measured, poured,
mixed, whipped, and variously sliced.

It may well be true that Tom and Scott use every single utensil
in Liza's kitchen. But it is equally true that they have a fantastic
time doing so.

Indeed, for me, the second great pleasure of the Lobster Pad Thai ritual (after the eating, at which we will arrive in due time) is watching these two commandeer the kitchen. Their style, in terms of grace and economy of motion, calls to mind Astaire and Rogers, though in terms of alcoholic consumption Martin and Lewis might be closer to the mark.

Scott does most of the blade work and it says something profound about both his skills with his trusty eight-inch Wüsthof Classic, and my own culinary incompetence, that I have watched the man julienne lemongrass for a full ten minutes.

Both chefs do a good bit of punning, with Tom—a longtime headline writer—taking the lead. (To give you a flavor of his style, consider this groaner, which topped the review of a particularly abject Chinese eatery: WONTON NEGLECT.)

These shenanigans compose a kind of theater in the round, given that the kitchen is the home's central hub, and given that their pace is, to put it charitably, a leisurely one. It is not uncommon to hear Liza and/or Karen observe that they could make the same meal in an hour, rather than six. Scott and Tom are entirely impervious to such kibitzing.

This is what I find so enchanting: that two men should lose themselves in the spell of collaboration. My own experience, growing up with two brothers, did not include group cooking. We preferred a regimen of beating one another to a pulp.

So Scott and Tom were having a swell time cooking, and I was having a swell time watching them and Liza and Karen were having a swell time both not having to cook and gently mocking their husbands for being slowpokes; the kids were climbing all over Erin. The afternoon was cooling off. The ginger had been minced, the scallions finely chopped.

"Is it time?" Tom said.

Scott nodded and went out back to fire up the propane-heated Turkey Fryer that he and had Liza bought a few years earlier (I believe I've conveyed that they're foodies). This could mean only one thing: the reappearance of the lobsters.

Yes, up they came from the basement. Scott carried two of them outside and lowered them, tail first, into the scalding water.

Erin, who is a vegetarian on moral grounds but eats seafood, wanted no part of this. None of the females did, actually. Scott and Tom were interested in a purely scientific sense: How many four-pound lobsters could fit in your standard Turkey Fryer? (Answer: two, and just barely.)

In the end, Jacob and I were left to watch the pot and its unhappy crustaceans. I am sorry to report that they did not die immediately. One in particular did a good bit of writhing before giving up the ghost.

"Is it still alive?" Jacob said.

"No," I said. "Those are just death throes."

"But it's moving."

"Yes, that's right. But sometimes an animal makes little movements after it has already died."

Jacob looked at me skeptically.

"Well, what's that stuff?" he asked finally.

The lobsters were emitting strings of pearly, coagulating liquid.

"That's . . . that's . . . I don't know exactly."

Jacob had been curious about the lobster boiling in the way of morbid four-year-olds, but this latest development exceeded his tolerance. He headed back inside.

The lobsters were dead now, no question. Their shells were turning a luminous red beneath a veil of briny steam. I had watched them perish. I felt bad about this. They were innocent creatures, after all. Terrifically ugly and potentially lethal, but only if I found myself on the ocean floor, a place I did not often find myself.

Tom and Scott appeared. Their central concern was timing. How long did it take to parboil a four-pounder? Scott poked at one of the lobsters. I decided that I probably needed a beer.

In terms of lobster guilt, the cooking phase was only a prelude. For the central scene of the entire pad thai drama resided in the gathering of the partially cooked lobster meat, which required the complete destruction of each animal's exoskeleton, and the scrupulous removal of every single morsel therefrom.

To bolster this effort, Tom had bestowed upon Scott several Christmases earlier an implement which has since come to be known (to them, at least) as *The Eviscerator,* a pair of truly fearsome kitchen shears used to cut through the shell of a lobster. Also used was the traditional claw hammer. The other members of the family gave the kitchen a wide berth.

I'm not sure that I can describe the action adequately, other than to say that it made open-heart surgery look relatively tame. This was nothing like the dainty dissections performed by casual diners on restaurant lobsters. It was carnage, an orgy of twisting and snapping and hacking and smashing and poking and the emission of numerous fluids.

To say that Scott and Tom enjoyed this ritual is to understate the case. They conducted their business in a giggling ecstasy. This was a treasure hunt, with gratifying elements of gross-out humor.

Tom peeled off the top of one tail to reveal a dark, veiny line.

"What's that?" I said.

"Back end of the digestive system," Scott said.

"It's full of shit," Tom said.

"The stutter," Scott said.

"The poop pipe," Tom said.

They had each drunk about a six-pack.

There was also a great deal of green gunk, which is called tomalley [insert your own pun here] and is technically, somehow, the lobster's liver. Scott would later inform me, rather against my will, that he and Tom sometimes smear tomalley on a piece of bread, a snack he describes as "pungently tasty." (On a related though unnecessary health note, Scott felt compelled to warn me that tomalley should not be consumed by pregnant women or children, because it contains toxins, which he claims, implausibly, can be counteracted by the consumption of beer.)

The harvest went on for nearly an hour, because the four-pounders were so incredibly large and because both men pride themselves on a thorough evacuation of all body cavities.

It is a strange thing to see the source of your phobia systematically disemboweled. It made me feel guilty again. These lobsters were senior citizens, after all. They might have been grandparents. For all I knew they had been involved in the labor movement. I saw them scuttling feebly along the ocean floor, muttering curses at the agile, young lobsters, lining up for the early-bird specials on krill.

It was time for me to go into the living room.

When I returned a half hour later, a large silver bowl sat on the counter, brimming with glistening lobster meat. It was more lobster than any of us had ever seen. We took turns lifting the bowl and trying to guess how much was in there.

The formal weigh-in: 5.7 pounds.

Dusk was now approaching. The shadows on the back lawn had grown long. Tom and Scott took some time to clean up the kitchen, then devoted themselves to the preparation of a batch of Vietnamese spring rolls, which were to be served in honor of Annabel's upcoming birthday, along with *nuoc cham,* a tasty lime-juice-and-fish-sauce dip, which the birthday girl (somewhat predictably, according to Tom) refused to eat.

This was, in its own way, an involved process, one that required wrapping noodles, shrimp, vegetables, and cilantro in fragile rice paper. I was even more impressed by the notion that an almost-eight-year-old child would request such a delicacy. My own ideal meal at that age consisted of Chef Boyardee Beefaroni, Ho Hos, and Orange Crush.

With the spring rolls done, Tom and Scott turned to the main event: stir-frying. Owing to the sheer volume of the batch, this had to be done in two shifts. Scott made sure the right ingredients were going into the wok at the right intervals and Tom stirred, somewhat frantically. First peanut oil and the lobster (the smell was dizzying), then ginger, lemongrass, chili paste, shrimp paste, sugar, rice stick noodles, fish sauce, lemon and lime juice, scallions, and egg.

The formal recipe calls for this stew to be dished up in separate bowls, with peanuts, bean sprouts, and cilantro. Then, and I quote, "Garnish with lime wedge and sprigs of Thai basil and *crisscross the lobster antennae over the top.*" (Italics mine.)

Thankfully, Tom and Scott dispensed with the froufrou approach and simply made up two huge, communal bowls. We gathered on the screened-in porch. For a few moments, we could only stare at the lobster pad thai. It was like the gastroporn on the Food Network: too beautiful for our mouths.

Then someone (I suspect me) spooned a portion onto my plate and all hell broke loose.

I must note here that I am generally not a fan of pad thai. Because often, in restaurants, the pad thai has been sitting around for a while and it gets dried out and—owing to some strange alchemy of, I think, the rice noodles and the fish sauce—smells like old socks.

This pad thai, however, was so fresh, so exquisitely prepared, as to explode on the tongue: the aromatic herbs, the loamy snap of the bean sprouts, the citrus juices, the chewy noodles, the crunchy peanuts and, at the center of the action, the sweet succulence of the lobster. I can't begin to describe the experience of this pad thai; words are inadequate, because all of these flavors and textures were being experienced simultaneously, actually interacting in the course of each bite.

And here's what made the whole thing so special: Tom and Scott were right in front of us, downing impressive quantities of wine and beaming. They had cooked this feast for us, for our enjoyment, and just as much for themselves, for the sheer pleasure of a thing created together.

It made me think of all the stories Tom and I had worked on over the years—more than a hundred. It was what Tom thrived on, the chance to guide a process, to help headstrong schmucks like me get my sentences in order, to usher beauty into the world.

And I thought of all the Monday nights we drove out to the Miami Shores Bridge Club for three hours of cutthroat duplicate under the yellow lights, how deftly Tom played, and how patient he was in the face of my incessant overbidding.

It made me a little choked up, to think of all the history between us and how we could never have that back.

People were offering toasts now. To the intrepid chefs. To the lobsters. To The Eviscerator. We had been at the table for nearly two hours. The candles were burning down. The kids had gone to bed. I was on my fourth serving.

There was some debate over whether this was the best pad thai Tom and Scott had ever prepared. I did not see how one could make a better pad thai, and I said so. Then, after checking with the proper authorities, I began to eat directly out of the giant bowl.

The rest of the evening begins to get a little blurry. I believe I suggested that Tom and Scott consider opening a restaurant dedicated exclusively to lobster pad thai (suggested name: *Booth & Claw*), though there is some chance that I merely thought this to myself.

I know there was a dessert and that it involved chocolate. We eventually went inside and played a rather silly game of something or other. For the most part, we sat in stunned gratitude, digesting.

The next morning, Erin and I had to return to Boston. We did so reluctantly, and only after securing a large plastic container stuffed with pad thai. It was half-gone before we left Maine.

Alabama's Best Covered-Dish Dinner

by John T. Edge

from *Food & Wine*

John T. Edge—director of the invaluable Southern Foodways Alliance and author of *Southern Belly: The Ultimate Food Lover's Companion to the South*—has an instinctive appreciation of whatever it is that makes Southern cooks special. His fly-on-the-wall reporting style lets the cooks' magic reveal itself naturally.

In the Northwestern Alabama Towns of Tuscumbia, Sheffield, Muscle Shoals and Florence, known collectively as the Shoals, a community of homegrown artists, designers and cultural provocateurs gathers each month for a potluck dinner. By and large, they are not cooks by trade. Instead, they are cooks by habit and social inclination. Surety with a cast-iron skillet is bred in their bones.

This place made these people. The Shoals was once a textile center; the forebears of these artists and designers were cotton farmers and laborers who earned their wages with their hands. When the mills closed, blue-collar jobs with benefit packages and pensions vanished. But an appreciation of handwork remained. Nowadays, among this diverse coterie, respect for that tradition serves as common ground. Honoring handcraft is a common cause. And food—culinary handwork—offers a reason to gather, a catalyst for conversation.

The group is deeply Southern, but the people defy stereotypes. Metal artist, builder and hunter Audwin McGee of Tuscumbia is the man behind the juicy garlic-rubbed pork roast at the center of the table. With his fiancée, Sandi Stevens, a lithe Alabama-born gymnast and sculptor, he's this month's host. To a casual observer, his second-story loft, set amid a row of redbrick storefronts in downtown Tuscumbia, calls to mind downtown Manhattan, but it's bona fide Southern. "Cleaning up before renovation," says McGee of the hardwood-floored rectangle that once served as storage space for a dry goods store, "we found dozens of blue-and-white-striped seersucker suits."

The flow of the dinner is easy. No one stands on ceremony. No one raises a toast to signal either the beginning of the meal, or the end. Across a table piled high with Southern sacraments, the friends talk about their mothers' recipes for leaf-lard piecrust and their fathers' formulas for barbecue sauce. They talk about great local cooks. About the men who gather on fall mornings to stir giant pots of chicken stew for church fund-raisers. About the women at Florence's Hollywood Inn who fry cornmeal-dusted okra to a peerless crisp. And, yes, they swap recipes.

Natalie Chanin, who hails from Florence, baked the downy buttermilk biscuits that everyone is slathering with butter. She's the designer and entrepreneur behind Alabama Chanin, who, through her former label, Project Alabama, sold the runway critics on densely patterned and elaborately beaded dresses stitched by local sewing circles. "Love your thread," Chanin was fond of telling the women who joined together at her country ranch house headquarters. "Love your thread." With Chanin are her boyfriend, Butch Anthony, a laconic and dry-witted artist whose work—cake stands bolted together from cast-off garden implements, serving bowls cleverly crafted from cow vertebrae—defies easy categorization, and Thom Driver, who helped style Chanin's Project Alabama catalog.

Angie Mosier, proprietor of retro-hip Blue-Eyed Daisy Bakeshop in Palmetto, Georgia, is a welcome interloper. She earned her entrée by pan-frying chicken drumsticks and thighs. Mosier also brought a tin of pecan sandies and creamy lemon chess pies. She got to know the Shoals crowd when the University of Mississippi–based Southern Foodways Alliance, of which Mosier is the board vice president, teamed with Chanin to collect oral histories of area cooks and showcase their stories and recipes in Chanin's Project Alabama catalog and on its Web site.

The cheese grits casserole—so light it might as well be called a soufflé—is a specialty of Billy Reid and his wife, Jeanne. From a second-story atelier set in an antebellum Florence home, he designs eponymous lines of clothing that evoke sepia snapshots of a vague Southern past. Yet Reid is quick to buck convention. At his Florence shop as well as at boutiques in Charlotte, North Carolina, and Dallas and Houston, he mixes and matches genres, displaying Alabama-designed and Italian-made wingtips atop gilt-rimmed cake plates that look as though Reid lifted them from his great-aunt's china cabinet.

Charles Moore, a Tuscumbia native who documented the civil rights movement for *Life* and the eldest of the group, has come, too. Along with local photographer Robert Rausch—bearer of a broccoli casserole bound with homemade cream of mushroom soup and topped with a crumble of Ritz crackers—he's taken on the task of documenting dinner.

At the table, it becomes clear that while these Southerners are rooted in place, they are not bound by it. As the biscuits are passed and the fried chicken is reduced to a jumble of bones, Chanin tells the story of quitting her life as a stylist in Vienna to hone her kitchen skills while working as a cook on an island in Los Roques, a Venezuelan archipelago. "The fishing families on the island couldn't pronounce *biscuit*," she says, "so they started calling what I baked *pan de* Alabama." McGee is full of stories from a trip to Mozambique, where, along with fellow Alabamians, he has been developing a sustainable hunting preserve and pondering how to develop the East African nation's tourism industry.

In the tradition of the church suppers of their youth, everyone talks at once, and almost everyone returns for seconds. As Chanin recalls her early days in New York City, snipping apart and then stitching back together T-shirts to make contrarian couture, the men debate the relative merits of two local steak houses. There's no clear victor apparent until Chanin steps in. "Dale's still gives you a glass of cold tomato juice to start your meal," she says. "It's really old-school." And the debate is settled, for now.

About the time Mosier slices into a chess pie and passes plates to all, a bottle of bourbon appears. Someone suggests a dessert wine as the proper accompaniment but is shouted down as three fingers of bourbon go into each diner's glass. In time, the group adjourns to the sleeping porch, and conversations trail off as everyone watches the moon rise alongside the Tuscumbia water tower.

∞∞

Supercrispy Pan-Fried Chicken

Instead of deep-frying chicken in a vat of oil, Angie Mosier prefers pan-frying, which creates delightfully crunchy and moist chicken without requiring quite so much oil. "For a covered-dish dinner, there's nothing better than a tray of drumsticks, which are easy to eat standing up," she says.

16 pieces of chicken (preferably drumsticks and thighs)
6 cups buttermilk
3 cups all-purpose flour
4 teaspoons salt
2 teaspoons freshly ground black pepper
1 teaspoon cayenne pepper
1 ½ quarts vegetable oil, for frying

1. In a large bowl, toss the chicken pieces with the buttermilk. Cover with plastic wrap and refrigerate the chicken for at least 8 hours or overnight.

2. In a large, resealable plastic bag, combine the flour, salt, black pepper and cayenne. Set 2 large wire racks over rimmed baking sheets. Working in batches, drain the chicken, scraping off most of the buttermilk against the side of the bowl. Add the chicken to the bag, a few pieces at a time, and shake to coat completely. Transfer the chicken to the racks, pressing the flour to help it adhere as you remove the chicken from the bag.

3. Pour 1 inch of oil into each of 2 large cast-iron skillets and heat to 350°F. Add about half of the chicken to the oil, being sure not to crowd the skillet. Fry over moderate heat

until the chicken is golden, crisp and cooked through, 20 to 25 minutes; an instant-read thermometer should register 165°F for thighs or drumsticks and 160° for breasts. Line the racks with paper towels and drain the chicken. Continue frying the chicken in batches, being sure the oil temperature stays at 325°F during frying. Serve warm or at room temperature.

SERVES 12–16

Buttery Buttermilk Biscuits

When she was growing up. Natalie Chanin ate homemade biscuits every day. "Now, I suppose, people don't make them from scratch as much," she says. "They seem like some kind of luxury." In truth, Chanin's light, flaky biscuits are incredibly easy to make—just don't overwork the dough or the biscuits will get tough.

2 cups all-purpose flour, plus more for rolling
2 teaspoons baking powder
1 teaspoon salt
1 stick plus 2 tablespoons unsalted butter—1 stick cut into
    cubes and chilled, 2 tablespoons melted
¾ cup buttermilk

1. Preheat the oven to 425°F. In a large bowl, combine the 2 cups of flour with the baking powder and salt. Using a pastry blender or 2 knives, cut in the cubed butter until the mixture resembles coarse meal. Add the buttermilk and stir with a fork or wooden spoon until a soft dough forms. Turn the dough out onto a lightly floured work surface and knead 2 or 3 times, just until it comes together.

2. Using a lightly floured rolling pin, roll out the dough ½ inch thick. Using a lightly floured 2 ¼-inch round cutter, stamp out biscuits as close together as possible. Pat the dough scraps together and stamp out more biscuits. Transfer the biscuits to a large baking sheet. Bake for about 20 minutes, until the biscuits are risen and golden. Brush the hot

biscuits with the melted butter and serve them hot or at room temperature.

MAKES FIFTEEN 2 ¼-INCH BISCUITS

Lane Cake

Lane cake, an Alabama specialty, was created by a woman named Emma Rylander Lane, who wrote a cookbook called Some Good Things to Eat *around the turn of the 20th century. Typically, Lane cake is a large white cake with a filling of egg yolks, sugar, raisins, pecans, fresh coconut and lots of bourbon. Here, it's frosted with silky vanilla buttercream. The bourbon in the filling is key—it helps cut the sweetness a bit.*

For the Cake
3½ cups all-purpose flour
1 tablespoon baking powder
¼ teaspoon salt
2 sticks unsalted butter, at room temperature
2 cups sugar
1 teaspoon pure vanilla extract
1 cup milk
8 large egg whites (reserve the yolks for the filling)

For the Filling
1 ½ cups pecans (6 ounces)
1 ½ sticks unsalted butter
12 large egg yolks
1 ½ cups sugar
1 ½ cups unsweetened shredded coconut
1 ½ cups golden raisins, coarsely chopped
¼ cup bourbon
For the Buttercream
2 sticks unsalted butter, at room temperature
1 teaspoon pure vanilla extract
¼ teaspoon salt

1 pound confectioners' sugar, sifted
¼ cup half-and-half or milk

1. Make the cake: Preheat the oven to 325°F. Butter three 9-inch round cake pans. Line the bottoms with parchment paper; butter the paper and flour the pans. In a large bowl, whisk the flour, baking powder and salt. In a standing electric mixer fitted with a paddle attachment, beat the butter and sugar at medium speed until light and fluffy. Beat in the vanilla. At low speed, beat in the dry ingredients and the milk in 3 alternating batches; be sure to scrape the side and bottom of the bowl.

2. In a clean bowl, beat the egg whites until soft peaks form. Beat one-third of the egg whites into the cake batter. Using a rubber spatula, fold in the remaining beaten whites until combined. Divide the cake batter among the prepared pans. Bake for 25 to 30 minutes, until the cakes are lightly golden and springy to the touch. Let the cakes cool in the pans for a few minutes, then invert them onto wire racks to cool completely. Peel off the parchment paper from the bottoms.

3. Meanwhile, make the filling: Spread the pecans on a baking sheet and toast for 10 minutes, until fragrant. Let cool, then coarsely chop. In a medium saucepan, melt the butter over low heat. Remove from the heat and whisk in the egg yolks and sugar until smooth. Return the pan to moderate heat and cook the filling, stirring constantly, until slightly thickened and an instant-read thermometer reads 180°F: be sure not to let it boil. Remove from the heat and stir in the chopped pecans, coconut, raisins and bourbon. Transfer to a bowl and let cool.

4. Make the buttercream: In a medium bowl, beat the butter until creamy. Add the vanilla and salt, then gradually beat in the confectioners' sugar, being sure to scrape the side and bottom of the bowl. Add the half-and-half and beat the buttercream until fluffy, about 1 minute.

5. Assemble the cake: Place a cake layer on a serving plate and top with one-third of the pecan filling, spreading it

almost to the edge. Top with a second cake layer and another third of the pecan filling. Top with the last cake layer. Using an offset spatula, spread a thin layer of the buttercream all around the cake, being sure to fill in any gaps between the layers. Refrigerate the cake for 10 minutes, to firm up the buttercream.

6. Spread the remaining buttercream evenly around the side of the cake only, leaving the top with just the thin layer of buttercream. Spread the remaining pecan filling over the top of the cake. Let the cake stand at room temperature for at least 4 hours before cutting.

SERVES 12–16

The Age of Casseroles

by Irene Sax

from *Saveur*

The former food editor of New York's *Newsday*, Irene Sax spins a little culinary history in this magazine essay, taking us back to a pre–Julia Child era of home cooking. As one who was there, Sax recalls those times in nostalgic, mouthwatering detail.

It must be years—no, decades—since I last made a casserole: I mean an all-American one-pot meal of ground beef, elbow macaroni, and canned tomatoes or of tuna, noodles, and a white sauce. But there was a time, back in the 1950s, when casseroles were standard fare in my kitchen. I made them not only for family suppers but also on the occasions when, after much polishing of wedding present silver, ironing of napkins, and brooding about hors d'oeuvres, I put together a grown-up dinner party.

In those days I lived with my husband and three small children in Rochester, New York, where snow fell from November through April. We had four rooms in university housing and, unable to afford restaurants or babysitters, swapped dinner party invitations with other couples just like us. But don't imagine that these were slapdash affairs. We read the magazines; we knew how things were supposed to be done.

In the winter, the sun set at around four in the afternoon and the kids went to bed at six. That left me an hour to dash around, scooping up toys from the living-room floor and giving the bathroom a quick, pine-scented once-over. I'd shove my jeans into the hamper, dive into the loose Guatemalan dress I used as a hostess gown, and then stick the shepherd's pie that I'd prepared earlier that day into the oven. By the time the guests arrived, at seven (often with a sleeping infant they'd lay in the center of our bed), there were candles on the pullout table and ice in the ice bucket.

I can't believe how much we could drink in those days: not just martinis and Manhattans but strange concoctions that we got from cocktail books and from my splattered copy of *The Joy of Cooking*. We'd sip our rob roys and sidecars, smoke our Pall Malls, and eat deviled eggs while the women talked about their children and the men about their jobs. When I finally carried the shepherd's pie to the table, all steamy and crusty, and served it with garlic bread, a green salad, and glasses of Gallo white, I knew that we were living the good life. That's because, back then, casseroles, traditionally used for making food go farther in hard times, were actually considered chic.

Today, of course, casseroles are hopelessly out of style, done in by a combination of prosperity and the availability of ever more convenient supermarket foods. But while they've become dated, they are by no means dead. Despite ups and downs in prestige, casseroles have always enjoyed a solid grassroots popularity.

For one thing, they can be delicious. Omit the garlic salt and Durkee fried onions that blighted your grandmother's hot chicken salad, and you may be surprised at how good it tastes. For another, virtually anyone can make them. Recipes for casseroles tend to be easy and forgiving: everything goes into the dish and the dish goes into the oven, where it may stay for anywhere from minutes to hours.

Perhaps best of all, casseroles are truly and traditionally American. Look in any local charity cookbook, and amid recipes for today's tomato-and-basil salads you'll find casseroles or, depending on the region, "hot dishes." Many of these recipes are forever attached to the home cooks who invented them: it's not just any old noodle surprise casserole; it's Aunt Millie's noodle surprise casserole. In older books, Aunt Millie was often the family's live-in cook. In the oldest books she might have been an ex-slave. Casseroles are who we are, or at least who we used to be.

The name casserole, like much of our culinary heritage, is

European, taken from the heavy, covered French pots of the same name. The word itself probably comes from the archaic French term *casse* (pan), and the dish is related to ones like cassoulet. In this country, by the end of the 19th century, the old-world stews and braises that are the American casserole's forebears began to evolve into one-pot mixtures of protein, starch, sauce, and, often, vegetables. James Villas, author of *Crazy for Casseroles* and one of the few contemporary food writers who admit to loving them (he calls them "the true cooking of America"), says they've been popular in the South since Reconstruction, when women were suddenly faced with the challenge of feeding their households with limited supplies of food and no kitchen help.

Recipes for dishes called casseroles started to become common in American cookbooks during the First World War. But it wasn't until the Depression and, soon afterward, the food shortages of the Second World War that casseroles turned into the objects of a national enthusiasm. Marian and Nino Tracy's *Casserole Cookery*, for instance, an iconic book published in 1941, went through 13 printings in the next ten years.

The main impetus behind the popularity of casseroles was thrift. Casseroles are as close as you can get to bottomless pots, meals that are easily stretched to feed extra mouths at church suppers or fund-raisers or when unexpected company shows up. When meat was rationed during the war, a housewife could expand her family's allotment of protein by adding beans, noodles, or rice, along with a liquid, to produce a hearty meal. She probably also figured out quickly that casseroles provided a great way to use leftovers, meat or otherwise. A famous post-Thanksgiving dish, known as, among other things, turkey-stuffing strata, combines leftover turkey and stuffing moistened with leftover gravy.

If casseroles saved money, they also saved time and effort. The mother who toiled all day on an assembly line or in an office could put everything into she pot and refrigerate it before she left for work in the morning. When she got home and the whole concoction had had a good day's rest, it went into the oven. And, since the cooking pot could be placed directly on the table, there was one piece fewer to wash when dinner was over.

How did such earnest, honest, utterly cozy family dishes become the stars of my dinner parties in the late 1950s? Well, after the war, the food sensibilities of average Americans were refined significantly. Perhaps that had to do with the fact that returning soldiers brought home a taste for then exotic fare like pizza, but more likely it was because America's interest in the world outside its borders was growing—our insularity was dissolving. Strange as it seems today, casseroles had a romantic, earthy aura that evoked European meals. In his 1955 *Casserole Cookbook,* no less a gastronome than James Beard calls them "an ingenious European idea with a unique American twist," lauding the ability of French peasants to give "inexpensive odds and ends of food . . . an almost miraculous savor."

And remember that the men may have come back after the war, but not the household help, who had graduated to blue- and white-collar jobs. Middle-class women who through the early 20th century could count on at least one "girl" to help out at dinner parties were forced to do it all on their own. What could be more efficient and impressive than a casserole? Frugality was no longer a concern: some postwar books contain recipes featuring crabmeat, lobster, or steak. Given their capacity for surviving long delays, finished casseroles could remain in a warm oven while the host poured another round of daiquiris. They were considered respectable party fare well into the 1960s, when Julia Child's flutey voice first emanated from television sets, instructing us in how to master the art of French cooking.

What happened? What changed all that? Blame the seductive powers of TV dinners and store-bought "dinner mixes," like Hamburger Helper. Blame the fact that Americans traveling to Europe in ever greater numbers got to taste the real thing. Or blame the new abundance and variety of fresh produce and the growing sense that baked dishes were heavy and slow and square when we were starting to admire speed and lightness and lemongrass.

You can also blame the laziness that was replacing thrift in many American kitchens: so many casseroles had degenerated into slapped-together mixtures of bouillon cubes and frozen and canned foods—they became a symbol of convenience, not quality.

Women who prided themselves on conquering Julia Child's notorious 13-page recipe for french bread might make tuna–noodle casserole for their families but wouldn't dream of serving it to guests on a Saturday night. That dish, and its sisters, came to be designated by the slightly condescending label "comfort food"—dishes that we confess, with a self-mocking smile, that we used to like back before we knew any better.

Maybe it's time to take another look. These days, we serve champagne instead of martinis, and the jug wine has given way to albariño. The Guatemalan dress is long gone, as are the cigarettes. And everyone is on a diet. But wouldn't it be lovely to go to a dinner party some wintry evening and watch your hostess carry in an earthenware pot of bubbling chicken divan with, of course, a green salad and a loaf of crusty bread?

—∞—

Shepherd's Pie

Shepherd's pie gets its name from the romantic notion that it was eaten by shepherds in the north of England long ago. We decided to make ours with lamb, keeping the spirit of the idea. When made with beef, this classic casserole is usually called cottage pie in England.

14 tbsp. butter
2 lbs. lamb shoulder, trimmed and cut into ½" cubes
2 leeks, white parts only, finely chopped
2 medium carrots, chopped
2 tbsp. flour
1 ½ cups beef stock
1 tbsp. Worcestershire sauce
1 tbsp. finely chopped rosemary leaves
1 tbsp. finely chopped thyme leaves
⅛ tsp. freshly grated nutmeg
Salt and freshly ground black pepper
1 ½ cups frozen peas, thawed
3 large russet potatoes (about 2 lbs.), peeled and quartered
½ cup half-and-half

1. Melt 2 tbsp. butter in a large pot over high heat. Add one-third of the lamb and brown on all sides, 4–5 minutes. Using a slotted spoon, transfer lamb to a plate, leaving fat in pot. Repeat process 2 more times, using 2 tbsp. butter and one-third of the lamb for each batch. Add leeks and carrots to pot, reduce heat to medium, and cook until softened, scraping up any browned bits, 3–4 minutes. Return lamb and its juices to pot along with flour and cook, stirring frequently, for 1 minute. Whisk in stock, Worcestershire, rosemary, thyme, nutmeg, and salt and pepper to taste. Increase heat to medium-high; bring to a boil. Reduce heat to medium-low and simmer, covered, until lamb is tender, about 40 minutes. Uncover pot and simmer, stirring often, until thickened, 35–40 minutes more. Remove from heat, stir in peas, and set aside.

2. Meanwhile, put potatoes into a large pot and cover with salted water; bring to a boil. Reduce heat to medium-low and simmer until tender, 20–25 minutes. Drain and transfer potatoes to a bowl. Add 6 tbsp. butter, half-and-half, and salt and pepper to taste; mash smooth with a potato masher.

3. Preheat oven to 375°F. Transfer lamb mixture to a 2-quart casserole dish. Top evenly with mashed potatoes, making swirls and whorls with the back of a spoon. Cut remaining butter into small cubes; scatter over potatoes. Bake until golden brown and bubbling, about 30 minutes.

SERVES 6

Someone's in the Kitchen

The Great Carrot Caper

by Dan Barber

from *The New York Times Magazine*

To say that chef Barber knows his food is an understatement—at Blue Hill at Stone Barns up in Westchester County, New York, the menu is drawn from foods raised on its companion farm. It's an inspiring concept, even when it threatens to go awry . . .

Last December, right around Christmas, I received a small package from Jean-Marc Montegottero, an artisanal-nut-oil producer in Burgundy. The package contained a shoebox filled with dust. Flummoxed, I phoned his American distributor and importer and our mutual friend, Olivier Wittmann, to inquire about this strange gift.

The dust was almond residue, Olivier said, and he told me about a visit he made to Jean-Marc's on a cold October afternoon. As he walked up the path to his farmhouse, all he could smell was almonds. Figuring that Jean-Marc was making an almond tart for dessert, he opened the door to the kitchen and saw only a large *sautoir* of potatoes simmering gently in duck fat. Confused, he looked at Jean-Marc, who simply smiled. "Sit," he said. "Eat."

The potatoes smelled, and tasted, as Olivier would attest, like almond potatoes. Jean-Marc, a scrupulous recycler, collected the flourlike dust after pressing almonds for the oil and spread it over his potato field like compost. Through a kind of magical osmosis, the almond potatoes were born.

Jean-Marc's gift to me could not have come at a better time.

Fall harvest at Stone Barns was a waning memory. Dark clouds of root vegetables and cabbages were on the horizon. I seized on the nut idea—with carrots instead of potatoes. Almonds and carrots are a better pairing, I thought. (Was this becoming competitive?)

Getting the cooks excited about the connections to the farm became one goal of the project. (Carlo Petrini, the founder of Slow Food, has often said that we ought not to think of ourselves as consumers but more as co-producers who are connected to the food we eat. Here was our chance.) But even more, I wanted them to know that their chef was always pushing for creativity and experimentation. Ferran Adrià may have espresso foam and olive-oil capsules, I thought, but he doesn't have carrots pre-infused with almonds. At night I dreamed of being on the cover of *Gourmet* magazine, wearing a black cowboy hat and cradling a bundle of carrots. Headline: "Chefs as Farmers-Scientists: The New Frontier in Food."

In the days that followed, the farmers dutifully (and skeptically) planted Napoli carrots and spread the almond dust over the rows. Meanwhile, I told the staff—first the cooks, then the waiters, then anyone who would listen—that we were engaged in a very exciting experiment. "A revolutionary harvest," I called it. But I said nothing about Jean-Marc. The excitement of being a creator-farmer-mad scientist was too intoxicating; I couldn't admit to the truth that I was more of a lucky chef-gentleman farmer-copy cat.

I used the next nine weeks as a buildup to the harvest, taking the cooks and waiters down to the greenhouse and showing them the almond carrots. I explained that my plan was to do nothing with them in the kitchen, or almost nothing, just serve them shaved and perhaps with a splash of vinaigrette. This dish would be about the wonders of nature, not about the creativity of the chef (false modesty, of course: in proposing to do nothing to the carrots I hoped everyone would concentrate on the creativity of the idea).

The week before the harvest I intensified the campaign. I spoke about the carrots at every family meal and made sure the cooks went to the greenhouse to weed and care for what was about to make history. I even got the valets excited, proudly showing off our little Manhattan Project. "Jesus, it sort of already smells like almonds," I heard one of the valets say as he walked away. "God-damn genius," the other said.

The Friday night of the harvest we were overbooked. News of the almond carrots buzzed in the dining room. For some reason the vegetables arrived a bit late that day, and there was the usual mayhem in prepping for dinner. So I didn't actually try the carrots until service began. How did they taste? Sweet and crisp, very delicious. But not like almonds. Not even a faint whisper of nuttiness. And nothing that suggested nutfulness in the future.

Just then the orders began trickling in: "Ordering, Table 41, a fennel soup and three almond-carrot salads." And then, "Ordering, Table 31, four almond-carrot salads followed by. . . ." It had begun.

Stunned, I reached for a mandoline and a bowl. I shaved the carrots very thinly, tossing them with lemon vinaigrette, salt, pepper and . . . and I added a splash of Jean-Marc's almond oil.

"Taste these," I said, and handed them around to the cooks and waiters.

"Wow," said Karen, our resident waiter-scholar. "Unbelievable almond flavor."

"They taste like a bowl of almonds," said Duncan, the wide-eyed vegetable cook.

We sold 66 almond-carrot salads, exhausting the entire day's harvest to great fanfare. I spent the beginning of the night making the salads in a fearful state of self-loathing: Would I be discovered for a fraud, like some South Korean scientist, pulled in front of my deceived co-workers and accused of duplicitous claims?

But there were only compliments and applause, questions about how to get involved with the farm and comment cards in a bulk we had never seen, four big stars written across the bottom of many. It was a hugely energetic night, filled with the wonder of this gentle genetic modification that the entire dining room believed it was experiencing.

Mysteriously, my furtive, last-minute maneuvers can't account for the overwhelming response, and I should know: in the chaos of trying to make so many salads, I often forgot—or was guilt at work here?—to add the almond oil.

"Oh, that doesn't matter," said an amused Karen when I confessed to her—a mini *culpa* after midnight. "The myth outdid the truth, and you got your almond carrots."

Not long afterward, I received a call from a well-known New

York chef I hadn't heard from in years. He called to "catch up," and five minutes into the conversation he said, "Hey, so I heard you're growing some funky nut carrot up there." There was a long pause. "Any for sale?"

Almond-Carrot Salad

For the almonds:
¾ cup whole blanched almonds
2 teaspoons sugar
1 teaspoon ground cumin
1 teaspoon olive oil
Juice of half a lemon
Salt and freshly ground white pepper

For the salad:
½ cup golden raisins
¼ cup white *verjus*
1 pound carrots, peeled
2 tablespoons white balsamic vinegar
2 teaspoons lemon juice
1 tablespoon almond oil
1 tablespoon extra-virgin olive oil
2 teaspoons minced shallots
Salt and freshly ground white pepper
1 packed cup mixed whole herbs, including parsley, chervil,
    dill and mint

1. Prepare the almonds: Preheat the oven to 375 degrees. In a small bowl, toss together the almonds, sugar, cumin, olive oil, lemon juice and a pinch each of salt and pepper. Spread the almonds on a baking sheet and toast until light brown, 10 to 12 minutes. Let cool.

2. Make the salad: In a small saucepan, bring the raisins and *verjus* to a boil. Remove from the heat and let cool. Strain the raisins, discarding the *verjus*.

3. Using a mandoline or sharp vegetable peeler, slice the carrots lengthwise into ribbons, applying pressure on the peeler so the ribbons aren't too thin. Place the carrots, vinegar, lemon juice, oils, shallots, cooled almonds and raisins in a large bowl. Season with salt and pepper, mix to combine and marinate for 10 minutes. Gently toss in the herbs and serve.

SERVES 4

Spoon-Fed

by John Grossmann
from *Gourmet*

It's a kitchen axiom: Chefs must taste the food to know if it tastes right. That's the premise freelance food writer Grossmann explores in this close-up of Tory McPhail at Commander's Palace, the renowned—and at last reopened—New Orleans restaurant.

One teaspoon of lobster citrus fumé.
One cooked shrimp.
One thin slice of mirliton.
One teaspoon of rémoulade sauce.

Tory McPhail, executive chef at Commander's Palace in New Orleans, is working his way down a long expanse of hot and cold appetizer ingredients known as the garde-manger. He dips a small plastic spoon into a mound of shrimp mousse, then reaches for a small leaf of romaine lettuce. At 11:35 on a December morning, McPhail is tasting everything on the line, monitoring the sauces and the menu components prepped by his sous-chefs and cooks. Taste no. 14 this morning: a quarter teaspoon of sugarcane vinaigrette. No. 15: a teaspoon of house-made mozzarella.

I know, because I'm standing at McPhail's elbow, writing down every bite. What he eats. When. How much.

You can blame it all on those spoons. On a previous visit to the Commander's Palace kitchen, I noticed a handful of the prosaic plastic utensils poking out of the breast pocket of McPhail's chef's jacket and inquired about them.

"I go through as many as two hundred of them in a single day," he said, effectively opening the kitchen door on a little-known reality at many top-tier restaurants: The chefs who run them, who devise elaborate, multicourse tasting menus, often go several days without sitting down to a single meal themselves. Ultimate grazers, like McPhail, they eat standing up—a spoonful of this, a bite of that, tasting and retasting throughout the day to help ensure that everything leaving their kitchen meets the highest standards.

That realization stirred up a notion. "Would you be game," I proposed, "to let me document everything you eat in one day, from the moment you arrive in the kitchen until the moment you head home at night?" I also suggested that we should have the final list analyzed to see how many calories he took in, how much fat, how much cholesterol.

Neither of us knew of any study examining this particular occupational hazard of being a top chef, so, in the interest of science, McPhail said yes. But, frankly, he had another reason, too—and it was beginning to make the front of his forgiving double-breasted chef's jacket bulge. Fresh from cooking school in Seattle at age 19, five feet ten inches tall and weighing 160 pounds, McPhail started on the middle station of the garde-manger at Commander's in 1993. Little more than a decade later, after working in Palm Beach, London, the Virgin Islands, Las Vegas, and, since 2002, back at Commander's as executive chef, he could no longer ignore the impact of his career choice. In his early thirties, his waistline ever expanding, McPhail was nearing the 200-pound mark.

We agreed that I'd shadow him for a day, and then ask Debbie Strong, a nutritionist at the Ochsner Health System in New Orleans, to analyze my findings.

So here I am, the designated food diarist following in McPhail's wake, dodging hot pans and hustling cooks as the first lunch orders begin to pick up the pace in the kitchen.

Taste no. 22: the day's *amuse-bouche*—a poker chip-size oval of bread topped with crab mousse, a blue-crab claw, microgreens, and a drizzle of tarragon oil. Next, McPhail ladles about a tablespoon of seafood gumbo onto a saucer, blows on it, then tilts the saucer and swallows. "Every time, just like that," he says to the newly hired cook who made it. "Taste it fifteen times so you know what it's like."

"Yes, sir," the cook replies.

Between more tastes, McPhail turns to me. "That was something that Ella Brennan instilled in me when I started at Commander's Palace. She'd always come into the kitchen and ask: 'Are you tasting the food? Are you tasting the food?' She called it Creolizing a cook. You have to get that sense of seasoning that only happens here in New Orleans."

Taste no. 39 is a Key lime sorbet. "Oooh," McPhail says, nodding his approval, before filling a second spoon for another taste—the first bite of the day just for him. As on most mornings, McPhail informs me, he started his day with only a cup of coffee. No breakfast.

A few moments later, he snags a spoonful from a big container of truffled buttermilk mashed potatoes headed for the line. "Your potatoes are cold, bud," he informs his cook.

At 12:37 P.M., McPhail goes to the back door of the restaurant to inspect a delivery of jumbo lump crabmeat. Removing the lid from one of the plastic containers, he inserts a thumb and forefinger and pops a snuff-size pinch of the snowy white meat into his mouth. "Sweet. Good. Not too salty," he says, before poaching a second sample.

Returning to the bustle of the ramping-up lunch rush and checking tickets, he sees it's almost time to plate the tournedos entrées for a party of 23. Folding down a stainless-steel, Murphy bed–like worktable, McPhail helps assemble the plates. Taste no. 57 confirms that the mashed potatoes are now up to temperature. He spoons a big mound of an onion and roasted-mushroom mixture into a hot pan, stirs it a bit, then samples three mushroom slices plucked from the pan. He adds some salt and pepper. Samples another mushroom. Then, with the aid of the sous-chef across from him, he starts plating tournedos atop mashed potatoes. Then a blanket of the mushroom-onion mixture. Then a generous drizzle of a *marchand de vin* sauce, a red-wine demi-glace that he tasted earlier (and pronounced "rockin' "). As soon as the plates are topped with domes, a waiter grabs the tray. The process resumes.

By 1:09 P.M., after helping assemble the chocolate mousse cake desserts for the same large party, McPhail pops a nugget of cooked chicken into his mouth and pauses to pour himself a Diet Pepsi.

"How many tastes do you think you've had so far?" I ask.

"Sixty?" he ventures.

Like a veteran pitcher cognizant of his count, he's amazingly close. That morsel of chicken was taste no. 61. He's been in the kitchen an hour and a half. Most of his workday still lies ahead.

"I don't think the average chef in a small town does what we do in this kitchen," he says. "When you get to this level you have to be so detail oriented. There's a lot of pressure to make sure everything is right on the money. We're micromanaging every single sauté pan and every single salad, because the guests expect quality. The thing that helps us to do that is tasting our food."

Just then, the pastry chef hands McPhail a molasses drop cookie dusted with powdered sugar. Tonight it will complement a skillet-seared foie gras. McPhail breaks the cookie in two and eats one half, then the other. A local beekeeper hoping to break into the Commander's pantry has sent a sample of her honey. After a taste of the honey and a bit of the comb, he decides to incorporate both into a dish on the evening's still-evolving tasting menu. Now McPhail accepts a Southern Comfort eggnog shooter, a midmeal shot of alcohol intended, he says, to aid digestion "by boring a hole in the stomach."

"More alcohol and more sugar," he says, after a quick bottoms-up. A follow-up half shot wins his approval.

With the first dinner customers settling into the dining room, McPhail's tasting resumes in earnest. Taste no. 79: a few crumbles of Point Reyes blue cheese; no. 84: a candied pecan; no. 99: a bite of rabbit sausage; no. 104: a half teaspoon of homemade Creole mustard.

In addition to tasting the dishes he sends out this evening, McPhail also eats as part of the hiring process. Stopping by the salad station early in the evening, he asks a culinary school graduate named Mary to make him an appetizer of her choosing. "No truffles or foie gras," he says. A bit later, he tells another Commander's wannabe named Cory to make him an entrée.

Mid-evening, he's up to taste no. 159: a piece of Belgian endive plucked from a salad about to be plated. He scowls. "David, have you tasted this salad?"

"Yes, chef."

"Perfect," McPhail says with a "gotcha" sort of smile, playfully reinforcing the mantra of the kitchen.

His next bite is a forkful of citrus-vinaigrette-dressed greens from Mary's appetizer, which she has topped with a couple of prosciutto-wrapped shrimp. "Wow, that's lemony," McPhail says. Then Cory presents his entrée: tuna coated with brown sugar on one side, Creole seasoning on the other, and briefly seared. McPhail takes two bites of the tuna. Cory gets asked to join the *brigade*. Mary does not.

McPhail's last four mouthfuls of the day are as unpredictable as everything that's come before: two spinach leaves, spongecake, braised pork belly, and smoked-mushroom cream sauce. Tonight's final spoon count is 169.

In parting, I tell him I'll be in touch as soon as I get the results from our nutritionist-in-waiting.

Debbie Strong goes to work and begins to calculate the damage. Several weeks later, she breaks the news in a conference call with McPhail and me.

"Total calories: Three thousand four hundred and eighty two."

"That's a lot, huh?" asks McPhail.

"An active male like yourself should take in about twenty-five hundred calories a day," Strong advises.

"So I guess I'm off a bit," he says.

"That's putting it lightly," she continues. "And it's not just the calories. Over half of your calories are from fat, probably because of all the rich sauces and dressed salads you tasted." The bad news keeps coming: Nearly 70 grains of saturated fat—heart disease in a headline. "Like two and a half days' worth," Strong points out. Sodium—nearly 5,000 milligrams, about double the recommended daily intake. Cholesterol: 731 milligrams, twice the FDA guideline.

Since our day in the kitchen, McPhail has made a few changes. Three times a week he runs four miles; he squeezes in 450 sit-ups at least twice a week. And he's assigned more of the line tasting to his sous-chefs. "That's probably why they all have a little belly going on," he says.

In the last couple of months, McPhail has lost about 20 pounds. Apparently, our experiment was a real wake-up call—even in advance of the heart-stopping totals. "It was surreal," he says, "having you count all the foods I ate."

Surreal, perhaps, in terms of the out-landishness of the idea of recording the running total in a bustling restaurant. But all too real in terms of the results—and the unmistakable message for chefs who rise to success: A lifetime in the kitchens of fine restaurants is not without its health risks, even if you never sit down to a grand meal yourself.

The Harveys Circus

by Marco Pierre White and James Steen

from *The Devil in the Kitchen*

The story of how London became a gastronomic capital is largely the story of Marco Pierre White, told with riveting candor in his new autobiography. This excerpt focuses on the bistro where this outspoken, intense British chef first achieved rock-star status.

T he same two questions always crop up about Harveys. First, was I really so nasty to my chefs? Second, did I really kick people out of the restaurant?

Sometimes I bump into hugely successful, talented chefs who were my protégés and they say, "You were really nasty to work for but it made life easier afterwards." And they say that without a hint of irony. I've also come across punters who tell me they came to Harveys and say, "You kicked me out, but I suppose I asked for it."

Dealing with the staff issue, first. Yes, I was a hard boss. Even without my insistence on discipline, finding staff was difficult enough. At that time the majority of young chefs aspired to work north of the Thames, rather than south. They'd rather have done Belgravia than Bellevue Road. When they accepted the job, they were in for the shock of their lives. My unmanageable desire for perfection brought out a certain tetchiness in me. I expected my chefs and waiters to match my commitment, and I let them know that. My addiction to work, my constant craving for an adrenaline fix, set the pace, both front and back of house. I was working hundred-hour weeks, but they weren't slacking either. If joining

Gavroche was the culinary equivalent of signing up for the Foreign Legion, then taking a job at Harveys was like joining the SAS. We were a small unit of hard nuts.

In the early days, I allowed staff to sit down for a meal before service, but that didn't last long. Egon Ronay's glorious review a couple of months after we opened started off the nonstop bookings, which pretty much finished off the custom of staff lunches. There just wasn't time to eat. Jean-Christophe Slowik, or JC, replaced Morfudd as maître d', and one day he asked for a quiet word. JC was only in his twenties but had worked for Madame Point, widow of my hero Fernand Point, in France before doing a front-of-house stint with that genius Raymond Blanc. He was as young as the rest of us but had a wisp of premature gray hair. In his engaging, diplomatic and charming way, he explained that he had a problem. "What is it, JC?" I asked.

He said that he was having to take money from the petty cash box, nip to the deli a few doors down and buy sandwiches for his ravenous waiters. He asked, "Is it not odd that we work in a restaurant but have to buy lunch from somewhere else?" JC is good when it comes to making good points. JC was skinny enough and he added, "To lose any more weight, I will have to lose a bone." From then on I allowed staff to have a meal, a couple of times a week, before service.

I survived on a diet of espresso and Marlboros—my nutritional intake came from the morsels, nibbles and sauces I tasted during cooking. Most members of the team found that Mars and Twix were ideal for energy bursts. Then there were the plates that were returned to the kitchen from the dining room totally clean. For ages I thought the customers were so impressed with the food that they were devouring every last speck on the plate. In fact, it was the starving waiters who were responsible for the spotless dishes. As they left the dining room and walked along the corridor to the kitchen, they would polish off the customers' leftovers, guzzling the remains like famished vultures.

There was a look of horror in the eyes of JC's new waiters as they arrived for their first day at work. The sight that greeted them was one of waiters and chefs suffering chronic fatigue and hunger, all set to the soundtrack of a screaming boss. Even before service started and the first customers arrived, a new waiter would often make an excuse about getting something from his coat, only to scurry off and never return. These new waiters couldn't work a single hour, let alone an entire shift. Eventually JC accepted that many of the recruits would evaporate as fast as their enthusiasm and he worked extra hard to compensate for this problem.

In the kitchen, the first three weeks was the toughest period for the new boys. By the end of it they were usually fucked, having lost a stone in weight, gained a dazed expression and cried themselves dry. That was when the shaking started—and when many of them left. One day they were there, the next they were gone. If they could make it into the fourth week, they were doing well.

We were in the kitchen one night when Richard Neat mentioned something about feeling faint and then collapsed on the floor. He was having a panic attack between the stove and where the meat was prepared: the exhaustion had taken its toll. None of us knew what to do but one thing was for sure—the cooking continued around Richard's quivering body beneath us.

Then JC came into the kitchen carrying a tray and screamed, "Oh my God, look at Richard." JC phoned for an ambulance, which arrived within minutes, but JC was keen not to disturb the customers by letting them see the paramedics stomping through the dining room, so he directed them round to the back door. As the diners enjoyed their food, the ambulancemen tended to Richard. They had to strap him to the stretcher because he was having spasms. The next day, he was back in the trenches with the rest of us.

I make no apologies for my strict leadership methods and I have no one to blame but myself. However, I was, of course, the product of disciplinarians who included my father, Albert Roux, Pierre Koffmann and good old Stephan Wilkinson, my first chef at the George and the man who called me cunt as if it were my Christian name.

Normally only one person was allowed to speak during service, and that was me. Kitchen visitors said it was a bit like watching a surgeon in an operating theater.

Step now into my theater of cruelty:

ME: Knife. *[Knife is passed to me.]*
ME: Butter. *[Butter is passed to me]*
ME *[through gritted teeth]:* Not that fucking butter. Clarified fucking butter, you fucker.

Poor timing always upset me. If we were doing a table of six, for instance, and only four of the main courses were ready, then I was prone to flip. That's when I might send a chef to stand in the corner. "Corner," I'd say, jabbing a finger toward the corner of the room. "In [finger jab] the [jab] fucking [jab] corner." The chef would stand not with his face to the wall but facing me; that way he could pick up some knowledge while enduring his punishment. I remember one night, when I was in an intensely irritable mood, four chefs pissed me off, so each of them was sent to stand in a corner. When a fifth chef did something to annoy me, I shouted, "Corner. In the fucking corner."

"Which one, Marco?" he asked. I had run out of corners.

I went berserk if brioche wasn't toasted correctly. If it's toasted too quickly, you can't spread the foie gras on it; if it's toasted too slowly, it dries. It has to be toasted at the right distance below the grill, so it's crispy on the outside and soft on the inside. You don't scorch it and you don't dry it. Insignificant to you, maybe, but the difference between life and death to one of my cooks. If the brioche wasn't right, or if the vegetables had been chopped incorrectly, then someone was in for a nasty bollocking. "Do you really want to be the best?" I'd tell them. "If you do, that's fantastic; if you don't, then don't waste your time."

In order to achieve my dream I reckoned I needed a brigade with army-standard discipline and, as I had learned at Gavroche, discipline is borne out of fear. When you fear, you question. If you don't fear something, you don't question it in the same way. And if you have fear in the kitchen, you'll never take a shortcut. If you don't fear the boss, you'll take shortcuts, you'll turn up late. My brigade had to feel pain, push themselves to the limits, and only then would they know what they were capable of achieving. I was forcing them to make decisions. The ones who left, well, fine, at least they had decided a Michelin-starred kitchen was not for them.

Take a look at the ones who stayed, the ones who could take it and even appreciated it. Today, they are considered to be among

Britain's finest chefs and they all came from that cramped kitchen at Harveys. There's Gordon Ramsay, of course. Gordon arrived in January 1988 after phoning up and asking if there was a job going. At the time he was working at a restaurant in Soho and, during a break, had read an interview with me. He thought I looked wild and crazy and a bit like Jesus, and he felt compelled to pick up the phone. I hired him, and when he came, I treated him as I would anyone else. He would eventually leave my kitchen in tears, but would go on to win three Michelin stars of his own. There are other winners too: Philip Howard has two; Eric Chavot has two; and Stephen Terry has one. Meanwhile, Tim Hughes is now executive chef of the Ivy, Le Caprice and J. Sheekey. All of the chefs who went through Harveys will say they have never worked in a more pressurized environment, but I doubt any of them will say they regret the experience. Chefs love mania.

Gordon, Stephen and Tim shared a flat in Clapham, a couple of miles from Harveys, and I used to scream at them, "Did you bunch of cunts go home last night and conspire against me? 'What stupid things can we do to wind up Marco?' Is that what you all said to each other? Did you sit down together like a bunch of plotting cunts and say, 'What can we do tomorrow that will really piss him off? What can we do to really irritate him?' Did you, Gordon? Is that what you did, Stephen? Did you conspire against me, Tim? Because you are all being so fucking stupid today."

Other times the bollockings included physical abuse. I might severely tug a chef's apron, or grab a chef by the scruff of the neck and administer a ten-second throttle, just to focus him. One night I lifted Lee Bunting and hung him by his apron on some hooks on the wall. The cooks never knew what to expect from me—and neither did I. A film crew arrived for the series *Take Six Cooks* and happened to walk into the kitchen as I was throwing bottles of sauce and oil at an underling. The producer had to duck down to avoid being hit by flying glass. "I don't know if we can film in there," he told JC. "War zones are less dangerous."

Chefs who weren't sent to stand in the corner, throttled, or forced to duck to avoid flying sauces might even be chucked in the bin. We had a great big dustbin in the kitchen, which was filled with the usual waste produced in professional kitchens. The boys who were too slow, or simply too annoying at any particular moment, were dumped inside it. Arnold Sastry, the brother-in-law of comic actor Rowan Atkinson, was known as Onion Bhaji and he was regularly binned.

"Onion Bhaji in the bin," I might say, and the rest of the brigade would obey orders.

Why, you ask, did these poor young men continue to work for that bullying brute, Marco? Good question. And many of them not only continued to work with me, but stayed with me for years, right up until the day I retired in 1999. The thing is, a bollocking isn't personal. It's a short—sometimes not-so-short—sharp shock. It's an extremely loud wake-up call. It's smell-the-bloody-espresso time. In the heat of service, I didn't have time to say, "Arnold, would you mind speeding up a little, please?" I couldn't stop cheffing, couldn't take my mind off the game in order to say politely, "Gordon, when do you think you might finish the guinea fowl, old boy?" I had to be hard to deliver the message and the message was "Do it now and do it right." They all knew this and they all understood it. That is why, when a chef is receiving a bollocking, none of his colleagues jump in to defend him. The rest of the brigade look down and carry on with the job. Each one of them knows that sooner or later he will be the one getting a bollocking. I created fear but I don't remember anyone ever saying, "Marco, enough is enough. Pack it in." I'm convinced that a mile-wide streak of sadomasochism ran through the Harveys brigade. They were all pain junkies—they had to be. They couldn't get enough of the bollockings.

The Best Chef in the World

by Alan Richman

from *En Route*

Superlatives don't come easy to an acerbic
(and often controversial) food critic like Alan
Richman—but watch his resistance crumble
in this profile of Michael Troisgros from the
Canadian magazine *En Route*.

To arrive at Hôtel Restaurant Troisgros by train, as so many patrons once did, is to respect tradition. The local from ever-prosperous Lyon to once-thriving Roanne meanders through countryside and villages that seem to have changed hardly at all. Homes have lace curtains. Meadows are lush with wildflowers. The simple restaurant by the *paste de gare* in Saint-Romain-de-Popey awaits disembarking passengers, as the now grand Troisgros did decades earlier. Finally, the train glides into the Roanne station, located across the street from a building where, almost a half-century ago, a boy looked out the window of his room and contemplated where life might someday take him.

"I remember the steam whistle, so noisy, the smells from the charcoal. For years this is what I saw," says Michel Troisgros, now 48, a small, dark, slightly stocky man, who smiles often and would appear to be a very tough fellow if he did not. "I had only one idea, to take the train and go away. I was like a boy living on a harbour. It was the boat for him, but the train was the same dream for me."

So many relatives lived in those rooms above the restaurant: his father, Pierre, and his uncle, Jean, two of the most famous members of a generation of chefs who defined French cuisine; their families; the grandfather. "And don't forget the dogs and cats," Michel says. Clearly, the children longed to be elsewhere because that is where all but Michel went. His brother, Claude, well known and well travelled, is now a chef and restaurateur in Brazil. The one who came home when it was his duty to do so was Michel.

He has now been chef of the family restaurant for almost a quarter-century, which is not what he dreamed of doing, but he does not complain about what he has become. To me—someone who has eaten in every important restaurant in Paris and in the United States and at a ridiculous number of other gastronomic shrines— he has become the best chef on earth. Several years ago, I arrived here in the company of four wine collectors, gentlemen with far too much money to spend on leisure pursuits. We ate a $5,000 meal that included Troisgros' variation on Kiev: Instead of the old-fashioned preparation of deep-fried chicken and herb butter, his Kiev was a crunchy pastry shell stuffed with pigeon, black truffle, foie gras and spinach, the pinnacle of fried food. We liked it so much, we stayed an extra day and spent another $5,000, mostly for the incomparable pleasure of eating that Kiev again.

To dine at Troisgros is to experience all that classic French food once meant and to savour everything that modern French food has become. It is more than just magnificent cooking because for food to be great, it must be more than flavourful—even if that seems to be all that customers and critics nowadays demand. It must also pass another test, the verdict of history.

The cuisine of Michel Troisgros occasionally bends to the same South American rhythms as Claude's. It honours the backgrounds of his father (Burgundian) and his mother (Italian). I sometimes think his greatest single accomplishment is an amuse-bouche that was inspired by a visit to Piedmont: an elongated cracker spread with salted butter and topped with anchovies and black truffles, the anchovy inexplicably supercharging the truffle. I hesitate to tell him this because I do not think three-star Michelin chefs appreciate being celebrated for their pre-meal snacks.

Most significantly, the influence is Japanese, which has been a factor in the Troisgros family for decades, long before "fusion" became a culinary and not a thermonuclear term. The genius of this cuisine is not its complications but its clarity. On his menu, Troisgros' Japanese-influenced dishes, such as steamed sea bass fillet in an infusion of seaweed on koshihikari rice, sound elaborate. On the plate, they are astoundingly focused. Regardless of what he might affix to a basic French recipe, even a touch of the mustard-like, fiery Asian condiment yuzu kosho, every flavour comes pre-cisely to the point. No other chef prepares food of such towering ambition that is so deliriously easy to eat.

The link between the Troisgros family and Japan is pro-bund and is perhaps the reason the food appears to come from a common culture, not a mixture of two different ones. Japanese influences are even more evident at the restaurant of Hôtel Lan-caster in Paris, where he is the consulting chef. When Michel was a boy, in 1967, his father left for Japan to cook at the first French restaurant to open in Tokyo, a branch of Maxim's de Paris. Pierre remained there for a year, sending postcards to a son longing for his return. "I was only nine, but did not see my father for a year, and when he came back, it was on the train to Roanne. The door opened—I can still see it—and he was wearing samurai clothes. A few weeks later, cases of food started arriving from Japan. It was the first time I ever tasted ginger, sweet ginger in cans. There was soy sauce. There was none in France. It was all a shock. Then the Japanese started coming, not just chefs to learn here, but Japanese guests too."

Eventually, Michel did get to travel, mostly to apprentice in the great restaurants of France, but he felt a responsibility to return when his Uncle Jean died of a heart attack on the tennis courts in 1983. Of all the brothers and sisters, nieces and nephews, he had the fewest obligations. His wife, Marie-Pierre, agreed. "I know now," he says, "that being here was the sense of my life. I can tell that today." When he hesitates, I ask him if he ever envies Claude, who has taken culinary independence to the extremes. Wistfully, he smiles. "Sometimes," he says. "He is free. Claude can travel when his house is open. I can only travel when my house is closed. It is easier to have a restaurant in Brazil than in France."

The restaurant Michel Troisgros returned to, although leg-endary, would soon suffer. It was the same for most of the great countryside establishments of France. The TGV, the fast train, came along to link Paris and Lyon without stopping at Roanne. A new superhighway bypassed the city. He takes a piece of paper and sketches a map of the once indispensable RN7, now an outmoded road from Paris to Lyon. On or just off the road are Troisgros, La Côte d'Or (renamed Le Relais Bernard Loiseau) in Saulieu, Pic in Valence, La Pyramide in Vienne, l'Oustau de Baumaniere in Les Baux-de-Provence. These days, the chefs of those restaurants are revered; the late Fernand Point of La Pyramide is probably more celebrated than the Sun King. Back then, these establishments were merely fine places to dine, not shrines.

Michel recalls the restaurant he returned to as being more like an auberge, a simple inn and gathering place. The bar displayed basketball and tennis trophies, not cognacs in crystal decanters. "It was a place of warmth, where people were welcomed with all our heart. It was a modest place, except for one thing—the kitchen. I am not sure I would have had the courage to do what my father and uncle did."

The kitchen of Troisgros, all shiny steel, with electric burners and picture windows, seems entirely of today. It is actually of 1977, when Pierre and Jean had it built. Michel, pleased as always when he discusses his family, says how clever it was for his father and uncle to construct this expensive kitchen because the journalists came to write about it and to photograph it and to exclaim in wonder that great food could be cooked on electricity instead of gas.

"This was crazy to do in 1977," he says, "To do a kitchen so well built it is like a Rolls-Royce instead of investing in the hotel or in the comfort of the guests. But it was a great decision. The priority for them was the most beautiful and comfortable kitchen in the world. The stoves are still here, 30 years later. And now they are economical; the price of gas is so high."

The kitchen is essentially unchanged. It has a small table for guests. The walls are decorated with cartoons celebrating the once essential relationship between the restaurant and the railroad. In one, a waiter lifts a cloche, and under it is a section of track. In another, a conductor wearing a napkin around his neck cries out, "Roanne! Roanne!" In this kitchen, 20 cooks prepare food for an average of 60 guests per meal, not nearly as many as in the old days, when it seemed all travellers passed through the great textile centre of Roanne.

The dining room is more attractive than I remember from past visits, when it seemed like a holdover from the cosmetic excesses of the 1980s and '90s. It is serene and pale, dominated by a large black-and-white photograph of the gnarled branches of an old tree. I suggest to Michel that it has the feel of a traditional Japanese room, but he says, "I don't want Japanese architecture. I want refined and pure, simplicity and wood."

Much like the food and the ambience, the standards he upholds as a three-star chef have changed. They are more excessive than ever. Before each service, tablecloths are ironed to eliminate creases. Plates are wiped with vinegar to remove fingerprints. White peppercorns are crushed by hand. During meals, the kitchen becomes quiet, intense. The number one chef softly advises the number two, who gently corrects the number three— and you wonder why French food is so expensive. A young Japanese chef, the hardest working man in the kitchen, prepares lobster for a fricassee, picking away unseemly bits indiscernible to my eyes. (I wonder if I will ever again eat a crustacean hurled whole into a pot without fearing the presence of unpurged body parts.) The serenity is broken only by a captain or a chef calling out an order. The kitchen acoustics are perfect. The men in high positions are all baritones.

Troisgros is the absolute master of tricky fish. His sardine filet, marinated in vino santo vinegar, orange, shallots and almond oil, is soft and creamy, as I've found bony sardines never to be. He has brought back "aux amandes"—the seafood suffix that I Americanize as "almandine." His thick filet of sole almandine with leeks and mushrooms has a touch of ginger that accents the sweet and sour flavours of the almonds and the sherry vinegar. Fish prepared aux amandes is difficult to find, and to eat his preparation is to wonder what other culinary treasures of the past we unjustly ignore.

Lunch at Troisgros is, in some ways, a more formal meal than dinner. At least the patrons seem to dress better, especially the local businessmen and the aged couples arriving to celebrate special occasions. At one such meal, I walked into the men's room to find an elderly woman there. I backed out, although apparently not hastily enough to deter her from snarling at me. (I was not surprised since the French believe in blaming anything that goes wrong on the nearest American.) My appetite was unaffected. I ate vivid green asparagus prepared three ways: with mayonnaise and black truffles; with red pepper sauce and bits of red pepper; and with fresh mint and a mint-leaf garnish. Leg of lamb was accompanied by a mousseline of eggplant so rich, I might have preferred it as dessert.

Lunch or dinner, Michel is always there, nodding hello at every service because he says that is what customers demand of three-star chefs in the countryside. Sometimes, after a long day, he tries to call Claude. "I never know where Claude is," he says. "He is travelling a lot. I call Brazil; he is never there. Maybe he is in the deepest jungle. Maybe he is at the bottom of Argentina. He always answers me if I e-mail, but I never can find him on the phone."

He laughs with delight at the thought of such freedom, of having a restaurant that does not require the presence of the chef. He does not seem to mind that for him, such a life is not possible. He tells me that he still has two airline tickets to Sydney, Australia, dated 1983, one for himself and the other for his wife. That was the trip he was to take when his Uncle Jean died and he was called home. "It is just another dream," he says. "I still have the tickets. I will never use them."

Building the Perfect Pizza

by Laurie Winer

from *Los Angeles Magazine*

LA-based screenwriter/food columnist Laurie Winer nabbed a plum assignment— chronicling the return of La Brea Bakery's Nancy Silverton with her new venture Alessi. But this is more than a chef profile; it's a smart snapshot of idiosyncratic LA food culture.

Los Angeles, it seems, is a pizza desert. If you have enjoyed a thin-crust pie at Angelini Osteria or a slice of pepperoni at Casa Bianca, this will come as a surprise. But pizza mavens—and they are a vociferous lot—will tell you that you haven't enjoyed it as much as you thought.

You may also be new to the term "pizza cognition theory." It was first put forth by *New York Times* editor Sam Sifton. He wrote that the first pizza you eat as a child is what you recognize as pizza for the rest of your life. This is like saying we all marry our fathers; it's true for only those who suffer from arrested development. My theory of pizza cognition says that until you have had transcendent pizza, you do not know you have never had transcendent pizza. On this, any human being can be educated in a minute or the time it takes to bite, chew, swallow, and think.

At this point you may be feeling civic and wondering, "But what about Spago? Didn't it change the world of pizza?" The answer, according to Ed Levine, the author of *Pizza: A Slice of Heaven,* who has spent much of his life tracking down great pizza, is no. Spago pizza, aka California pizza, aka designer pizza, was famous not for its entirety but for such innovative toppings as barbecued chicken and smoked Gouda. It was created not by Wolfgang Puck but by Ed LaDou, who went on to develop the menu for the first California Pizza Kitchen, which, writes Levine, "introduced truly awful versions of California pizza to the rest of the country."

Like most L.A. bashing, derision for our pizza comes from New York, but not only from New York. The *Los Angeles Times* writer David Shaw, in one of his last pieces before his death a year ago, observed that L.A. may have good pizza—he named Casa Bianca, Antica Pizzeria in Marina del Rey, Abbot's Pizza in Venice, Mulberry Street Pizzeria in Beverly Hills, and Caioti Pizza Café in Studio City (run by LaDou)—but it does not have superb pizza. In fact, Shaw suggested, the one person who could possibly elevate pizza in L.A. was Nancy Silverton.

In June the Alessi restaurant at Melrose and Highland was in the process of becoming Mozza, a much-anticipated coproduction of Silverton and Mario Batali. Batali is the clog-wearing, red-bearded voluptuary whose outsize appetites (most recently memorialized in Bill Buford's best-seller *Heat*) and energetic, intense Italian cooking have earned him an international reputation. Babbo, his flagship New York restaurant, is still one of the most popular restaurants in the city after eight years. Apparently, Batali's seven-restaurant empire is not enough; he is expanding to Los Angeles as well as Las Vegas. Silverton's renown has to do with sublime desserts and sandwiches and with bringing great bread to Los Angeles; she is as taciturn and trim as Batali is voluble and large. Mozza is really her restaurant; it was Silverton, along with chef Matt Molina, who devised the menus (in the style of Batali), and the 28-year-old Molina will be doing much of the cooking. Batali and longtime partner Joe Bastianich lend their name, aesthetic, and business acumen to the place. Mozza is a big deal not only because it is Batali's debut here but because it is Silverton's first restaurant since opening (with her former husband, chef Mark Peel, and their partner, Manfred Krankl) Campanile and La Brea Bakery in 1989, two institutions that helped establish Los Angeles's reputation as a great food city.

Over six days in early summer, Silverton invited friends to the old Alessi space to taste the pizza she'd been perfecting for months. The restaurant looked forlorn as I approached it. Overgrown bougainvillea and trash clung to the building. I tried the door on Melrose—locked. I walked around to the door on Highland and pushed. I fell into a large, dingy space, and the first thing I saw was the actor Ray Romano chewing and staring thoughtfully at a pizza slice—it was blistered black around the edges and was white and creamy on top. The director James L. Brooks was leaning against a counter. Tables and chairs were strewn about, and a press of people stood near the pizza oven. They included producers Robin Green and Mitch Burgess, writer Margy Rochlin, *Los Angeles Times* contributor Amy Scattergood, boutique owner Caryl Kim, producer Phil Rosenthal and his wife, Monica, and Silverton's boyfriend, writer Michael Krikorian. Sitting were some teachers from the 24th Street Elementary School, whose formerly all-concrete grounds Silverton, writer Emily Green, and others are turning into a teaching and cooking garden.

I spotted Emily. "Who is this Ray person?" she asked me. Emily's TV gets one channel. I think it's 56. Just as I noticed that Emily had spoken while chewing, something she never does, Silverton appeared. In auburn sunglasses, her curly brown hair pulled up into a high bun, she wore a dark apron low on her hips over a summer shift. She offered me a slice. *"Lardo,"* she said. In her early fifties, she's one of those people who seem to regard "hello" and "good-bye" as time-consuming contrivances. That's when I took a bite and my pizza cognition changed forever.

It was a warm, crackling, well-salted crust topped by a buttery sliver of pork. The crust was a revelation—the ends were not an afterthought or something you'd leave on the plate but a treat you'd look forward to having all by itself, after the toppings had been eaten. Silverton had concocted it from American flour (the other ingredients are secret), allowing the dough to rest on and off for up to 40 hours and baking it for exactly three minutes in a 750-degree oven, charring it from top to bottom and blistering the ends while leaving the middle warm and breadlike but not doughy. On top, Silverton floated a stream of unearthly delights—cream and sausage and fennel pollen, squash blossoms and *burrata,* littleneck clams with Parmesan and pecorino, long-cooked broccoli, Gorgonzola with fingerling potatoes.

Everyone around me was serene. They were standing, sitting,

talking, but mainly they were eating. With concentration. I wondered about the purpose of the gathering. It was clear that Silverton, in private and in her obsessive way, was satisfied with her pizza. She wasn't seeking our input; there was nothing anyone could tell her that would make it better. She wasn't looking for praise; she knew how good it was. Although she was always in the kitchen or hovering on the edges of the room, she was at the center of the event. There would be no speeches made, no tinkling of a glass or thanks given. She mostly watched people eat her pizza. Feeding people the best food she was capable of, it occurred to me, was her way of showing and receiving affection, maybe even love.

Something else was going on as well. The room may have looked like a *Gourmet* photo op, the pizza may have been world class, but it was still just pizza. We were far away from the precious foodiness of it all, the need to know what the hell *sous vide* is or how foam is extracted from a tomato. Suddenly, in the way that the Zeitgeist can shift in a moment, it seemed as if we would all—eaters, investors, and chefs alike—be freed from the oppressiveness of contemporary food culture, a culture that asks more and more of us. When we go to the grocer, are we buying locally produced food? If not, are we contributing to global warming? Is our beef grass fed (good) or corn fed (bad), and has our free-range chicken ranged free or has it been stuck in a coop with an open door that no one ever told it about? On this day we were just eating pizza, and we were happy.

The New Yorker ran a cartoon a couple of years ago that showed a rich man in front of his giant marble fireplace saying to his wife, "I tried pizza today. I still don't understand what all the fuss is about." Okay, the joke isn't that funny, but my husband and I still quote it. If you don't get pizza, you don't get life. It's not necessarily perfect food, but it's food you can eat day or night, hot or cold, food that you can get delivered to your house no matter where you live. It's the first food you want when you've been out of the country. I don't care where it came from; it's the most American food there is.

"It's almost like finding religion when you discover how good pizza can be," says Ed Levine. "There are only maybe a half dozen practitioners who can really do it in the country." Levine's pantheon consists of six restaurants, all but one in the Northeast. His

Leonardo is Chris Bianco of Pizzeria Bianco (in Phoenix), the only *pizzaiolo* who has won a James Beard Award and who some have said is the best not only in the country but in the world. I don't have to mention that the world includes Naples.

There is a pizza orthodoxy, an accepted body of knowledge that states the following: Great pizza must be made in a coal- or wood-fired oven. (A brick oven no longer ensures quality, as many brick ovens are now gas powered.) It must cook at a high temperature for a short period of time. The best tomato sauce is made from uncooked canned tomatoes from Italy (Silverton uses San Marzano). The toppings should be fresh and perfectly local (but imported from Italy is acceptable). Most important is the crust. It needs to have the "hole structure"—you hear this phrase over and over—of well-made bread. By this definition, the thin crust is akin to a bread made by an artisan, which is why Silverton was destined to open a pizzaria.

Before La Brea Bakery, when Los Angeles was considered a bread wasteland, much as it is now considered a pizza desert, Silverton had a vision of what she wanted to do. She was in Berkeley, and she tried bread from the Acme Bread Company. She realized, she says, that the fast-rising recipes and standardized loaves she'd been making as pastry chef at Spago missed the point. The point was sublime, often irregular bread with "inner beauty." Making that kind of bread meant entering into a long, embattled relationship with yeast and flour, a relationship that would take over her life. "Strange as it sounds," she writes in *Breads from the La Brea Bakery*, "baking can be like a marriage: There's a lot of give and take. If you try to be too controlling, the bread rebels. If you ignore your bread and think it's going to be there when you decide to come back around, think again." Silverton often worked through the night, kneading, waiting, flouring, poking—like Debbie Reynolds dancing until her feet bled to perfect her numbers for *Singin' in the Rain*. Silverton went through 75 recipes before she was satisfied with her sourdough.

In 2002, her marriage to Peel was over; the year before, they'd sold an 80 percent share of La Brea Bakery for $56 million. (She is still the "public face" of the bakery and checks in almost daily on the breads and sandwiches in the store on La Brea.) Suddenly wealthy, she had a lot of free time on her hands. She lunched with friends. She entertained. She volunteered at the 24th Street School Garden Project. Mostly, she was looking for her next challenge. "I need that sense of accomplishment," she says. "I need that thing to be obsessed by. Otherwise I don't feel grounded." She started searching for a new space.

Batali had approached her about working with him at his newest restaurant, Del Posto, but she didn't want to move to New York. Still, the seed of the partnership was planted. While Silverton waited for a space to open up here, she began working at friends' restaurants for free. At Campanile, Silverton had instituted "Grilled Cheese Night," which made the restaurant a happening spot on Thursday nights. In that spirit she started "Mozzarella Monday" at JAR, the restaurant owned by chef Suzanne Tracht along with Phil and Monica Rosenthal. Monday went from being the restaurant's slowest night to one of its busiest. Soon she started working on Tuesday night, also for no pay behind the antipasti bar at La Terza. Behind a counter, Silverton has the aura of someone who has found a home for herself, a place where she can be near others but stay in her own world, preparing food with her hands, chatting, but only when she feels like it.

For one of the last tastings, Silverton invited 35 people to Melrose and Highland. The space was no longer Alessi but not yet Mozza; it was a skeleton of the restaurant that would be. (The pizzeria is scheduled to open this month, the osteria in the fall.) We were all in place, munching, trying to pretend we weren't waiting, Silverton included. On this day the master himself was expected; Chris Bianco would be flying in from Phoenix. Silverton sat on a bench, placid and watchful as usual, but maybe there was a slight flush to her cheeks.

Then Bianco breezed in. In his early forties and solidly built, he appeared boyish in his T-shirt and laceless sneakers. He threw a wave to Silverton and walked to the pizza oven. Silverton was chatting but keeping an eye on Bianco. He emerged a few minutes later and gave her a vigorous thumbs-up. "It's really, really good," he shouted across the room. I noticed he did not use the word *great,* which I thought implied some envy and was just another sign of how good the pizza was.

Seeing that I had a notebook, Bianco came over. Where Silverton endures interviews, Bianco adores them. In a Bronx accent, he dispensed a stream of pizza philosophy, half of it brilliant, half of it bunk. A dozen people stood around to hear what he had to say. "If I unleaven this crust," he began, "then we have pasta." No one knew what to say to that. Someone brought him another slice, and he ate. We waited. "I don't know anything except that this has integrity," he said. "The cell structure of it. I think of bass notes when I eat this pizza. I hope people eat it and submit to it, let it sink in."

Phil Rosenthal had his video camera out and was taping him. Bianco was ready to continue. "Pizza will fight you," he said. "You want to, and you can't master it. It's a relationship. You have a relationship with yeast. It's dysfunctional. It's chaotic." Silverton nodded but said nothing.

Everyone resumed eating, satisfied. It seemed that the maestro had spoken and had given his blessing. Perhaps that's what we'd been waiting for. But he was not done. "When we make pizza," he said, "we are like Roman soldiers making gruel. We are making something basic to our natures. When we sit down to eat pizza, we should remember that this will not be our defining moment, 'cause tomorrow the pizza will be different, and so will we."

No one was sure if he had finished. My mind was wandering; I had been thinking along similar lines. Perhaps it was my own vanity, but I was thinking that Los Angeles would never be the same after it tasted Silverton's pizza. It was as if I were seeing Disney Hall for the first time, and Disney Hall had cheese all over it. Then Silverton turned to me. The nature of her thoughts was less rococo. This was her moment, not Bianco's, and she was going to define it herself. She made sure I was looking at her and then looked away. "This is how I judge a great meal," she said. "When I'm eating it, I don't want to be anywhere else. That's how I want people to feel when they're eating my pizza." I nodded and kept eating.

Mr. Puck proved that he knew his Apple: out from the kitchen came a plate of pig prepared four ways, precisely the kind of unpretentiously rustic and absurdly rich dish that could make Johnny literally rise from his chair and yelp in delight. That's just what he did, before proceeding to correctly guess the farm in Pennsylvania where Mr. Puck had purchased his pork.

This was dinner with Johnny Apple, the *New York Times* correspondent, who died last Wednesday at age 71. Or, rather, one kind of dinner with Johnny Apple.

He was capable of eating lunch at a three-star restaurant in the French countryside and, after an interval of only three hours, dinner at a brasserie in Lyon, narrating each dish as it came, as he did while traveling in France with a *Times* correspondent a few years ago. He was flamboyant enough to commandeer a favorite Madrid restaurant during the 1997 NATO summit meetings, never mind that it was normally closed for lunch, and then direct a three-hour afternoon feast with Sandy Berger, the former American national security adviser. The event provided little news but many opportunities to sample bottles of 1975 Imperial Gran Reserva Rioja, as one of his guests later recalled.

He brought no less gusto to a fabulous neighborhood restaurant that served Serbian food and that he somehow snuffled out in the outskirts of Milwaukee. Or to the Palm in Washington for a steak. Or to whatever was served to him at the dining table of a friend, which made him less intimidating to cook for than one might think. Presented with flageolets at a dinner at a friend's house in Washington a few years ago, he scooped them up and roared his verdict: "Best I ever had on this continent!" The host beamed in appreciation of a nuanced compliment that said as much about the eater as the chef.

He was a gourmand, but he was not a snob, at least when it came to matters of food and wine. He loved it all, and he loved it in enormous amounts—and never more so than when he was sharing a table with his wife, Betsey, who shared his tastes, his sense of humor and his adventurous approach to food.

He was as happy eating chicken gizzards at a dusty dive he found in Nashville as he was slurping down dumplings stuffed with foie gras and shiitakes at Blue Ginger in Wellesley, Mass. He

Sharing in the Feast With Johnny Apple

by Adam Nagourney
from *The New York Times*

The word "gourmand" must have been invented to describe R. W. Apple, Jr., the omnivorous *New York Times* reporter who took on a food writing beat in his last decade, promptly making it his own. A fellow *Times* journalist remembers Apple for all of us.

The restaurant was Spago, in Beverly Hills, and Johnny Apple was in the house.

And everyone knew it.

It started with the maître d'hôtel, who fawned over us—make that: who fawned over Johnny—the moment he spotted that large frame pushing through the door. He guided us to a table in the center of the dining room (with a view, as Johnny noted upon unfolding his napkin, of Esther Williams, the 1950's Hollywood sensation, perched at the next table). It continued with the wine steward, who looked understandably intimidated as he came over to negotiate the wines we would be drinking that evening. Then, finally, Wolfgang Puck himself embraced Johnny as if he were the only person in his dining room, never mind that Spago was teeming with its usual roster of celebrities, along with the political crowd in town for the 2000 Democratic convention.

Johnny offered Mr. Puck a challenge—"We are in your hands," are the words I recall—and thus began a four-hour blur of plates and platters and bottles of wine the likes of which I had never seen before, or since, at a Puck restaurant. Two hours into our bacchanal loved his oysters raw and he loved them stewed and he loved them deep-fried. When he was the Washington bureau chief for *The Times* he had lunch with a few colleagues and Barbra Streisand at a suite at the Jefferson Hotel near the White House. Ms. Streisand has always had a strong interest in politics and in Johnny's writing, and knowing of his reputation she arrived with a bottle of a California cabernet.

As the story was later told, Ms. Streisand said, "When should we open it?"

"Any time before you drink it!" Johnny replied with a loud chortle.

In a business in which reporters tend to guard their personal opinions when writing about politics, Johnny compensated by having, and sharing, strong views on all matters having to do with food and wine.

Dining at the Summer Shack in Boston? One had to order Jasper's pan-roasted lobster. (Upon sitting for dinner he made clear that this was being attended to by Jasper White himself, and that it was not open to discussion.) In Cancún? There is only one place to eat: a pizzeria on the roundabout on the main drag.

In Des Moines, Iowa, during the 2004 caucuses, we had dinner at the 801 Steak & Chop House, where Johnny ordered pork chops. A young *Times* reporter, out to impress the boss, ordered a dozen oysters. Johnny shot him a withering, "what are you thinking of, ordering oysters at an Iowa steakhouse" look. The judgment was borne out with the delivery of a bland and watery plate of Wellfleets.

He scoffed at the notion that one should drink the best of the wine first. Save it for last, he said, and savor it like a dessert. So it was that he brought a 1964 Burgundy, a Vosne-Romanée, I believe, from his extraordinary collection (a bottle that he no doubt bought in the 1960s) to an engagement dinner of some friends—noting, but not bragging, that he had seen this same wine go for auction that week for about $650. He instructed the waiter to open it and put it aside until we had finished our meal. Never had I enjoyed a glass of wine as much as I did that night.

His very last e-mail message, sent the night before he died, was a response to a *Times* food writer looking for suggestions on pancake recipes for a magazine feature. "Just very quickly since I don't have my files here," Johnny wrote. "1. American pancakes—Overrated, as you say. You might try the Bongo Room, in Wicker Park, north of Chicago. 2. Don't forget Breton buckwheat crêpes. 3. From South Asia (states of Kerala and Tamil Nadu in India): they make great dosas."

Johnny was the person to call for a restaurant recommendation when heading anywhere around the globe. To his eternal credit, he never kept secrets; he wrote about the places he discovered and loved. I soon learned a trick to find his recommendations without pestering him: I would search Nexis using three elements: his byline, the name of a city and the phrase "my wife, Betsey."

Dining with Johnny had advantages beyond his elastic expense account. A newspaper restaurant critic strains not to be recognized. But Johnny made no secret of who he was (as if that were possible); he loved being recognized and feted as a celebrity. That was always a treat for his dinner companions: it meant a personal visit by the chef, the most intricate discussion with the sommelier about the most obscure wines, then a shower of dishes from the kitchen, most of them unavailable to the civilians in the house.

As a student working on my college newspaper I avidly followed Johnny's coverage of the 1976 campaign, during which he established himself as one of his generation's great political reporters. After I found myself working with him at the same newspaper, improbably enough, I could never decide what I found more unnerving: working at a desk next to him on election night, sitting next to him at a restaurant or, eventually, cooking for him in my kitchen.

But the last proved easy and immensely pleasurable; in truth, having Johnny to dinner proved to be a more profitable experience for the host than the guest. Johnny and Betsey came over a few months back, after he was ill but when he was weathering it well. He offered to bring wine, and, not having been born yesterday, I readily agreed. Johnny showed up not with one bottle of wine but 10. And not any wine but a 1982 Bordeaux, one of the best vintages of the past century, a Château Haut-Bages Averous Pauillac that he plucked from his extensive collection. "You can't take it with you," he said, cheerfully.

Nine of us managed to get through most of that wine that

night. I put one bottle aside, for the next time Johnny and Betsey came to dinner. That was, as it turned out, his last night in our dining room. But one evening before the end of the 2008 presidential campaign—an election that we will, sadly, have to chronicle without the presence of R. W. Apple Jr.—I will uncork that 1982 Bordeaux from the Apple cellar and raise a toast to a man who taught us all about writing and reporting, yes, but also about living. And living very well.

Dining Around

My Miami

by Anthony Bourdain

from *Gourmet*

His no-holds-barred memoir *Kitchen Confidential* made a star out of Anthony Bourdain; nowadays he's more often seen on television than behind a stove. But three things no one can question — the man can craft a sentence, he has strong opinions, and he knows food.

Like a heat-seeking missile, I can find my way to the finest steamed shark's head in Singapore or the best bun cha in Hanoi. Blindfolded, with one wrist cuffed to an ankle, I can drive you to the earthiest pig's-foot soup in the Dutch West Indies, or to the world's most sublime soup dumplings in Taipei. But in Miami, one of the most international of cities, I am pathetically up a creek. Which is why I was so easily led into the bizarro universe of Miami Beach's Afterglo, the alien spawn of "celebrity dentist" Dr. Tim Hogle and chef Michael Schwartz, formerly of the well-regarded Nemo. Afterglo specializes in what it calls "international beauty cuisine," and in the manifesto that precedes its menu, the restaurant promises to serve only dishes loaded with "syntropy," the "order-enhancing energy force" that, it insists, counteracts the evil "thermodynamic" effects of uglifying "entropy."

Several Nobel Prize–winning biophysicists are said to support Hogle and Schwartz's theories, but their names appear nowhere in the manifesto. I fought the urge to flee and instead read on. "A beautiful young person is the result of nature's genetic lottery," claimed one passage. "A beautiful older person, on the other hand, is a work of art. This work of art is you. And you are the artist."

As best as I can make out, the good doctor was telling me that by applying the principles of cosmetic dentistry to fine dining along with organic, low-glycemic, anti-inflammatory, low-acid, high-enzyme ingredients—Afterglo has managed to craft an entire menu of "beautritional" cuisine.

Beginning to consider my own "ongoing contamination and interruption of (my) body's beautifying energy supply" and unsure whether to order a meal or an early prostate exam, I turned the page in search of food. I found a multicar pileup of mixed metaphors and descriptive sourcing that read as if an unholy group of hippies, fusion-happy chefs, and eugenicists had spent a week together in the desert, eating mushrooms and "conceptualizing." Salad selections bore names like Way to Glo, A Beautiful Mind, and Sing Like No One Is Listening, and featured such raw ingredients as burdock root, hemp seeds, red *tosaka* and *ogonori,* organic sun-dried *goji* berries, ginkgo, and red-clover sprouts. The woman sitting next to me wondered aloud if we might be offered after-dinner high-colonics.

We settled on Here Comes the Sun for the table, and I chose the Grass Fed Vietnamese-Style Bison Ceviche appetizer and a special entrée of braised short rib. "Here Comes the Decorating Kit" was more like it. The dish consisted of chewy segments of seeded flatbread and a "sunshine dal" that looked and tasted like wallpaper paste. My bison, however, was flavorful and well textured, lightly cured and dressed with a classic Asian garnish of lime, lettuce, sprouts, and "wild jungle peanuts." The Broken Arrow Ranch Venison Tataki, teamed skillfully with a crunchy medley of raw apple, spiced pumpkin seeds, arugula, and crushed juniper berries, was good enough, yet like a lot of the more competently prepared dishes, it was smothered by the décor and the pomposity of a Greater World View. The Mahogany-Glazed Alaskan Black Cod, served with a New World/Old World fusion of yuca *croquetas,* pickled pearl onions, cilantro aioli, and the inevitable microgreens, was fresh and well cooked. My short rib, however, was woefully undercooked, dry, and tough, and tasted both cloyingly sweet and unpleasantly salty. The restaurant's press kit proudly claims that "unnecessary high heat is avoided" so that "essential beautifying ingredients" can be preserved. Funny, I thought that high heat was desirable so that caramelization could occur and flavor could be preserved. But no less an authority than Einstein is invoked in the Afterglo press materials. And I ain't no Einstein.

I hate to kick a bunch of obviously skilled cooks in the teeth. I'm sure their intentions are honorable. But a cook's responsibility is not to make you beautiful. It's to give you pleasure. I strongly advise the far-too-talented-for-this cooks of Afterglo to flee. Immediately.

The following day, desperation for an honest meal drove me to a forlorn strip mall past the airport, where I'd heard you could get decent Salvadoran food. I'd spent 80 bucks on a cab to get there, and my kitchen Spanish wasn't up to allowing me to actually read **El Atlakat**'s menus, one Salvadoran and one Argentine. But at least I knew what a *pupusa* was, and so I placed my order. I heaped the soft white disk of cornmeal stuffed with cheese and *loroco* (an asparagus-tasting flower native to Central America) with a spicy pickle of carrots, onions, and chiles, and drizzled the mass of it with hot sauce. It was tasty and filling, and I was momentarily happy. So happy that I ordered a taco, a corn tortilla rolled like a cigar around piquant chicken-leg meat, deep-fried and served with sour cream. I washed it down with a cool, fruity *horchata,* and last night's nightmare began to recede.

Now I was on a roll. The next day I stumbled into **Selva Negra,** a Nicaraguan restaurant where I was willingly and non-judgmentally overfed. Sitting in a heavy wooden chair among left-over Valentine's Day decorations, fake flowers, and three television sets showing Spanish-language soap operas and soccer games, I gorged on a platter of *antojitos nicaragüenses*—thick, juicy slices of dark brown *morcilla* (blood sausage); sweet plantains; spicy home-made chorizo; thick blocks of boiled yuca; unapologetically crispy, greasy *chicharrones* (fried pork skins); more rolled, fried chicken tacos; fork-tender hunks of spicy roast pork; and rough slices of grilled skirt steak. Plus fried *maduro* plantain chips, tortillas, beans, and slaw. Straightforward and decidedly not "beautritional," this food felt somehow lighter and freer than the upscale fusion fest; it was certainly a hell of a lot more fun.

Though pleased with myself for having found Selva Negra, I still needed help. And I knew no one better for the job of navigating lesser-traveled Miami than my friend Linda Bladholm, a local journalist who investigates such things for a living. After I made a quick distress call, she agreed to meet me that night in North Miami Beach—at a strip mall, of course—on the West Dixie Highways for a Japanese family-style dinner at **Hiro's Yakko-San**. "You're going to love this place," she said. "All the sushi chefs come here after work." More-encouraging words have never been spoken.

An authentic joint with minimal atmosphere, an uncompromising Japanese menu, and a roster of daily specials scrawled on blackboards, Hiro's opened five years ago—the sister restaurant to three local sushi bars (one of them next door). Miami sushi chefs looking for a taste of home find much to love at this place, and have been known to fill it late at night drinking Japanese beer, or sake from tall husks of bamboo, and getting rowdy. Our bare table was soon covered with the kind of no-nonsense fare you find at the small Japanese bars called *izakaya*. We ate chewy, rich strips of beef-tongue steak; some raw cold-water uni (sea urchin roe); grilled pork belly with *ponzu* sauce (an argument-ending defense of high heat and the glorious effects of caramelization); chicken-liver *nira itame* with chile and bean sprouts that brought me back to late-night places in Osaka; and deep-fried bok choy and *age nasu*—fried Japanese eggplant with bonito shreds and ginger—that was like a gentle whiff of the Tsukiji fish market. Having also requested the meal of choice for tippling off-duty sushi chefs, I finished the night by tucking into a steaming bowl of udon noodles with crispy pork. After a few bamboo lengths of sake, I drifted off to my happy place—that idiotically grinning fugue state I find myself in usually only in faraway towns, shoeless and wearing a sarong.

At one point, Linda mentioned **Sam Jack's Specialty International**, an African grocery store hangout, where the pepper pot soup, she insisted with an evil smile, would be right in my comfort zone: "There's still fur on the cow's feet."

Sam Jack's looks exactly like what it is—a provisioners-warehouse–grocery store for Miami's West African population.

Here, in a featureless area of Opa-Locka, you'll find groups of Nigerian and Ghanaian men sitting in chairs out front in the parking lot or leaning on parked cars drinking milk stouts and bottles of Guinness while listening to music from home at an ear-splitting volume. Inside the dim and dusty warehouse, shelves are stocked with dried fish, cassava flour, palm oil, and canned goods. There's a counter and one table usually filled with a group of men who know each other well. One or the other will occasionally rise to dance alone when the mood strikes. And presiding over all this from behind the wooden counter is the very large, very welcoming Sam Jack. Told that I wanted the famous pepper pot, he reached into a chest freezer, removed a preportioncd plastic container, and popped it into the microwave. Then he found me a chair, a cold Guinness, and a plastic spoon.

They call it pepper pot for a reason. It's spicy. *Very* spicy. And filled with all sorts of wonderfully gristly bits. The traditional African concoction features goat meat, a cows' foot, salt, onion, and potash (for tenderizing). It's stewed in commercial bouillon (Maggi brand seems to be the West African favorite), and they add chiles, ground crayfish, bitter African leaves called *ukazi,* and *uva uziza* seed, which has a smoky, allspice-like flavor. I gratefully slurped down my broth and chewed my meat and gristle. No fur here.

Linda had warned me that because a lot of these small restaurants move around frequently or close, it's always best to call first. I didn't, of course, and many times, after driving around in countless circles, I found my destination either shuttered or gone completely. But it was on one of those occasions that I found the most pleasant surprise of my trip, just a few blocks from Afterglo. **Antojitos de Mi Tierra** is a brightly colored Colombian nook that looks so wrong and yet tastes so right. Its "dining room" has only seven bare tables, and its "lounge" consists of one stool next to a chest freezer offering serve yourself "fruitsicles."

To a mainly Colombian clientele, Antojitos sells simple but very decent *salchipapas* (fried potatoes with sausages), empanadas, *morcilla,* fried fish, fried plantains with cheese and guava, *buñuelos* (fried *croquetas* of cornmeal and cheese), and *arepas* (buttered corn pancakes with sausage, cheese, or shredded chicken). But I fell hard for the unlikely and horrifying sounding *choriperro,* the best-selling version of their Colombian hot dogs. Who would have thought that a *perro* (dog) of Colombian chorizo sausage on a fluffy, oversize hot dog bun, topped with cheese, onion, ketchup, Russian dressing, chopped potato chips, and pineapple jelly would be so fine?

But the single best thing I had in Miami was the *mondongo* that came next: a mammoth bowl of steaming, tender squares of tripe and ripe plantain swimming in a hearty, spicy, electric-green cilantro-loaded broth, accompanied by rice, salad, and sweet plantain. A few mouthfuls of *mondongo,* and I knew where I was. I was in Miami, in a country not quite my own. I was seated at a proud table expressive of another place, of another people, some far away and others close by. I was being fed well. All was right with the world.

Then There Were None

by Dara Moskowitz Grumdahl

from *City Pages*

Despite several national food-writing awards, Dara Moskowitz Grumdahl remains passionately rooted in the Minneapolis-St. Paul culinary scene, where her spirited, witty, clear-eyed columns and restaurant reviews tend to keep things lively.

I went through all the stages of grief when chef Doug Flicker called to tell me that Auriga was closing. Denial: You can't be serious, you made it this far—you outlasted Five Restaurant & Street Lounge, you outlasted Restaurant Levain, both of which closed in the last few weeks; the customers will come back, they have nowhere else to go—just hold on!

Then, anger: What the hell is wrong with people that the Cheesecake Factory is packed and Auriga can't make it! And: What the hell is wrong with me, why didn't I write about how great Auriga is more recently, and stop this? Truth be told, I had Auriga on deck for a re-review rave next month, but I spent the last year putting it off, waiting for the pastry person to stabilize, waiting for the new front-of-the-house guy to get settled, and now it turns out that all that waiting was waiting exactly too long, and how I hate, hate, hate myself.

Next? Bargaining: Look, if you just let people know Auriga is in bad shape they will come in droves; I will write about you, everyone will write about you! In the end this conversation between Doug and I turned into nothing but a professional mess, with the chef comforting the restaurant critic with brave words: "Plenty of other restaurants have opened and closed," Flicker assured me. "The world will continue to spin."

But will it? Will it really? I'm not so sure.

Auriga played a unique role in Minneapolis. It was the chefs' think tank, the place young cooks went for inspiration and established chefs went to see what the kids cared about. As Jeff Pierce, of the restaurant supplier Great Ciao, told me, "We used to say, only kind of tongue-in-cheek, that if we wanted to launch something in this market we'd give it to Doug or Steven Brown for two weeks as an exclusive, and then everyone in town would clamor for it." Speaking of Steven Brown, he's out of a job too: Restaurant Levain closed on New Year's Eve.

This caps an altogether brutal season for Minneapolis fine dining: In the fall, Seth Bixby Daugherty left his chef job at Cosmos to pursue the work of his heart, improving food in the school systems. Who to blame for that? Why, look no further: "When I saw your story ["Carrot Invitational," 8/23/06] I said, What am I doing? That's who I am. That's what I should be doing," Daugherty told me. "Do I want to spend the next 10 years working a hundred hours a week, or do I want to follow my heart, and spend time with my kids? Life's too short. I read the story, I gave notice." Which prompts me to ask: What the hell is wrong with me? I set out to improve the restaurant scene in this town, and instead I execute surgical strikes on its top talent? Ahem. Then of course there was the late 2006 scandal of Five, of the zillion-dollar build-out and sky-high ambitions, which bought out chef Stuart Woodman, fired him, and then promptly collapsed, leaving a zillion-dollar empty shell.

"I didn't know that we were living in a gilded age, like, two years ago, but I guess we were," chef Marianne Miller told me. Remember Miller? She was chef at high-flying Red, and then Bobino, but both went out with the grace of the Hindenburg, so she now cooks only at private events for wealthy folks. As of February 2007, something like half of the best chefs of the Twin Cities are unemployed or simply not cooking in restaurants: Doug Flicker, Steven Brown, Stuart Woodman, Marianne Miller, Seth Bixby Daugherty.

So, what happened? In the case of Auriga, it turned into something of a battle between the restaurant and the building that housed it: In the winter the heating bill would shoot up astronomically, and the restaurant got socked with a number of massive costs for building repairs. "We had a horrific year last year, and, while we probably could have struggled along for a few more years, we decided we'd rather not go out owing our suppliers and the government, we'd rather go out with our heads held high," Flicker told me. That point about wanting to go out without owing the suppliers is a bigger one than it might seem, for two reasons. One, because it tips a hat toward a future—keeping honor with your suppliers is important if you ever want a restaurant in this town again. Two, and this is not a good thing, it gestures toward a Minneapolis restaurant scene that is very much an interconnected organism—an interconnected organism which just took a serious body blow.

What composes such an organism? First, there are the suppliers: the farmers, the foragers, the olive oil and cheese sellers, the wine importers, and so forth. When a restaurant closes, all those people lose out, in terms of customers, in terms of bulk purchasing power, and more. I talked to Pat Ebnet, who owns Wild Acres, a locally famous humane outdoor poultry operation in Pequot Lakes, and he explained that when a restaurant closes he can lose money every which way from Sunday. There's the product he's delivering to a locked door, sure, but there's also the pheasants or chickens in various stages of growth for future orders, the feed he's bought to raise those birds, the advertising the restaurant provides for that farmer to reach other chefs or retail accounts, and more. "The Syscos and Westlunds of the world have deep pockets, and they can just leave product in the freezer," explained Ebnet, but farmers like him process to order. So, the producers with the highest ethics, the most sustainable practices, and the highest quality take the biggest hit when leading restaurants die: Minneapolis's fine-dining infrastructure just got walloped.

Another karate-chopped arm of this interconnected organism? Our next generation of chefs. The line cooks at Auriga, Levain, and Five are just the people who would have been opening new restaurants here in the 2010s. Auriga had a staff with young cooks who are already veterans of some of the most important restaurants on earth: the Fat Duck, Allinea, and French Laundry. They were working at Auriga specifically to learn how to run an independent restaurant in Minneapolis. Instead they learned how to close one.

I asked some of the other orphaned Minneapolis chefs, Steven Brown, Stuart Woodman, and Marianne Miller what they think about the future of fine dining right now. "I don't want to be overly dramatic," said Miller. "But if Auriga can't make it, can any of us? The only jobs right now seem to be in the corporate structure of a multi-unit restaurant, and I'm anti- the globalization of fine dining. Once you know how to cook, you can't unlearn it and do a bad job because you're using someone else's guidelines, and that's what the corporate thing is. I'm not giving up yet. I'm going to wait it out and I'm see what happens."

Also waiting it out is Stuart Woodman, formerly of Five, but he is also the chef boasting the most impressive cooking résumé Minneapolis has ever seen, including the job as opening sous chef at Alain Ducasse at the Essex House. "I talked to someone last week who said, 'You're leaving town, it's too small,'" Woodman told me. "Well, that's a great rumor, but we love it here, our five-year-old loves it here, and we're committed to staying. I've turned down some job offers, a great one in California, but I'd really like to open something here that was more focused, and controlled. People say: You were on the cover of *Food & Wine* and a few months later you're canned! Yes, that was great, but the reality is that a lot of restaurant stuff takes place on a lot smaller scale than people realize." Meaning: The cover of *Food & Wine* might not matter as much as your heating bill.

Okay. Heating bills. A basic economic fact of life. But Steven Brown, the chef lately gone from Levain, pointed out any number of other economic facts that might be informing this current restaurant massacre. Perhaps the real problem has been that places like Levain and Auriga have been engaging in an experiment to pay the full, real, unsubsidized costs for food, and it killed them. How so? Okay. In a fine-dining Minneapolis restaurant, they pay all their workers a living wage, they buy local, sustainably raised meat and produce when they can, and usually California organics otherwise, and so forth.

For argument's sake, let's make up a competitor: Quick Cafe. Quick Cafe hires quasi-illegal workers to work in its restaurant (i.e., those with suspect documents, the only ones who will accept tip-free minimum wage) and in that restaurant they plate and serve food prepared at a California commissary by other quasi-illegal immigrants. That Quick Cafe food is sourced from ingredients including old California dairy cows pumped full of heaven knows what hormones, antibiotics, and so forth—old California dairy cows that are themselves a backhanded government subsidy because of the milk price supports which discriminate against Midwestern dairy farmers. Once turned from government-supported dairy cow to bucket of heat-and-serve food, said "food" is driven across the nation in trucks fueled by gas kept at artificially low prices, and, at the end of the day, paired with a soda made with government price-supported corn syrup, for a $4.99 value meal.

"People think fast food is the only thing *Fast Food Nation* covers," Brown told me, summoning Eric Schlosser's damning portrait of American food production. "But it goes beyond fast food, to restaurants you think are nice, and it's also just insidious in all kinds of other ways. We have these expectations we don't even know we have," Brown explained. "A hamburger is supposed to cost $5, a glass of wine is supposed to cost X, and if it costs more, we feel we're getting ripped off. But every other segment of our [food] economy besides fine dining is propped up by illegal labor, factory farms, and so on. So someone like Tim Fischer [a local pork producer] is out there trying to sell his meat, and people are like: Why should I spend $10 a pound when I could spend $3 a pound at Sam's Club? So what was wrong with Levain?" Brown continued. "Partly it was that people come and get this great stuff that costs an arm and a leg, and then they get in their car and say, 'My wallet is empty, but that sure was good, next year we'll come back!' And the next day they're back at McDonald's or Sam's Club." All right, that's an incredibly depressing thought—perhaps our de facto subsidized economies of factory farms and poorly compensated labor have become so much the norm in America that no one can go against them. That's pretty bad.

Now, let's make it worse. It hadn't occurred to me until Brown pointed it out, but while so many independent places are trucking along on their old independent business model, a new breed of restaurant has arrived among us: The institutionally subsidized one. 20.21, the Wolfgang Puck Restaurant at the Walker Art Center; Cue at the Guthrie; Jean-Georges Vongerichten's Chambers Kitchen at the new Chambers Hotel—all of these hot new restaurants have their rent, their heating costs, and so forth folded into the budget of another institution that meets its expenses in ways other than selling plates of chicken.

When I spoke with Marianne Miller, she joked, "Can't the government subsidize restaurants?" Perhaps, in a roundabout way, with all the fancy financing that went into places like the Guthrie and the Walker, it is. Look for this subsidized economic reality to dominate this year's coming ritzy crop of new hotel restaurants. I used to think that a stand-alone restaurant was simply an architectural term; now I see it's an economic model.

Now, if that doesn't depress you enough, I'll heap some more on. It goes without saying that part of the reason that it's so distressing to lose our great restaurants is that it makes Minneapolis seem kind of podunk, cow-town, ambitionless, pathetic. We like to think of ourselves as a little more San Francisco, a little less Grand Forks. But what if we fail to understand the real difference between us and San Francisco—that they have gazillions of gazillionaires, and we're just middle-class? Maybe when we compare our food scene with the ones in New York and California, we're assuming that they operate under the same rules of business that we do, that they read a profit and loss statement the same way we do. But maybe they don't.

In Minnesota, restaurants need to operate in the black. Yet consider the best restaurant in America, French Laundry. To get it started, Thomas Keller signed up 48 investors for the 17-table venture—that, in case you don't feel like doing the math, is almost three investors per table. However, even though the restaurant has been packed since the minute it opened, according to a *New York Times* story a few years ago, it still hadn't paid back its investors, and the investors don't much care. Are we ever going to compete with that? If one of the requirements of having a great food scene is the ability to operate in the red indefinitely, we never are.

Frankly, the only real hope I see is that no one is leaving town: Flicker, Brown, Woodman, and Miller all say they love it here, and plan to stick it out—we're hanging on here by the skin of our quality of life.

Of course, I don't mean to give short shrift to the great, independent, home-grown fine-dining, or simply fine restaurants we have left: La Belle Vie, jP American Bistro, Vincent, Lucia's, Restaurant Alma, Café Brenda, Spoonriver, Sapor, Cue, Fugaise, the Dakota, 112 Eatery, the Town Talk Diner, Solera, the Modern Cafe, the Corner Table, the Craftsman, Bayport Cookery, and, in St. Paul, Heartland, Zander Cafe, Cafe 128, Au Rebours, and W. A. Frost. We should certainly all support these places, and whomever I've left out, to the best of our abilities—but it seems Polyanna-ish to say that that alone is the answer. Perhaps I'm just stuck in that stage of grief called "going endlessly over things that can't be changed," but this all just seems awful to me. I cherish the idea of meritocracy, and what seems to be happening in our city right now is that the best and brightest are our vulnerable outliers, and have gotten mowed down first. If it's as bad as all that, what does the future hold?

To answer that, I called up Doug Flicker again, seeking more. "Everything is born, and lives, and dies," he told me. "Hopefully sooner than later, we'll open something new. I will evolve; hopefully everyone will evolve. When we opened Auriga we wanted to change something, we didn't want to be here for the rest of our lives. At the time we thought it would go for 10 years and we'd move on, and that seems to be coming true, a few months early. It's not a failure to close—because how do you define success? I was married here, Mel was married here, Scott was married here," said Flicker, naming two of Auriga's founders. "There have been babies born, countless first dates. . . . The bottom line is, I'm proud of what I've done here; as hard as it is to tell people that they're out of a job, it's been nice working with so many people. I feel a little like a grandparent or something, I look out and feel good about all the things I've gotten to do. There's a part of me that will die along with this restaurant. . . ." he trailed off. "I don't want to stop cooking, and hopefully after all the dust settles I'll start looking at places. I wish it was as simple as pointing a finger and saying, this was the cause, that was the cause, but it's not. A lot of things have changed in Minneapolis, not just competition, but what it takes to do business. It's time to reinvent myself again, to get some piss and vinegar back in me, readjust, fuel the fire."

All I can do right now is pray that this is just that for our city too, a time to fuel the fire, and not as awful as it feels.

Precision Cuisine

The Art of Feeding 800 a Night in Style

by Melissa Clark

from *The New York Times*

Melissa Clark has observed many a kitchen at work, as a chef, a caterer, and a cookbook writer collaborating with Daniel Boulud and David Bouley. In this inside look at some extremely high-volume eateries, she deftly cracks their code for maximum efficiency.

In the arena-size basement of his stadium-size restaurant, Buddakan, the chef, Michael Schulson, translates the graceful choreography of the usual professional kitchen into something best compared to a fast-paced team sport. When you're cooking for 800 a night, finesse and spontaneous creativity necessarily morph into raw athleticism and well-drilled precision.

Think of it as extreme cooking. The rules go like this: Working at top speed, frenzied cooks in white jackets must flash gargantuan amounts of scallop-fried rice, taro lollipops, edamame dumplings and shiny Peking duck over leaping flames without burning up themselves, the scallops or the kitchen.

Passed on to Mr. Schulson, the expediting chef—or ringmaster—the piping-hot food is appraised, tasted, fluffed, rearranged and then either approved or rejected (he has about eight seconds per plate and a 10-percent rejection rate). Accepted dishes earn his bellowing cry, "Runners! Get me runners!" He screams this over and over all night long (there are never enough runners), always followed by "yo, yo, yo, yo" (in lieu of names he has no time to remember), and, "go, go, go, go," sending the runners on their way.

Navy-clad muscle-bound runners balancing trays piled with the steaming plates fly out of the kitchen. Scaling narrow staircases, darting down disco-lighted hallways, and skidding past tipsy patrons in miniskirts and stilettos, they barrel through three levels and as much as 16,000 square feet to reach their goal: a hungry table of 14.

In a typical evening at Buddakan, this is played out approximately 133 times in a five-hour time span.

Pushing the limits of what a restaurant kitchen can do, big-box eateries—those serving 600 to 1,000 customers a night—are being forced to become increasingly inventive and resourceful in how they run their kitchens, or else face drowning in the unending chaos of those vast numbers.

For Buddakan, part of its salvation lies in vigorous speed. Another factor is the sheer numbers of employees.

In addition to the 24 line or main cooks, there are four dozen prep cooks rolling dumpling skins, pinching the heads off bean sprouts and peeling fresh water chestnuts during the day, and several wandering sous-chefs on duty at night, ready to jump into the fray wherever needed.

There's even one person whose sole job is circulating in the 3,500-square-foot kitchen to empty the garbage cans into one of the two refrigerated garbage rooms the restaurant had built.

But Buddakan's crowded, frenetic model represents just one of many approaches. Peek into the kitchen at Vento or Blue Fin, two restaurants in the B. R. Guest group, and it's a completely different scene, closer to tournament dominos than a rugby match. All screaming is turned down to a hushed silence but for the click-clacking of dishes and clanging of pans. Outsize gestures and flamboyant maneuvers are replaced with the precise, methodical movements of the two expediters (one for appetizers, one for entrees), intently focused on a five-foot-long sheath of order tickets, which they arrange into numbered blocks grouped by order time, and constantly reshuffle. The aim is to coordinate everything so that the appetizers arrive between two to eight minutes from when a table orders, with the entrees following 15 minutes later.

Although they serve the same number of people a night as Buddakan—give or take a couple hundred—Blue Fin and Vento employ about half the number of cooks.

For them, the key is in their particular style of expediting. It's a routine that has been honed over the years to such a fine tool that, Blue Fin's executive chef, Paul Sale, said, if the appetizer expediter "dropped dead right now, I'd still know that mussels were missing from table 117."

An adjunct part of the system is making sure that each cooking station is equally busy throughout the night, and never backed up at vital moments, say, during Blue Fin's pre-theater rush, when the restaurant might have 600 "covers" (or diners) in two hours. If a cog in the machine gets stuck (perhaps by a rejected order of over-cooked halibut), it is up to the expediter to urgently grease it, by repositioning problematic tickets into their own panic section where they will receive special attention.

Since the distances in mega-restaurants can be expansive, communications devices, like walkie-talkies, headsets and computers, are useful.

In the kitchens themselves, the more advanced and highly specific gadgetry is used in food prep. For Buddakan's lacquered ducks, whole defeathered birds have their skins ballooned out (to separate the fat from the meat) with an industrial-strength air compressor. The birds are then slow-roasted in a specially designed duck cooker that's unfortunately somewhat apt to catch fire. At Blue Fin, one piece of big technology is an $18,000 rice washer that helps out the sushi chefs.

However, as it is with all games of skill—whether dominos or sports—for high-volume restaurants serving high-quality food, it's the strategies, rather than any clever gadgets or pieces of equipment, that make or break them.

A well-designed kitchen is paramount too, but here bigger isn't necessarily better. At the Italian restaurant Vento, Brett Reichler, a corporate executive chef for B. R. Guest restaurant group, motions his arms around the relatively small size of a kitchen that cooks for 600 people a night.

"Just making it bigger wouldn't make it any more efficient," he said. "A guy shouldn't have to move too far to complete a dish. If I have to take two extra steps for each dish, that's a thousand steps at the end of the night.

"We want to move as little as possible to get the job done," he added.

The same quest for efficiency underlies yet another big-box kitchen maxim: have as few hands touch the plate as possible.

Unlike a classic brigade de cuisine, where the fish cook sears the tuna, passes the plate to the vegetable cook who adds the freshly sautéed snow peas and sends it down the chain to the saucier, who drizzles on the ginger glaze, at Vento and Buddakan et al, each cook builds a dish from start to finish.

For any classically trained chef, it's an adjustment that takes some getting used to.

Mr. Sale of Blue Fin admitted, "I had to completely change the way I was used to cooking to make it work."

The approach to writing menus changes, too. Dishes need to be streamlined and simplified so that most of the preparation can be done in advance; when an order comes in, the chef can quickly cook the protein and heat the made sauces and garnishes.

As Mr. Reichler of Vento said, "Pan sauces made à la minute are just not going to happen here like at Le Bernardin."

The only dishes cooked completely to order are those made in a wok, which has many advantages over the Western-style burners. Not only does it get much hotter and thus cook the food more speedily than a frying pan, it also holds more volume. At Buddakan, the wok cook can put out four orders of scallop-fried rice in the same three minutes it takes a cook on the standard burner to whip up one order of sizzling short rib with mushroom chow fun and the mysterious "crispy stuff" mentioned on the menu.

Wok cooking, and being able to send the food to the table family style for sharing, are two reasons many of the giant restaurants (Buddakan, Ruby Foo's, Japonais, Buddha Bar, Megu, Tao) are Asian. It makes it possible to get a lot of food out to the tables quickly.

Family-style dishes also encourage the expediter to send out dishes as they are ready instead of waiting for all the entrees for the entire table. This gives Mr. Schulson at Buddakan another measure of control. If the cook in charge of the minced pork lo mein is in the weeds, as they say, Mr. Schulson can still instantly send that hungry table of 14 their sweet and crispy jumbo shrimp and jasmine-tea-scented chicken.

Just as soon as he can find a runner, that is.

The Greatest Restaurant on Earth

by Ivy Knight
from www.gremolata.com

> Although she's a working restaurant cook, Ivy Knight finds time to write outspoken reviews and essays for Web sites like eGullet and Toronto-based gremolata.com. She's also a competitive extreme pillow fighter— but that's another story.

On a sunny spring morning I'm on Queen Street in Parkdale, in Toronto, in Canada. The sun actually shines here sometimes (quelle surprise!), so I left the sled dogs at home and opted not to wear my favourite lumberjack ensemble. I'm not heading to the beer store for a couple of two-fours of Molson or to the butcher for a few pounds of back bacon. I'm just standing here, waiting for the doors to open at St. Francis Table. Waiting with me are Sean, Alice and Larry, three volunteers from different backgrounds who have given their time to this enterprise for a combined 10 years.

St. Francis Table is a restaurant staffed by volunteers to serve the people of Parkdale who are in need. Do *not* confuse that with a soup kitchen. Here the customers pay for their meals and are seated at a table with a server to wait on them. They pay only a dollar, but that single dollar is enough to make them feel less like they're getting a handout, and more like they are functioning, contributing members of society.

Brother John, a member of the Capuchin Brotherhood, an offshoot of the Franciscan family, gives me a bit of the history on the restaurant. They opened their doors in December of 1987, after a survey showed that food service for the poor of Parkdale was the number one need. "We felt that the city didn't need another soup kitchen." says Brother John. He stands at the door during meal service in his long, brown hooded robe, looking like Friar Tuck without the frothing mug of ale, greeting each customer, most of them by name, as they arrive. This restaurant has provided over half a million meals since it opened.

"From day one we had patrons owing for meals. At the end of the month every single patron was paying up. We took this as an early indicator of their appreciation for what we do here."

The restaurant is privately funded, relying on the charity of private individuals and businesses for income. It serves a three course lunch from Sunday to Friday adding a three course dinner from Monday to Thursday, with often more than a hundred customers per service. That's a lot of food and a lot of labor. They offer a drop-in space for the St. Francis Table patrons—a warm and welcoming environment for folk to get off the street for a while.

St. Basil the Great Catholic School provides student volunteers. As part of the curriculum in Grade Twelve every student will pass through St. Francis's doors. Today there are four girls, Ivana Cotic, Diana Chiodo, Sarah Migliaccio and Patricia Rubino. Both Sarah and Patricia have been here before and were surprised by the space.

"I expected it to be more run down, I thought it would have been more like a cafeteria" Sarah admits. "I also never thought I would like serving so much." All the girls seem to love it here. Adds Ivana, "We've only been here an hour and it's so comfortable it feels like we've been here forever."

It's a very friendly place. In the spotless kitchen, Head Chef Sam Kumarasamy puts the girls to work cutting French fries. "We make our own fries here," he tells me. "The students really like to do a job different from their daily life, it makes them happy and they learn new skills. This is not only about feeding the poor, this is about bringing people together. These girls will now have a better understanding of people they see on the street. They will see them as human beings because of the experiences they've had here."

Volunteers Rosa, Lily and Alice are cutting veggies for salad while Larry prepares the tuna for tuna salad sandwiches. I'm happy to see he's using Hellman's and not Miracle Whip. If I had my way, Miracle Whip would be wiped off the face of the planet. It's disgusting.

Today is Wednesday, so it's tuna salad sandwiches and fries for lunch. Larry obviously knows a thing or two about the perfect tuna salad—he's been making it every week for seven years. The menu is totally up to Sam for the remainder of the week. Right now he's bustling around making sure everything that needs to get done is getting done.

"My work is to keep everything organized and running smoothly. We have about two hours prep time and then we open the doors for service. The customers, they don't like to wait. Everything has to be ready when they get here."

Sam shows me the dishwashing machine which they bought from Diversey Lever, who now donates all the necessary detergent and chemicals, and maintains all of the equipment at no charge. He takes me to a large standup fridge, filled with cakes and pastry.

"Fortino's supermarket donates all day-old pastry and if Dufflet Pastry has a damaged cake they freeze it and give it to us. We're happy to have so many desserts to offer our customers."

I realize just how much these people and this calling means to Sam, who's aware of how the little extras can make a meal mean so much more than just refuelling—everybody needs a treat.

Most of the rest of the food is purchased, with Sam buying all the meat and produce himself. "Through experience I finally found the best butcher, Mr. Limo at O Nosso Talho (Bloor and Dufferin). Sometimes the bank card has no money in it and he says 'Don't worry about it, pay when you can.' He gives us very good deals."

We go downstairs to dry storage where two teenage boys are loading bags with dry pasta to be taken to the food bank, where all the excess donations are sent. There are rows of shelves filled with non-perishable items. Brother John tells me how one parish in Woodbridge put out a call for everyone to make lasagnas. "We got over three hundred lasagnas which are stored in the walk-in freezer. We just put the word out for what we need and usually end up with three or four times more than what we asked for, so we pass it along. Between volunteers and donors, we're blessed every day."

This place is definitely an exception to the rule when it comes to feeding the poor. If it were like this everywhere we wouldn't see Christmas in July posters for food bank drives.

St. Stephen in the Fields Church may be losing its meals program, which provides free breakfast to approximately two hundred people every weekend. The Anglican Diocese wants to boot everyone out and sell the prime piece of real estate to the highest bidder. The church was built in 1857, a food bank was started in the 1970s, the church is now serving 7,000 meals annually to the people in the community. Robin Benger, who runs the Sunday breakfast program, tells me "The church is locked in the final stage of the battle to stay alive. I'm carrying on regardless. I'm committed to making sure those people get a free meal once a week for as long as I can provide it."

Back at St. Francis Table, Sam shows me a shelf filled with boxes stamped with the American Airlines logo, containing stainless steel knives, forks and spoons. "These were donated after 9/11 when they switched to plastic. Our customers feel like they are flying first class when they use this cutlery."

I meet Brian in the kitchen, a retired elementary school teacher. He's been volunteering here for two years. "This is the one thing on my schedule that's etched in stone. It's different from other places; there's a lot of respect for the customers. They say it's really nice to be served rather than have something put on a tray. You get to know the people. Some have mental health issues, there but for the grace of God are we. These people have lives and they're intelligent, they just happen to be in reduced circumstances."

I'm introduced to Cassie and Noreen who are support staff for the Community Living Toronto Youth 2 Work Program. They are here with Sean, Andrew and Zinaida. "I come in and job coach for youth with intellectual disabilities," explains Cassie. "These three have all expressed interest in food. I'm here to teach them new skills. We have youth working everywhere. We train them on the job so it doesn't take time away from the regular staff. We stay on the job with them and slowly phase out until they are working independently. Once the customers come in, Andrew busses tables and Sean and Zinaida wash dishes. It's about allowing them to be who they are and focus on what their goals are. We don't say

'Loblaws has a placement, you're going there.' You see a lot of growth, they're being integrated into the community. It makes them proud and gives them a feeling of self-worth."

Sean, who looks a little like Alex P. Keaton, smiles broadly to himself, he looks up and says, "This is my favorite place."

Everything's ready and the doors open. Ivana has taken her first order. "I'm so nervous, I keep asking my friend what I should say," she confides as she picks up a plate for her customer. Rosa and Alice stand behind the steam table filling orders. The servers run to get cutlery and drinks while Lily mans the coffee service. People are streaming in. It looks like lunch in any busy restaurant, with no suits and cell phones—a noticeable and welcome difference. There are a few guys who look like roadies for the Grateful Dead, some flower children gone to seed, some seniors. Everyone quietly eats their lunch, sometimes talking with their table partners. No one is falling over drunk or screaming obscenities. It's calmer than I would have thought possible.

Gerry McGilly has been the administrator here for six years and we go to his office to talk. He got into this from a social justice point of view.

"I was doing street outreach, helping people find housing and a housing project was originally planned for this site so I was brought in. There wasn't enough money for the housing project, so a meal program was implemented instead. You can't fight housing and social justice problems so easily but you can feed people easily. The lunches here tend to be more about getting the food out and keeping it simple for the volunteers. For dinner, Sam gets a little more creative and offers more options." Gerry enjoys working with the Capuchin brothers. "They're like the hippies of the Christian world. They have a joyful way of looking at things. People are more important to them than rules and regulations. The focus here is to try and find what we have in common, not what makes us different."

For small charities, a twenty year life span is the norm; donors lose interest, your volunteers, who are usually retired people, are unable to come anymore. I ask Gerry if this concerns him. "We're not worried. The religious connection allows us to get a lot of volunteers through the local Catholic schools and the Centre for Student Missions, who send kids from all over North America to spend a week volunteering here and understanding our mission."

It's a mission that provides something rarely seen in situations where the poor and disenfranchised are concerned: nourishment and dignity for the customers, a deeper understanding of their fellow man for the student volunteers, and a greater sense of self and place in the community for those involved in the Youth 2 Work program.

I've worked as a cook for the past six years. I've been in plenty of kitchens filled with screaming, freaking madmen racing the clock to get the food ready and out to the customers who are paying a small fortune. The kitchen at St. Francis has to get the food out for sure, and they have to get it out to customers who are paying *their* small fortunes. These customers have had their palates honed by near starvation—the most important part of their day is this meal. That's pretty intense pressure, but I don't think I've ever seen a kitchen full of people enjoying themselves so much.

No stress. Kindness and goodwill permeate the place. Every chef I've worked with over the years has said that the secret to good food is the love you put into it. If that's so, St. Francis Table is serving the best food in the world.

Are You Lonesome Tonight?

by Gail Shepherd
from *The Broward-Palm Beach New Times*

In her current gig as dining critic for this Ft. Lauderdale–based alternative newsweekly, Gail Shepherd dines out more than most of us do—and not always with a companion. Here's how it played out for her in one restaurant.

There's something human beings really hate to do all by ourselves. We don't like to dine alone. When we venture out to eat, let us have at least one other sentient being beside us at table even if, in a pinch, it turns out to be someone we don't much like.

Dining alone is scarier than intensive psychotherapy—all your worst fears are forced to the surface. Am I conspicuous? Are people staring? Am I hogging more than my fair share of space? Does my waiter resent me? Do I look like a loser? What should I do with my hands? And most metaphysical of all, in this yawning absence, this silent hour, do I really *know who I am?*

Women particularly, in our post-feminist age, still rarely go out to eat alone. Even when traveling for business, we mostly order room service, subsisting on tepid burgers and soft-boiled eggs. As for me, I've dined on my own at very posh restaurants precisely twice in my life, and both times, the experience was surreal and dreamlike. And ultimately wonderful. At 19, in San Francisco, I once got gussied up and took myself out for an expensive, leisurely meal at a well-known Polynesian-themed restaurant. The odd thing is, I remember every bite I ate (crab Rangoon, pepper steak), exactly what I was wearing (a cream-colored silk skirt), and even what chair I sat in (the great, balloon-shaped butterfly chair in the corner). The waiters looked after me, bemused and solicitous, not sure if I was a whore, a crazy heiress, or just another lost soul.

There's a strange sense of "last meal"-ness to the experience of dining alone, an intensity and focus, as if at the end of it, you're going to quietly fold your napkin and go throw yourself off the nearest bridge. But in that void of white tablecloth and empty chairs, you have no choice but to pay attention to your food (which may be why the *Guide Michelin* surveyors famously work solo). You note the feel of table linen, the sheen of flatware. You study the four furled pink rosebuds in the glass vase; absorb the murmur of waiters and wine stewards as they pad around behind you; notice the precise, measured way your wine glass is refilled. The light from high windows turns your pinot noir the color of a liquid blush. Eating alone slows time. It almost, but not quite, conquers it.

Sitting with me, myself, and I on a recent evening at the Restaurant at the Four Seasons Resort in Palm Beach—feeling a little bit smug and not at all lonesome—I wondered why I don't do this more often. For one thing, your final bill is half what it would be if you were eating with somebody else. You can hie over to the snootiest places with the best chefs, get waited on hand and foot, and nibble the most delectable morsels. When you dine alone, that glass of good champagne is within reach, and nobody is going to judge you for ordering it. You can say "yes" to the half ounce of osetra (at the Restaurant, it's $75); you can OK the seven-course tasting menu with wine pairings. You consult with no one but your own conscience—and maybe the wine steward. My friends, it is bliss. I'm strongly urging you to give it a whirl.

The Restaurant at the Four Seasons is a fine place to take your first solo flight. Chef Hubert des Marais is one of our great celebrity chefs; at the tender age of 31, a little over a decade ago, he was fingered by *Food & Wine* as one of 10 Best New Chefs in America. During his long stint at the Four Seasons, des Marais has put in a splendid garden at the resort, where he plucks fresh herbs and tropical fruits for his "Southeastern Regional" menu; he's been known to purchase fruit too from local residents' backyards. Des Marais frequently goes sea fishing with resort guests and cooks up their haul, and he seemingly has more southeasterly regional ideas than he can shake a stick at. The seven-course tasting menu, for instance, changes daily. The night I was there, my waiter said he'd worked at the Restaurant for ten years and couldn't remember seeing any dish repeated more than once or twice.

The à la carte menu is laden with tropical touches: avocado and sunchoke, banana blossoms, basil pesto sorbet, alligator pears, hearts of palm. You'll find guava and passion fruit reductions, boniato fries, and Old South standards like red-eye gravy polished to a new gloss with heirloom tomatoes. The best representation of Chef Hubert's whimsy, though, is in his tasting menus. You can choose three-, five- or seven-course tastings ($65, $85, $105, respectively), with or without wine pairings ($85, $115, $150 for a three-ounce pour with each course). Go with the pairings if you dare (my waiter, probably worried about my blood alcohol level and the ever-industrious South Palm Beach cops, advised me to drive home along A1A and advised me, please, not to go over 35 miles per hour).

After settling in at a window-side table overlooking the sea, nestled in softest linens, my brocade back-pillow adjusted, my handbag perched on its very own padded stool at my feet, I decided on five selections. The meal would begin with a crab and leek fritter *amuse bouche*. There was chilled grilled summer tomato soup with a morel mushroom dumpling to follow. Then a piece of annatto-basted Florida mahi mahi with yucca frita and fresh passion fruit reduction. A pan-seared Peking duck breast with caramelized peach and red curry vinaigrette came next. Then tenderloin of bison with braised beluga lentils and roasted figs in truffle jus. The evening would conclude with a chocolate and orange parfait on cocoa nougatine and a scoop of coconut ice cream. I planned on espresso afterward, to accompany the little tray of sweetmeats.

The service at the Restaurant is beyond courtly. It's in fact so pitch-perfect that it made me glow with pleasure. Every server, from the bread man to the wine steward, uses your name (your last name, that is, as in: "Welcome to Restaurant, Ms. Shepherd." Or "May I pour you more water, Ms. Shepherd?" Or "Pardon my reach, Ms. Shepherd."). I was offered newspapers and magazines (the solo diner's first resort, which I refused). My napkin was placed in my lap. My chair adjusted just so. I was visited by a head-waiter, a waiter, a wine steward, a food runner, a bread server, and a table busser, all of whom cared *deeply*. My flatware and service plates were changed and updated with great precision. It was a ter-rific performance.

As for my five courses, one was ho-hum; the rest were stellar. The tomato soup was mysterious and smoky, topped with a petite, warm morel dumpling and mined with emerald-green herbal infusions. It was flecked here and there with the most delicate little basil and oregano sprouts, dusky, peppery, and sweet. A 2002 Ech-elon chardonnay was served with it. But the second course, mahi mahi, fell completely flat. The fish had purportedly been basted in annatto, a subtle flavor that I certainly couldn't detect, and the fil-lets were perched on mealy, dry yucca fries. The wine, a sauvignon blanc from Robert Pecota, was the one pairing I didn't find con-vincing. Even so, when the mahi was followed by rare duck breast with a grilled peach, all was forgiven. Here was a dish I'll remember forever: the duck breast pink and moist and fatty, set against a perfumed, warm peach flecked with lots of cracked pepper and coriander seeds, topped with a tiny sprig of flowering mint and surrounded by a moat of red curry vinaigrette. It was the perfect iteration of summertime. The Alderbrook pinot noir served with the duck had unfortunately gone off, but when I pointed this out, a new bottle was opened with great bustle and profuse apolo-gies. And the new pour was delicious with what I had left of the bird—light-bodied and exuding warm cherry and spices.

The most tender, dreamy, and luscious tenderloin of bison was brought out next, on a bed of tiny dark "caviar" lentils alongside melting roasted figs in a bottomless, velvety truffle jus. What a superb bite this was—the textures of the meaty bison and sweet figs set against the fragrantly earthy lentils. Along with it came my favorite wine of the evening, a smooth, rich, round and very drinkable 2002 Italian Campofiorin Masi that made an ideal accompaniment for this aromatic dish.

Dessert was lovely to look at, better to dig into—an expensive-looking square of rich chocolate that seemed to emanate light, perched on a buttery nougat and festooned with tall, dark choco-late squiggles like a lady's hat. A strip of orange marmalade flecked with fresh mint separated dark from light: a tiny round of refreshing coconut ice cream to take the edge off the chocolate. The Quady Essencia orange muscat served with it ("Orange and chocolate always compliment each other so well," the steward confided as he poured) was delightful.

By the time the tropical fruit gum drop, the butter cookie, and the chocolate candy arrived, I'd lost any trace of self-consciousness. I was in exactly the right place at exactly the right moment. Clearly, I belonged here, sipping my cup of bitter espresso, savoring the deep and luxurious easiness of my own company. I was someone I could do this with again, sometime.

Mood Food

by Tim Gihring
from *Minnesota Monthly*

> Senior writer and arts editor for this glossy
> regional monthly published out of the Twin
> Cities, Gihring approached this food writing
> assignment with a very specific focus—with
> delicious results.

I am not feeling sexy. Bundled in long underwear, hiking socks, and a ski hat, I'm all set to seduce a yeti. My date is almost certainly wearing two pairs of everything I am. If we tried to kiss, we would bounce off each other like billiard balls. If ever there was a time for an aphrodisiac, this is it.

Aphrodisiacs remind most people of powders purveyed in naughty magazines or in the back-alley shops of Hong Kong, which take something like rhino horn or tiger penis—name your phallic symbol—and grind one species after another toward extinction for the sake of well, extinction's opposite. Most of it sounds like more hooey than a pick-up line. But could a billion Chinese be wrong? That's what I was supposed to find out, by visiting local restaurants and sampling not some Love Potion No. 9 but foods said to inspire romance. And although I was bringing along my girlfriend, not a stranger who wouldn't realize what hit her till she woke up in Mexico smelling of whale vomit (yes, another reputed aphrodisiac), the test would be true: if any dish could assist in the shedding of even one layer in a Minnesota winter, we'd have ourselves an aphrodisiac.

We begin at Ginger Asian Bistro, which occupies an old house near the crossroads at 50th and France in Edina. Ginger is one of the world's most venerable aphrodisiacs. The famous French courtesan Madame du Barry is said to have served ginger to all of her lovers, including King Louis XV, who was reportedly reduced to a state of utter submissiveness. The substance is said to stimulate the circulatory system, get the blood pumping. Or, as our waitress says in halting English, "It opens you up. If you're on the cold side, this will help you heat up." Though, she adds, "if you're on the hot side, this won't help much." Nearly everything on the menu comes with ginger; I ask for the dish with the absolute most. "We can always add more," the waitress offers. "Spice things up a bit."

We order vegetable dumplings with ginger sauce, a ginseng-ginger soup, ginger-broccoli tofu with red peppers, and something called the Pineapple Festival—the dish most laden with ginger. It turns out to be sweet-and-sour chicken spilling out of a decapitated pineapple—the plumy head rests beside it on the plate with a pink umbrella stuck in like a flag, as though Barbados had conquered this fruit for beach bums everywhere. Each bite tastes like a tropical romp in a hammock, and suddenly I'm noticing the chopsticks, wrapped in napkins and standing straight up at each table setting, which reminds me of the Washington Monument, the Foshay Tower, and ancient obelisks. Did anyone ever ask women whether they wanted these giant phallic symbols erected in public, I wonder aloud. "No one asked women a lot of things," my girlfriend says. I ask her if she's feeling anything. Nope.

For dessert, we try chocolate fondue at Barbette, the cozy Uptown bistro that may be the best casual date spot in Minneapolis, if only because its perfectly warm lighting could make even Dick Cheney look like a softie. From the dark booths to the chocolate served to us in a mug, everything here seems to be melting—including my girlfriend. She confesses that dipping strawberries, apple and banana slices, plus bits of a lemon-ginger scone, in chocolate, is having an effect. The fondue, a virtual cocktail of serotonin stimulators and phenylethylamine (the supposed "love chemical" that peaks in the body during orgasm), is bringing her over to the "hot side." Evidence shows that the phenylethylamine in chocolate is unfortunately metabolized before it ever reaches the brain, but no matter, we're being drawn together—even as we notice the couple beside us falling apart. Eventually they leave, but not together; the woman is in tears. We can't help wondering if a little warm chocolate might have helped.

On another freezing night, we test that most clichéd of aphrodisiacs: raw oysters. There's nothing romantic about devouring the squishy cold blobs. And it's only sexual if you think like ancient frat boys, who apparently thought that slurping flesh from shells was rather like getting up close and personal with, let's say, Georgia O'Keeffe's flower paintings. There's a macho vibe at the oyster bar in the Oceanaire, the area's premiere seafood establishment, which flies in a dozen oyster varieties daily to the Hyatt Regency hotel in downtown Minneapolis and displays this challenge, attributed to Jonathan Swift, on a wall: "He was a bold man who first swallowed an oyster." Many of the male servers sport mustaches and talk to diners about oysters the way baseball coaches soothe rattled pitchers: with a firm hand on the shoulder and a go-get-'em attitude. "Tear it up!" our waiter tells us as he brings over a dozen mollusks, mostly the East Coast variety, which are generally more firm and briny than the fishy-tasting West Coast kinds. And so I tear in, even as my girlfriend, who's attired in a cute sweater covered in tiny hearts, wonders what's in it for her.

Perhaps to get her in the spirit, our server offers her a Flirtini, a martini made from pineapple juice, vodka, and champagne. Instead, she orders a cognac cocktail that could've curled the man's mustache. She hasn't touched the oysters. Then we notice a couple at the other end of the oyster bar, celebrating their minutes-ago engagement; within the hour, the man's shirt is halfway unbuttoned. The waiter tells us he once saw a woman come in alone, devour three dozen oysters, and jump all over the stranger beside her. I look at my own shirt, tightly fastened, and wonder how many slimy goobers it might take to change that. My money is on the cognac.

Wedded Bliss

by Jason Sheehan

from *Westword*

As a former chef, Jason Sheehan can analyze what's on his plate in amazing detail—but his essays in this Denver alternate newsweekly go far beyond mere meal description, bringing to life the whole rich experience of eating out.

Laura staggers as we step through the double doors and into the Royal Peacock. She doesn't swoon, exactly, but there's not much in this world that can make her swoon. She misses her footing a little, and then a huge smile spreads across her face, and her eyes go wide as though she's just experienced a sudden and unexpected spiritual enlightenment. She inhales deeply, her nostrils flaring, and takes my hand.

"Can you smell that? Isn't that your favorite smell in the world?"

Back at the house, she'd been in a lather, skipping from the bed to the closet to the computer, where the Royal Peacock's menu was up on the screen. She'd been planning her assault for most of the afternoon, throwing around words that I didn't even know she could pronounce, translating for me a language that, for her, is pure sensuality: Jaipur masala, ghoste ka salun and Rajasthani rajput thali, describing not just a vegetarian combo plate, but the smooth sweetness of creamed spinach, the yellow stain of turmeric, the arcing burn of dry cumin and fresh coriander, the texture of mashed, baked raisins on her tongue.

"Look at this," she said, pointing to a special of caribou in a sauce of coconut and sweet potatoes that had been one of the Peacock's game specials for April. "I can't decide what to eat. I want everything."

She bounced up from the computer and went to the closet. I edged toward the bedroom door, trying to make a quiet escape. "You're going to change, right?" she asked. "And shave?"

I said no, that jeans and boots and a button-down Oxford would be just fine for a Sunday night in Boulder. She pulled clothes out for me, anyway. "I like this place, Jay," she said. "And they're so nice. You should respect that."

Apparently, respect would be shown by me wearing khakis and white linen and not my grungy work boots, by not spilling the saag or eating inappropriately with my fingers, by not mispronouncing "shajahani" or stepping out for a smoke between courses or doing any one of the myriad things I regularly do to embarrass myself while dining out.

Laura was back at the computer, silently mouthing the names of various dishes, tasting the words on her lips. I kissed the back of her neck, and she waved me off.

"Go brush your teeth," she said. "We have to go. Now."

In the warm, dim, tattered dining room of the Peacock, Laura takes my hand. She comments on the smell. It is Nag Champa incense and curry. It is old carpets and fresh cinnamon. It is twenty-year-old tandoor smoke. It is warm and cloying and sweet, and, as in those old cartoons where the hungry dog is hooked in the nose and lifted by the tendrils of smoke coming from a fat T-bone cooking somewhere off-screen, it has a potent and undeniably attractive force. Laura floats to our table behind Laxmi Lalchandani, the niece of Shanti Awatramani, the man who runs the Royal Peacock, wrote the menu that's stood unchanged since the '80s and still cooks some nights. I swear Laura's feet aren't even touching the ground. She glows like she's swallowed a string of Christmas lights, and before she sits, she runs her fingertips across the scratchy, industrial poly-blend tablecloth. The menus are faded, printed on loose paper folded inside covers upholstered in threadbare purple cloth with beaded peacocks on the front. We order bottles of Kingfisher lager, and Laura looks at the pictures of elephant-riding warriors hung above the windows, the scenes from the Bhagavad Gita, princes and princesses locked in permanent embrace, Shiva with arms outstretched, one foot forever descending.

"It's just like I remember," she says. "Nothing has changed."

Everything has changed.

I first heard of the Royal Peacock almost ten years ago. I was in the Southwest only by dint of powerful drugs, poor life choices and my legendarily bad sense of direction. Leaving Buffalo and headed for Rochester one night, I'd somehow found myself in Santa Fe. There was a New Year's Eve party going on around me, and I was on the phone with Laura, in Colorado, whom I hadn't seen since being thrown out of college (for the first time) years before. We made plans to get together, and did. It was a classic boy-meets-girl, boy-loses-girl, boy-ends-up-staying-in-girl's-new-boyfriend's-basement-for-a-week-and-stealing-her-away-while-boyfriend-is-at-work kind of story. Pure American romance. And though we never made it to the Royal Peacock then, I remember Laura telling me about her favorite Indian restaurant in Boulder. We talked of biryani and saag, but mostly ate takeout Chinese food and made long drives to Johnson's Corner for coffee, cigarettes and pie. Back in Santa Fe, regrouping, we ate eggs and chile. Staying at her parent's house outside Philadelphia, we ate roti canai and bastilla and she made me herbed chicken and pasta. In our tiny apartment in Rochester with the hardwood floors and the cockroaches, we would lie tangled in blankets beneath the cracked windows, and I would ask what I could do to make her happy.

"Go to the Royal Peacock in Boulder and get me saag paneer," she would say, and I would get up, get dressed.

"Anything else?"

"Bombay paratha. And make sure they don't forget the raita."

She would talk with her eyes closed, lying on her side, half-dreaming, and the strength of my love for her could be gauged by how far I got before she called me back. When we fought (and we fought a lot, still do), we would make amends with promises of food. Lutece, La Tour d'Argent, the Spring Mill Cafe, croquettes from the Gateway Diner, samosa with tamarind chutney from the Royal Peacock.

Living in Albuquerque, we played the same game. Sometimes

we would drive to Boulder—six hours booming across the desert and up into the mountains in a series of highly undependable vehicles—meaning to go to the Royal Peacock but never making it, always ending up at Juanita's or somewhere else. The Peacock became part of the mythology of our relationship, a story we told each other, a make-believe perfect destination. It had everything to do with love and sex and food and mileage—the four cardinal points of our eventual marriage.

After we moved to Denver, we could finally go there whenever we wanted—but still didn't. We talked about it all the time. We scheduled it, then bumped it, then rescheduled it and bumped it again. Frankly, I was flat-out fucking terrified that after eight years of anticipation, we would go to the Peacock and it would be terrible. Nothing like Laura remembered, like nothing I had imagined. And then where would we be?

Now, sitting at our table wreathed in good smells, we order. Carefully. We drink our beers and tell Peacock stories to each other all over again, and then the food begins to arrive. Laura takes a samosa. I spoon out a bit of murgh chaat—sliced yellow tomatoes, cold chicken and cubes of cucumber in a cool yogurt sauce spiked with mango powder. After eight years of talking about it, together we finally taste.

And together we are gone. The chaat isn't just good—it's beyond fantastic and actually stuns me for a second, freezing me in a pantomime of bliss with my eyes closed and my jaw locked and my lips pursed as though waiting for an invisible kiss. The yogurt is milk-thin, savory, fruity and deeply sweet, the tomatoes crisp and juicy, the cucumbers astringent and refreshing like spring rain. And the chicken, impossibly, has kept both its flavor and its texture in the face of a dozen competing sensations.

Across the table, Laura groans quietly, opens her eyes and looks at me.

"Is it good?" she asks.

"You have no idea."

When she smiles, it's so wide that I'm afraid the top of her head is going to fall off.

The rest of the night is a blur of singular impressions. We trade plates. The samosa are almost too hot to eat, but I pull one in half, and the smell of cumin and fennel rising from the potatoes and peas inside the pastry shell hits me like a slap. Laura laughs when she tastes the chaat. When Laxmi returns, she's carrying salvers piled with dal and saag and golden saffron rice, ajmer murgh and rogan josh with cilantro and delicate vegetables in cream sauce, and kheer and raita, of course, all in lovely tin and copper bowls. She also has a tray of naan and Bombay paratha—unleavened wheat bread filled with a thin layer of potatoes and spices. Approaching, she looks like a Balinese dancer, arms raised, hips cocked to swivel around an empty chair, nose stud winking.

We eat quickly and shamelessly, stuffing ourselves while everything is hot, scooping up pinches of saag paneer with pieces of naan torn from the puffy round, as well as bits of lamb in a fiery sauce the color of old brick that comes on like lightning, burns and then vanishes, leaving behind just the essence of smoke and a tingle of barely remembered pain. The creamed, spiced sweet potatoes taste of Thanksgiving in strange latitudes, the sabji kari like an exotic vegetarian heaven. The dal is thick and starchy, its lentils perfectly cooked. The saag is incredible, packed with so much heavy cream and clarified butter that each bite melts away to nothing. The ajmer murgh—tandoori chicken breasts swimming in a spinach and cream sauce—is less complicated than the saag, but with a depth of smooth sweetness that seems to go on forever. It's one of the best things I've ever tasted, worth an eight-year wait. The first bite compresses the time between my lying on the old boyfriend's floor and just now to an instant, a blink.

Laura and I have been eating Indian food together for a long time, but I finally understand what she was asking for in Rochester, dreaming of in Albuquerque, trying to explain to me from Boulder to Philadelphia and back again. It wasn't food she was after, it was this sensation of perfect, timeless bliss, of tasting something that comes as close to perfection as any human endeavor can.

I flag down Laxmi and ask for chai. It's a family recipe, passed down from her aunt through all the female blood relatives. She claims it is the best chai in the country, the best that can be had without going to Bombay—where the family comes from and where she grew up, among the hotels and resorts that Shanti

Awatramani's family ran. When she sets the cup down in front of me, the steam seems to have a weight. It's so heavy with spice it can barely rise.

Laura is beaming, pop-eyed, lost in reverie, home again among flavors whose memories were all she had to live on for far too long. With a fork in her hand, a spot of spinach on her lip and a blush of heat and spice in her cheeks, she is more beautiful than I have seen her in a long time. She digs through her rice pudding looking for raisins and shares them with me.

In the parking lot outside, she dances to the car, spinning in circles like a six-year-old who's had too much candy. Laura is a woman more likely to punch a nun in the face than to dance. At our wedding, I had to bribe her just to get her up for one song. But here, she dances. And I lumber, stuffed and half drunk on spice and memories, carrying a heavy bag of takeout.

Late that night, long after Laura has collapsed, stunned into sleep, I go down to the kitchen and assemble a second feast of dirty, spicy rice and cold tandoori chicken stained a pale red, and murgh and sweet potatoes and blazing hot biryani and naan smeared with honey. The first time, I waited eight years before trying this food; now I barely wait four hours before having it again. I eat by the light of the TV, lying on our couch in our house, amazed all over again, sucker-punched by a cuisine I thought I knew. In the morning, Laura will likely kill me for eating all the leftovers—but then, this relationship has always been based on food. Food started it, food sustained it, food kept us together through some very strange years. No doubt, food will be the end of it as well.

But not until morning, at least.

Post-It Love

by Brett Anderson

from *The Times-Picayune*

For Brett Anderson, post-Katrina New Orleans is no longer a place for critically rating restaurants. It's the bigger story he's compelled to write, of a city rebuilding itself and a dining scene that's coming back restaurant by restaurant.

From December 1946 through August 2005, the Camellia Grill was about as steady as a restaurant can be. It's the restaurant you came to at the river's bend, near the end (or is it the beginning?) of the streetcar route. You'd often wait in line to enter, as you'd expect to at a landmark, for breakfast, lunch, dinner or whatever you call a meal consumed during the last moments of consciousness, with only one eye open, at an hour that beat cops advise honest citizens to be home in bed.

In the past year the Camellia Grill has gone from a famous diner to a mystery hiding in plain sight, partially wrapped in Post-It notes.

"Came from Florida for pecan pie. Sorry we missed you!"

"What are you waiting for?"

"Need workers? I'll work! Put up a hiring sign. I miss you!-Sexy Nola Lady."

The notes were brought to my attention last spring, about the time I began trying to determine why the Camellia Grill, despite being on high-and-dry ground, surrounded by reopened businesses, has remained closed since Hurricane Katrina.

The notes cover the outside of the diner's vestibule. Many are written on heart-shaped paper ("Miss you!-Julie"). Some messages reference others:

"I never got to try y'alls red beans and rice."

"I never got to try 'em either!"

The tableau reads like bathroom stall graffiti risen to a higher purpose. The shared longing in the hand-scrawled words ("miss" by far the most recurring) softens the blow of finding the restaurant shuttered. ("Please unlock" reads a note near the doorknob.) While nowhere near as satisfying as finding Harry Tervalon or Michael Carbo, longtime fixtures behind Camellia's counter, doling out plastic straws to customers with the sort of flourish dapper waiters generally reserve for fine silver or champagne flutes, the messages are welcoming in their own way.

They are mash notes to restorative griddle fare ("I need a fried egg sandwich and some chocolate pecan pie!") and restless ambiance ("I miss all the smoke and grease and shouting across the room") that double as invitations to join the chorus. The messages have been compounding for weeks. Try not putting pen to paper after reading a few yourself.

The Camellia notes are also an expression of what people are asking all over town: What's up with the Camellia Grill? When will it reopen?

Here's what I know: nothing.

Michael Schwartz, the restaurant's owner, has been missing in action since Katrina. And I'm not the only one who has been looking for him.

When I told Camellia's lawyer, Mark S. Stein, that I field questions about the restaurant seemingly every day, he told me he did as well. This was a few weeks ago. Stein told me he'd be talking with the restaurant's owner in a day or so and would call back with any information. He never did. He also hasn't returned several phone messages since.

When I contacted the "block captain" on Schwartz's street in May, he told me people had been inquiring as to Schwartz's whereabouts since fall. At least one person was interested in purchasing Schwartz's house, he said.

Soon, a handful of other curious neighbors were brought into the discussion, and in the flurry of e-mails that followed, rumors and theories were shared. Many of these stemmed from a well-publicized petition filed in 2003 by three of Camellia's creditors who sought to force the restaurant into Chapter 7 bankruptcy.

The dispute was resolved, according to a 2004 *Times-Picayune* story that quoted Mitchell Hoffman, a Camellia attorney at the time. Several messages left for a New Orleans attorney by that name have gone unreturned.

Schwartz's neighbors believe he has relocated to Mississippi or Tennessee. Wherever it is, he hasn't been the only person related to the restaurant who has proven difficult to find.

My effort to contact Harry Tervalon set me on a dead-end trail to Texas. I got a hold of Michael Carbo. It wasn't the Michael Carbo I was looking for, although he was familiar with the long-time Camellia employee.

"I go to the Camellia Grill. We call each other cuz," the wrong Michael Carbo said of the Michael Carbo I thought might know something about the status of the restaurant. "He's black, I'm white."

Phone calls to the households I thought might be home to former Camellia managers, waiters and cooks all came to similar, if less amusing, ends.

I was optimistic that Priscilla Hagebusch would offer something—if not answers then perhaps prose that gave voice to what we'll call the Camellia Lovers' Predicament. In 2001 she'd penned a poem mourning the cloth napkins the Camellia had replaced with paper. (TLC Linen Services was one of the creditors who filed the 2003 bankruptcy petition against the restaurant.) But I couldn't find Hagebusch, either.

There seems to be consensus among the Camellia devoted that if the current owner doesn't reopen the restaurant it ought to be sold to someone who will. A 1996 *Times-Picayune* story marking the Camellia's 50th anniversary suggests that Schwartz would be willing to move the property. Schwartz said in the story that he was trying to sell. Asking price? In "the mid seven figures."

In fact, in the late 1990s Ti Martin tried to add the Camellia to her family's restaurant portfolio, which includes Commander's Palace. "It didn't work out," she said.

In May a concierge from Le Pavillon called to say one of the hotel's wealthy customers had expressed an interest in buying the diner. Could I help put him in touch with the current owner?

In early June, I felt on the verge of a breakthrough. A Metairie lawyer who'd e-mailed about the Camellia forwarded our correspondence along to a local real estate agent and a woman who he said ate at the Camellia on its opening day as a little girl. I never heard back from the latter. The former, however, knew just about everything there is to know about the Camellia—save for what the future holds.

Which is a shame. The notes stuck to the windows of the diner don't prevent a visitor from peering inside. The 29 stools are there, arranged around a counter with a meandering contour that seems to mirror the nearby river's. One of the message writers is right: "Those stools look lonely."

Fast Food

Don't Call It a Hot Dog

by Joe Yonan

from *The Boston Globe*

This was one of intrepid food reporter Joe Yonan's last pieces for *The Globe* before moving down to Washington to become *The Washington Post*'s new food section editor. Boston's loss is the DC area's gain.

To hear a native Rhode Islander tell it, the most colorful moniker for the state's stubby little hot wieners, laden with meat sauce, mustard, onions, and celery salt, is too colorful for a family newspaper. "Off the record, then," he said. "You wanna know what we call 'em?"

Of course. But I've done some research. I know that here in the littlest state, what are sometimes called New York System wieners are an only-in-Rhody obsession right up there with cabinets, coffee milk, Del's frozen lemonade, and jonnycakes. And I know that they go by many a name.

Gaggas, right? Sure. Destroyers? Uh-huh. Belly-busters? Close, he says, but not quite. So I give up: What, then, does John Rossi call them?

"Some people call 'em belly [expletive]," said Rossi, smiling, "because they're good going down, but four hours later they start to come back." In Rossi's experience, the only remedy for such a thing is a few big swigs of Coke about an hour or so after consumption.

Rossi should know. He's been consuming wieners for more

than four decades. "I was born in 1960, so I've eaten them since 1962," he said at the counter of Olneyville New York System in the Olneyville neighborhood of Providence. Moreover, to Rossi, two wieners don't even qualify as dinner, not even "all the way." On this Friday night, they're a mere appetizer for the cheesesteak he's now devouring. "If I wasn't getting the steak, I'd get four wienies," he said.

This little wiener—whatever you do, don't call it a hot dog—has flourished in Rhode Island for almost a century, ever since Greek immigrants who ran similar operations on Coney Island moved north and attached the New York name to their new shops in apparent hopes of gaining credibility with the locals. The name and style stuck, and today from Warren to Warwick, Cranston to Newport, and Providence to Woonsocket, dozens of restaurants with names like Wein-O-Rama, Weiner Genie, Rod's Grille, and Sparky's New York System, Sam's New York System, Original New York Systems, Ferrucci Original New York System, and, yes, just plain New York System sell them for barely more than a buck apiece.

Ask a Rhode Islander who makes the best wiener, and the answer will probably be whatever place he or she had them growing up. Lisa Hamilton, associate editor of *Rhode Island Magazine*, prefers those from Rod's Grille, but that's because she hails from Warren.

The opinions are held dearly. People even disagree on how to spell wieners. Hamilton says her magazine stopped including wieners in its "Best of Rhode Island" awards for a few years because of the contentiousness (read: hate mail) that resulted.

Besides the traditional squared-off shape of most of the wieners (a result of cutting, not tying them off) and the meat-sauce topping, it's the method of assembly that truly distinguishes them. The old-school short-order cooks prepare them "up d'ahm." They hold one arm out, palm up, and line up the buns between wrist and elbow, then quickly put a wiener in each, squirt on the mustard, dollop the meat sauce, spread the onions, and sprinkle the celery salt. At the best places, all that can happen in a matter of seconds.

"You have to get 'em out as fast as you can," said Nick Barros, one of the cooks at Olneyville, where the Showtime series *Brotherhood* has filmed some scenes.

His fellow cook, Robert Zanni, talks up his co-worker's arm as if Barros were Curt Schilling. "I have short arms," he said. "But this gentleman, he can put on 15, then he stacks 'em—he can do up to 45!"

Actually, that's not exactly right. "I've done 50," Barros said.

On the other side of town, at Original New York Systems, when our group orders five wieners all the way, Norman Robb cradles a stainless-steel sheet for his assembly. Why not the arm? "Because the Health Department says don't do it," he said with a grin. "And because I don't know you."

This place, owned by the great-grandson of its founder, just celebrated its 79th anniversary. Robb has worked there for 19 of those years, and old habits die hard. "I have people who come in and say they won't buy 'em unless I do 'em on my arm," he said. "And then what am I supposed to do?"

Robb and fellow worker Raymond Colaluca are full of stories about founder Gust Pappas and celebrity visitors such as Louis Armstrong, who came for wieners at 2 A.M. one day in the early 1950s.

Musician David Byrne famously worked here in the 1970s, and some say the trademark chopping motion he performs in his oversized suit in the video for the Talking Heads' song "Once in a Lifetime" came from his experience assembling the wieners. "When he goes like this," Colaluca said, looking about as far from Byrne as can be imagined, "he's putting on the mustard, putting on the meat sauce, putting on the onions."

Like Olneyville, Original New York Systems is open until long after Providence's clubs close, which explains the wieners' reputation as post-imbibing, pre-hangover food. As such, the grease content is high, particularly in the meat sauce, which consists of ground beef, fat, and seasonings no one will divulge. "That I can't tell you," Colaluca said.

At the sunny Rod's Grille in Warren, the meat sauce is less greasy , but co-owner Sandra Rodrigues, whose grandfather Mariano started the place 50 years ago, won't divulge much about her grandmother's recipe. "I've seen some of the other recipes in the paper, and hers is definitely different," Rodrigues said. "What's different about it I'm not allowed to tell."

At Olneyville, Rossi remembers skipping church with money his mother gave him for the offering and instead spending it on 25-cent wieners. "It was sinful," he admitted. For its part, Original New York Systems made news this year when a unit of Rhode Island soldiers serving in Iraq wrote to ask for a taste of home; the restaurant sent all the makings except the actual wieners. "That's on account of the pork," which Muslim dietary laws prohibit, Colaluca said. "We didn't want to start another war."

In Search of the Transcendent Taqueria

by Bill Addison

from *The San Francisco Chronicle*

Between a four-year stint at Atlanta's alt weekly *Creative Lounging* and his new top slot at *The Dallas Morning News*, pastry-chef-turned-dining-critic Bill Addison spent nearly a year feasting at ethnic eateries for *The Chronicle*'s highly-regarded food section.

C all it "trial by taqueria."

I was six weeks into my new job as a staff writer for the *Chronicle*'s Food section when my editor, with a glint in his eyes, proposed an assignment: Go out and, as an extension of this year's Bargain Bites (look for it this Sunday in the *Chronicle Magazine*), explore the Bay Area's taqueria scene. Visit as many as you can, he urged.

Sure, I was game. I'd moved to town just three days before I started work. Tackling taquerias would be a good way to learn the region, right? Burritos are nationally known as the soul food of San Francisco, but how many burrito joints could there possibly be?

It took only a perfunctory Internet search to puncture my naiveté. The Bay Area has hundreds of taquerias.

I made it to 85 in 10 weeks.

Taquerias are an indelible part of the Bay Area's food culture. They provide their customers—blue- and white-collar workers, college students, families of all backgrounds—with the region's indigenous fast food. They're a near-ubiquitous presence in almost every area, neighborhood and town.

And, whoa, do they encourage fierce loyalty and ferocious

debate. The focal point of that debate, though, is centered on the foil-wrapped, barrel-shaped burrito. "It's basically the No. 2 plate at a Mexican restaurant rolled into a flour tortilla," quips Jonathan Gold, food critic at *L.A. Weekly* and a former restaurant critic for *Gourmet* magazine. "But you wouldn't believe how many letters I get from readers asking where to find San Francisco–style burritos in L.A."

Burrito disciples generally acknowledge El Faro in San Francisco's Mission District as serving the first "super burrito" in 1961. The simple yet genre-defying addition of rice, sour cream and guacamole to the basic meat, bean and cheese format sparked demand for a new breed of bet-you-can't-finish-it sustenance. The "Cylindrical God" has since become a worshiped local art form. Two Web sites started in the last year alone—Burritoeater.com and Burritophile.com—devote themselves to taquerias' Topic A.

Steve Ells, founder and CEO of Chipotle Mexican Grill, was so inspired by taquerias while working as a line cook at San Francisco's legendary Stars restaurant that he opened his own variation on a burrito joint in Denver in 1993. Today, the chain has more than 530 locations nationwide.

But local burrito fans are quick to point out that nothing beats a hometown construct. "We're spoiled," says Dan Johnson, a founding editor of Burritophile.com, which encourages users to post their own taqueria reviews. "Your average burrito in San Francisco would be something that in any other city would knock your socks off."

"And they're cheap," adds Cate Czerwinski, another Burritophile editor. "You don't hear as much discussion about who serves the best foie gras because not as many people can afford it."

Quesadillas, flautas, enchiladas, tortas and tamales are all standard taqueria dishes. But I noticed immediately when I started this quest (which excluded taco trucks, a subject unto themselves) that although the actual physicality of taquerias varies enormously, their kitchens are designed to expedite two menu items: burritos and tacos. The meat choices are essentially the same: carnitas (braised, well-browned pork); carne asada (grilled steak); al pastor (barbecued beef or pork) and chicken—stewed, roasted or grilled. The service is mostly the same, too: unapologetically speedy.

To cut the salty richness of the food, the beverages of choice include horchata—the milky sweet, cinnamon-scented rice drink —and juicy agua frescas made with in-season fruits. I came to savor the ephemeral moment when the cashier would slowly, carefully ladle my tamarindo or watermelon agua fresca from a barrel-shaped plastic jar before shooing me on my way.

Despite these apparent similarities, however, the food at one place is never quite the same as at another. The taste of a burrito can vary based on the texture of the meat, the seasonings in the rice, and how precisely the tortilla is folded around the ingredients, among other things. La Cumbre in the Mission, for instance, chops an actual piece of steak for its carne asada burritos and tacos. That results in an entirely different—and, in my opinion, notably superior—eating experience than scooping pre-cooked meat from a steam table, as many taquerias do.

Soft tacos, depending on a taqueria's idiosyncrasies, also morph in unexpected ways. There's no denying the appeal of Taqueria Vallarta's straightforward rendition of meat, salsa, onion and cilantro, but sometimes an unexpected twist—like how Taqueria La Morena in South San Francisco adds both pico de gallo and fiery hot sauce to its bean-laced tacos—can prove unexpectedly satisfying.

As for crispy tacos? Well, I realized how hard it is to be critical when your kisser's full of crunchy fried tortilla and gobs of guacamole.

Using your eyes and nose is the ideal way to scout out a neighborhood's most promising taquerias. El Farolito was one of the most oft-mentioned spots in the dozens of e-mails that the *Chronicle* received after we asked readers to tell us about their favorite taquerias. Colleagues and the online sites I scoured for suggestions also gave it high marks. But it was the line of eager customers outside El Farolito—and the smoky smells wafting out—that best tipped me off to the probability of a fine burrito in my future. Beware empty taquerias. They are usually vacant for a reason.

For every one burrito like El Farolito's that sent gluttonous thrills down my spine, I ate 10 that made me want to jog to the nearest sushi bar and scrap the whole project. They may all look the same in their silver foil, but underneath the wrapping each burrito is a microcosm of individuality. And a surprising number of things can desecrate a cylindrical god: Stale rice. Un-melted cheese. Under-salted beans. An over-steamed or blatantly unheated tortilla. Old, gray meat that had lingered on the steam table, though, was the most common sacrilege. Carnitas and carne asada shouldn't simply taste like vague, high-on-the-food chain protein. They should have a distinctive meaty robustness that helps them stand out from the other ingredients.

Yet quality ingredients alone don't necessarily translate to a good burrito. Construction and proportion are just as essential. Bay Area–style burritos evolve as you eat them. One bite may be full of guacamole and rice, but the next might include a hunk of pork with an extra nip of jalapeño, the next a slick of melty cheese. The more you eat, the gushier it gets.

Still, the first mouthful of a burrito reveals more than you might expect. Is it nothing but tortilla or rice? Then the ingredients probably haven't been distributed evenly. Cold spots—those unappetizing patches that yield nothing but blobs of sour cream—may lurk.

Every burrito enthusiast develops a list of adamant aversions, and mine is to lettuce. I know others will disagree, but I think lettuce turns a burrito's innards into a swampy mush. "Sin lechuga, por favor" has become my most oft-used Spanish phrase.

Tacos, likewise, have taken some divergent local twists. What was originally a two- or three-bite nosh has blossomed at some taquerias into full-blown knife-and-fork food. Beans are the most common addition to the basic meat-on-corn-tortilla premise, although I encountered a few overzealous places that slathered on rice, cheese and—grrr—lettuce to a regular taco. Happily, many taquerias also prepare tacos much closer to their Mexican roots—two small corn tortillas topped with a judicious handful of meat anointed with a splash of salsa, and perhaps chopped onion and cilantro. A bracing squeeze of lime at the table is all they need.

Those few places that did have me swiveling my head between bites of burrito and taco—burbling murmurs of astonishment and appreciation—automatically made it into my top 20. Yet even when I did uncover these dual pleasures, I found an almost unvarying trend: Among taquerias with two or more locations—I counted at least 25 such ventures—one restaurant makes markedly better food than its siblings. The recently renovated Half Moon

Bay location of Tres Amigos, for example, cranks out suave carnitas and saucy chile verde. Yet, a later visit to its San Mateo branch revealed strangely minced carne asada and virtual mud puddles of cold spots in the burritos.

Sometimes busy-ness—or the lack thereof—plays a factor. I gladly braved the masses for the astutely crafted tacos at Taqueria San Jose's cowboy-ish Marin location. But the tepid chow at its overly sedate Mission spot wouldn't warrant a return visit.

All this running around helped me observe how deeply the taqueria culture is embraced by the entire Bay Area. El Farolito in San Francisco might be construed as a hipster hangout, while Cactus Taqueria in Oakland gets viewed as a family restaurant destination. But the food they serve has the same fundamental soul.

The burrito's universal appeal, it turns out, unites the community in unspoken ways. And the fun of glimpsing all these different folks enjoying burritos and tacos side by side eventually became its own motivation for ferreting out the region's best taquerias. It also taught me that there isn't any predictable rhyme or reason for where an outstanding taqueria might be uncovered.

I found my Holy Grail one night late in my search. My quest was winding down, and I'd hit most of the must-try spots by then. Or so I thought—until I stumbled across Sancho's in Redwood City.

I ordered my usual: A carnitas super burrito and two tacos— one carne asada, one al pastor. When my food was up, I plunked down at the table and dug in.

And kept digging in.

It was my fantasy burrito. Everything about this creation tasted eloquent. The tortilla was crisp; the carnitas fell apart in leafy chunks; the refried beans melded with the cheese and guacamole; the salsa had a smoky, concentrated taste. And the tacos were tiny parcels featuring succulent chopped meat—and no beans.

I had a similar end-of-the-trek epiphany at Taqueria Reina's in San Francisco's South of Market neighborhood, owned in part by the people who run Taqueria Cancun. Not only did the thoroughly amalgamated carnitas burrito burst in all the right ways, but the cabeza (head) taco steered clear of the fattiness that often characterizes that cut of meat.

On the whole, transcendent tacos like those made at Sancho's and Reina's proved harder to find than deftly made burritos—that is, until I discovered the wonder of crispy tacos. Cactus' taco, made with Niman Ranch meats, put me in an ecstatic trance. What marvels of engineering crispy tacos are: A pliant outer tortilla surrounds a second, crispy deep-fried tortilla that heats the cheese into oozing lava. Grace notes of guac and sour cream mingle with the piquant meat. It's a chain reaction of decadence.

A crusade to continue my crispy taco adventures—after an underwhelming meal at Nick's Crispy Tacos near Russian Hill—led me to the hallowed and heavily debated doors of La Taqueria in the Mission. It's famous for its conspicuous absence of rice—a direct revolt against Bay Area dictums. I have no beef with La Taqueria's meat-dominant burritos and tacos, except perhaps for the relatively steep prices. Cheese, guacamole and sour cream are all extra, so two fully loaded crispy tacos and a small tamarindo agua fresca cost $13.24. In the realm of taquerias, that's a sizable chunk of change.

Yet the adoration this place elicits can't be easily discounted. "Man, there's a whole lot of love going on in this burrito," said a guy sitting behind me into his cell phone. Crunching on my tacos, I knew what he was feeling. The finest of these unpretentious foods can evoke a brimming sense of well-being. I understand now why taquerias inspire so much loyalty.

In the past week, as I completed this project, everyone I know was saying to me, "I bet you'll be happy to never eat a burrito again in your whole life!" Truth is, my editor has created a monster—or, more accurately, a Pavlov's dog. Every time someone mentions burritos or tacos, I salivate on cue. And start contemplating my next taqueria destination.

SELECTED HIGHLIGHTS ALONG THE WAY

Taquerias, I quickly discovered on this trek, are worlds onto themselves. Here are some highlights:

First Love. During my inaugural week of the hunt, I watched a mountain range of carne asada slowly sizzling on the grill through the window at El Farolito on Mission Street. The restaurant may as well have installed a neon lit sign on its facade a la Krispy Kreme: Hot Burritos Now. I quickly joined the line out the door. Observing the cooks and savoring the results of their labors helped me set benchmarks for the weeks of eating ahead. The staffers started a burrito by griddling its tortilla on both sides—a good sign—but didn't put the cheese on the tortilla while was it still on the griddle. I hoped the whole package would ultimately be hot enough to melt the cheese inside. The late-night crowd didn't mislead: El Farolito's burrito delivered. My initial nibble included husky, well-seasoned steak and a silken sliver of avocado—not the thin guacamole that most taquerias make. The tortilla had a flaky crispness, and I could feel through the aluminum sheath that the burrito was hot throughout. As I ate my vertical meal, I found that—hallelujah—the shreds of cheese had indeed melted. Shiny wads of foil littered the tabletop by the time I chomped this baby down to its floury, creamy nub.

Stand-up Tacos. One night, a taqueria lead in South San Francisco proved a dead end, so a friend and I wound up in the Mission, aimlessly wandering to see what we could suss out. That's when I came upon the nighttime taco stand that Taqueria Vallarta sets up in front of its door. Meats—including choice offerings such as sesos (beef brains), lengua (beef tongue) and cabeza (beef head meat, usually cheek)—were arranged around a circular grill. The cook tosses the diminutive tortillas on the grill, dabs a little meat fat on them and then turns the tortillas over to heat on the other side. He layers slices of translucent cooked onion with the meat, adds salsa and passes them to you on a paper plate. You can go eat them inside, or amble down the street eating your tidy, savory bundles. Vallarta also makes wonderful gushy burritos accentuated by robust carnitas. That's an anomaly—I found most taquerias do either burritos or tacos well, but rarely both with equal finesse.

Far-flung Favorite. "Where?" my San Francisco friends demanded when they inquired after my favorite taqueria find. "Sancho's. In Redwood City," I'd repeat confidently. Then I'd tell them the taqueria's story. As often happens in any facet of the restaurant industry, Adam Torres took a circuitous path before he became Sancho's chef and owner. "I owned a taqueria in Mountain View in 1998 during the dot-com boom," says Torres. "But I didn't really know much about food. Someone offered me a pretty penny to buy it, so I took them up on the offer." Torres used the money to send himself to the California Culinary Academy in San Francisco. His first job out of school was working as a line cook at Boulevard, followed by a stint at the Village Pub in Woodside. But he felt he was missing something, so he moved back to Redwood City and, with financial help from his father, opened Sancho's. "Now I know what's going on in the kitchen," Torres says. "I personally watch over the food, taste everything every day, and show my staff what makes food taste good."

A Chipotle Off the Block. There's some outspoken dissent about Chipotle Mexican Grill, the national chain with only one San Francisco location and a handful of others in the Bay Area. Detractors say they don't want to eat "corporate burritos and tacos" from a company owned by McDonald's. Well, I happen to like grabbing lunch at Chipotle. I just don't approach it like I'm eating at a taqueria. I order Chipotle's "burrito bol." It starts with a bed of cilantro-lime rice. I ask for toppings of pinto beans, salsa verde, cheese, a modest slick of sour cream, a hefty dose of guacamole, and half carnitas-half beef barbacoa, both of which are made with Niman Ranch meats. Then I douse it all with lime and Tabasco. It's a satisfying collision of Mexican-themed flavors. McDonald's is divesting its interest in Chipotle, according to Chipotle spokeman Chris Arnold. The company plans to be operating independently by the end of October. Will the move curry favor among the Bay Area's independent-minded diners?

Thankful Mouthfuls. Over the course of my quest, a few unusual dishes stood out. Taqueria Express in the Tenderloin serves lamb burritos and tacos, which lend a pleasantly gamy twist to the flavor mix. Cate Czerwinski of Burritophile.com recommended a plantain burrito at Cuco's in the Lower Haight that redefined euphoric carb loading. But my most baffling burrito was at Pancho's in Laurel Heights. Its "special carnitas burrito" included juicy pork that melded with refried beans to form a gravy-like sauce inside the tortilla wrapper. The rice, I was certain, had been flavored with celery seed. In the context, the pork could have been mistaken for dark meat poultry. Why was the flavor so strange and familiar at once? Then it came to me: It tasted like Thanksgiving turkey and stuffing. Was it hallucinatory palate-fatigue after a full day of taqueria sampling? I can't say. But I've grown so fond of the idea of a Thanksgiving burrito that I'm reluctant to return to Pancho's to either confirm or contradict my experience.

Porno Burrito

by Jonathan Gold

from *LA Weekly*

> They don't give the Pulitzer Prize to just any
> journalist—but Jonathan Gold earned his fair
> and square, wearing out the freeways and
> pavements of Los Angeles to ferret out the
> best unheralded food spots. His appetite is
> discriminating, and completely egalitarian.

Today's subject: the potato taco or, to be more specific, the wonderment of civilization that is the potato taco at El Atacor #11, a taquería chain's grungy outpost on the fringes of Glassell Park. You have, no doubt, tasted a potato taco, perhaps the basic model of the starch bomb tricked out with chopped onion and a bit of salsa, or perhaps one of the fancy examples of the breed, cooked with the roasted-chile mixture called *rajas* or embellished with all manner of sautéed vegetables.

On most taquería menus, *tacos de papas* are what you eat when you happen to be a vegetarian yoked to a companion whose needs include drippy hunks of steamed cow's intestine, or when the severity of your hangover precludes even a token three or four tacos made with turtle or spicy pork *al pastor*. As with the original po'boy sandwich in New Orleans, which was stuffed with stale French fries and sold to striking newsboys whose poverty drove even the cheapest meat sandwich out of reach, the potato taco is inexpensive and filling, engineered to stave off hunger for just a while longer. Nobody has ever driven across town for a potato taco, no matter how artfully combined with sautéed zucchini or golden achiote.

I was tipped off to El Atacor #11 by an unsigned e-mail a couple of months ago, a message instructing me to Google the phrase "porno burrito." I did. A healthy percentage of the results pointed toward the restaurant. The potato taco may be El Atacor's enduring glory, but its fame in the online world comes mostly from its Super Burrito, a foil-wrapped construction the size and girth of your forearm, which drapes over a paper plate like a giant, oozing sea cucumber or, perhaps more to the point, like an appendage of John Holmes. It is impossible to look at a Super Burrito without marveling at the flaccid, masculine mass of the thing. It is probably even harder to bite into it without laughing. (There are mock-porn videos on YouTube of what I assume is the Super Burrito being sensuously consumed, tortillas stretched with firm, white teeth, the distended tube making its way down any number of eager throats.) The Super Burrito, a standard composition of beans, rice, sour cream, guacamole, meat, lettuce, etc., is a formidable item of food and a proper subject of veneration, but it may be more admirable as an object than as an actual burrito.

The chokingly fragrant menudo leaves no doubt as to the part of the animal from which the meat was excavated—menudo may be L.A.'s favorite hangover remedy, but it is hard to imagine confronting this menudo on a stomach trembly with drink. The tacos made with *carne asada,* beef tongue, *carnitas, buche* and such are perfectly fine, but lack the particular energy snap that marks the very best tacos. (They are cheap, though: Family packs include 25 tacos for about $20.)

The *tacos de papas* at El Atacor #11, however, are different beasts entirely: thin corn tortillas folded around bland spoonfuls of mashed spuds and fried to an indelicate, shattering crunch. The barely seasoned potatoes exist basically as a smooth, unctuous substance that oozes out of the tacos with the deliberate grace of molten lava. The glorious stink of hot grease and toasted corn subsumes any subtle, earthy hint of potato, and *tacos de papas* evaporate so quickly that you are thankful they come 10 to an order, slicked with cream and thin taquería guacamole, piled together in a foam takeout container like so many lunch-truck taquitos. Ten *tacos de papas* may seem like an excessive quantity, and you could probably share an order if you were in the mood, but I have seen families of five sit down to five separate orders, 50 tacos in all, and afterward there wasn't a crumb or a spatter of sauce to be seen.

Las Fabulosas Taco Trucks

by Robb Walsh

from *Houston Weekly*

The Houston food scene is a mighty big beat for one reporter to cover—but Robb Walsh does it all, from regional and national food trends to specific restaurant reviews, both high- and low-end, always capturing the human side of things.

The *bifstek* taco at the Jarro trailer on Gessner came with Angus sirloin, sliced paper thin, without a thread of gristle, grilled well-done, and layered on two lightly fried corn tortillas. On the stainless steel counter that runs along the front of the trailer, there were salsas and condiments in six decorative, three-legged Mexican bowls.

I grabbed a fat lime quarter from one bowl on the shelf and squeezed it over the top of the steak. I skipped the bright orange *chile de árbol* salsa and the neon green serrano slurry. This time I wanted to try a dark chocolate-colored salsa made with dried chiles in oil with a dash of orange juice for sweetness. For a topping, I spooned up some *escabeche,* onion slices marinated in lime juice and flecked with Mexican oregano and chile powder.

This steak taco was one of the hundreds of tacos I'd eaten in the last six months while writing the Taco Truck Gourmet blog for HouStoned. And it was also my last, as the blog had run its course. With a note of nostalgia, I folded the two tortillas around the meat and condiments, cocked my head to one side in the time-honored taco eater's pose and took a huge bite.

The meat was so tender, it dissolved on my tongue. The juicy beef melded with the familiar flavors of corn tortilla and lime juice. The raw-flavored dried chile salsa came on like mole poblano's punk-ass cousin. And the juicy raw onions added some crunch.

Yeah, baby.

One morning six months ago, I tried to get breakfast at the famous taco trailer called Taqueria Tacambaro behind Canino's on Airline Drive ("Taco-Truck Gourmet," August 24, 2006). The proprietress, Maria Rojas, didn't have any egg tacos. She said she only had fajitas. I pointed to a pile of white things on the griddle and asked her what they were.

"Mollejas," she replied, which is Spanish for sweetbreads. The incongruity of eating a dish I associated with French haute cuisine from a taco truck made me grin. Just for kicks, I ordered a taco stuffed with sweetbreads and topped it with raw onion, cilantro and salsa. The fluffy, barely-cooked-through sweetbreads, hot off the griddle, were the best I have ever eaten in Houston.

Maria Rojas said she served the same food at her taco trailer that you'd find at the little *puestos* (food stalls) in the *mercado* of her hometown of Tacambaro in Michoacán. She chose her location near the fruit and vegetable stands of the Farmers Marketing Association on Airline Drive because it's the closest thing to a Mexican mercado you can find in Houston.

I might never have tried the taco de mollejas at Taqueria Tacambaro, if they weren't one of the only things available. The experience convinced me that there were some hidden treasures out there. So I decided to make a concerted effort to find the best taco trucks in the city and write about them.

I already knew there was nothing inherently wonderful about taco truck food. It can be better than, worse than or just the same as the food in a taqueria or a Mexican restaurant. But there are some fundamental differences.

Taco trucks are operated by immigrants for immigrants. This makes them a fascinating culinary phenomenon, first of all, because they're serving some items no other venues offer, and second, because they challenge high-minded ideas about authenticity.

Taco truck fare is defined by the Mexican-style taco, which is comprised of two lightly fried corn tortillas stuck together, then filled with some kind of meat. The price ranges from $1 to $2 each, with the vast majority falling smack in the middle at $1.50.

Optional toppings include a first tier of raw onion and chopped cilantro, which is generally free. For the second tier, an additional option of lettuce and tomato, there is generally a small charge. Jalapeños, sometimes pickled but more often roasted, are also available for a pittance. Salsas range from the simple to the elaborate; they are always free and always applied by the consumer.

Variations include other corn dough platforms, such as *gorditas, chalupas* or *sopes,* which go for $2 to $3. Flour tortillas are sometimes available for an extra 25 cents, and they are occasionally homemade. The oversize Mexican sandwiches called *tortas* are $5 or $6. I've also seen Frito pies and nachos on taco truck menus, but Tex-Mex crispy tacos and cheese enchiladas are notably absent.

Even though the cooks and the customers are mostly Mexican immigrants, it would be a mistake to assume that taco trucks serve authentic Mexican food. Goat is the most common meat in the Michoacán Mercado stalls, according to Maria Rojas.

On Houston taco trucks, fajita meat is by far the most common offering. You can get it on tacos, quesadillas, gorditas, tortas and scrambled with eggs on a breakfast taco. That's because the city's meat purveyors sell low-end beef for fajitas from as little as $1 a pound.

Nor can you say that taco truck food is all Americanized. Maria Rojas's tripe and sweetbreads tacos are exactly the kind of food that newly arrived immigrants will go out of their way for. Curiously, cutting-edge culinary types like Mario Batali and Anthony Bourdain are big into offal dishes, too. And, of course, so are the French.

Since few of my dining companions like sweetbreads and tripe, I took a French friend of mine, an artist named Bernard Brunon, to Taqueria Tacambaro. He was utterly amazed. And then he started taking other Frenchmen and visitors from France to eat tripe tacos there. Now photos of Taqueria Tacambaro are turning up in French art publications. I predict this taco trailer will someday be listed in French travel guides.

The Jarro taco trailer on Gessner has become legendary among taco truck owners. This is the most successful taco truck in the city. It does so much business that its owner, Guillermo "Memo" Piñedo, has opened a freestanding restaurant right beside it.

There are guys who eat lunch at the trailer during the week and then bring their families for a sit-down meal in the restaurant on the weekends. Jarro also serves tacos *al pastor,* made with marinated pork, and the Yucatecan specialty *cochinita pibil,* which is marinated pork cooked in banana leaves. While you can get tacos al pastor at almost any taco truck in the city, Jarro's steak tacos and the cochinita pibil are unique. And so are the unusual salsas.

"There weren't any taco trucks around here when we started," Memo says. "Now there are taco trucks all up and down Gessner." They are trying to duplicate Jarro's success. "But they don't get it," he continues. "It's the quality of the food, not the location, that made this taco trailer successful."

Guillermo Piñedo and his wife once ran a three-location chain of Jarro Café restaurants in Mexico. The original was in Mexico City, and the other two were in the beach resort communities of Ixtapa and Cancún. The devaluation of the peso in the Carlos Salinas era crippled their finances. Then Memo Piñedo was kidnapped.

"That was when we decided to get out," Señora Piñedo remembers.

The original idea was to come to Houston and open a restaurant. But the Piñedos didn't know much about the city, and that made it difficult to pick a location. The real estate negotiations, financing and permit processes were also daunting. A friend of theirs who worked as a chef at a Houston restaurant suggested they consider a taco truck instead. At first they dismissed the idea.

There are no taco trucks in Mexico, so it was hard to imagine. But their friend drove them around to see a few in Houston and they began to realize the brilliance of the concept. Memo saw that if your location wasn't working out, you could just move somewhere else.

The Piñedos invested $25,000 in a trailer and another $5,000 for everything else they needed. Their $30,000 investment was a tiny fraction of what it would cost to start a restaurant. And they had no loan payments to make. They paid several hundred dollars a month to rent a location in front of a liquor store on Gessner, but they had few other expenses.

Business was slow at first. "Memo only sold three kinds of tacos," says Señora Piñedo, "steak, cochinita pibil and al pastor."

The "bifstek" sold at most Houston Mexican restaurants is tough as shoe leather and riddled with gristle, so nobody was interested in a steak taco from a taco truck. And few of the laborers and immigrants who make up the majority of taco truck customers had ever heard of the slow-cooked Mayan pork dish called cochinita pibil.

"I ended up giving a lot of tacos away for free," Memo recalls.

And there were the weird salsas. Taco trucks, like taquerias, usually offer red and green sauce. Heat levels vary, but you seldom taste anything as hot as Jarro's orange chile de árbol or bright green serrano salsa in Houston. His friends pleaded with him to offer conventional fajita tacos and regular salsas, Memo recalls.

"Owners of other taco trucks asked me why I was paying $2 a pound for sirloin when you could get fajita beef for 75 cents. I said, 'America has the best beef in the world; why not put it on a taco?' They thought I was crazy. But I wasn't going to sell what every other taco truck was selling," says Memo. "I was going to sell the kind of food we had at our restaurants in Mexico. I was going to do it my way."

Within three months, word of mouth about the sirloin tacos and the super-hot salsas had spread, and the Jarro taco trailer on Gessner was swamped with customers. "I had to hire four workers to keep up with the orders," Memo says. Jarro taco trailer workers all wear uniforms, and the trucks are sparkling clean and painted in striking black with very professional graphics.

Behind the Jarro Café, there are two brand-new taco trailers that Memo has recently ordered. He intends to expand his brand with franchisees. Why franchise taco trailers instead of restaurants? "Because the trailers are cheaper, easier to run and more profitable," Memo says.

"It's crazy to have a taco trailer out front in the parking lot competing with your restaurant, huh?" Memo says with a laugh. But there's no way he would close it. The trailer makes as much money as the restaurant.

Why don't the taco trailer customers come inside?

"There are lots of reasons," Memo explains. Some loyal outdoo customers are laborers who don't have time to change clothes and clean up. It's also faster outside, and it's 25¢ a taco cheaper.

"It's my drive-through window," he jokes.

The taco truck has a long history in Texas. Cowboy chuck wagons, which were often manned by Mexican *cocineros,* appeared on the scene in the 1860s. Spanish vaqueros used mobile kitchens mounted on oxcarts on the earliest trail drives in the 1700s. Tamale carts and other mobile food vendors were also very common in Texas before the sanitary laws of the Progressive Era were enacted in the early 1900s.

But the first actual taco *trucks* in Texas were Model T Fords. One such early taco truck can be seen in a 1939 black-and-white photograph by famous Texas WPA photographer Russell Lee. The photo is titled "Mexican lunch wagon serving tortillas and fried beans to workers in pecan shelling plant, San Antonio, Texas."

In the photo, a Hispanic man squats in the back of a Model T pickup truck with a cardboard box full of tortillas. His customers take the tortillas and make "self-serve" tacos from a selection of fillings in metal pots arrayed along the edge of the open tailgate. It's a unique solution to the lack of hand-washing facilities—the taco truck vendor never touches the tacos.

Modern taco trucks are a variation of the panel trucks known in various parts of the country as "maggot wagons," "grease trucks" and "roach coaches." These mobile canteens were easily adapted to the street food traditions of the Latino communities of the Southwest, where they became known as *loncherías.*

In Texas, the taco trailer is increasingly popular as a lower-cost alternative to the taco truck. The trailer is hauled back and forth to a commissary by another vehicle, generally a heavy-duty pickup truck. Jarro Café buys their trailers from a fabricating company in Monterrey, Mexico. The simplest design can be purchased for as little as $15,000.

In 2003, a rash of complaints about Houston taco trucks triggered a crackdown by the health department. Angry restaurant owners who considered the trucks unfair competition went to the press with accusations that the trucks weren't following the city's sanitary standards. Reports of illnesses were rumored. Television crews caught a few infractions on video. Since then, Houston taco truck operators report that enforcement has stiffened.

The rules require taco trucks or trailers to show receipts for daily trips to a "commissary," which is the only place where they're allowed to discharge greasy wastewater, fill their tanks with potable water from an approved source and undergo required maintenance. There are 12 such commissary locations in and around Houston.

Every taco truck or trailer in Houston must obtain a license from the appropriate health department in order to sell food. The mobile kitchens are subject to the same sort of inspections as restaurants. There are around 800 mobile food-service operations inside Houston city limits, and 600 in the nearby suburbs.

So what's the best taco truck and the best taco in Houston? I am calling it a tie between Taqueria Tacambaro and its tacos de mollejas and the Jarro trailer and its phenomenal Angus sirloin tacos and stunning salsa bar.

If you have never eaten at a taco truck before, either one of these is a good place to start. "Some people avoid taco trucks because they think they are dirty," says Piñedo. "Go take a look inside our trailer. It's cleaner than a lot of restaurants. There are clean taco trucks and dirty taco trucks, just like there are clean restaurants and dirty restaurants."

"When I was a little girl, we visited some relatives in San Diego," says Ms. Piñedo. "We got chips and sodas from a big stainless steel food truck that parked at a construction site nearby. It was so clean and shiny. I said, 'I wish we had those trucks in Mexico.' Now we own one. The food may be Mexican, but taco trucks are totally American."

"It's a restaurant without the headaches," says Memo. "When I came here, it was my dream to own a restaurant. Now I want to sell the restaurant and buy more taco trailers."

LAS FABULOSAS TACO TRUCKS . . . DELICIOSO!

Our Top Picks
There are some *muy sabrosos* tacos out there if you're brave enough to eat at a taco truck and don't mind ordering in Spanglish.

1521 Gessner
What to get: Don't miss the steak (bifstek) taco made with thin-sliced Angus sirloin. Also recommended: the Campechana (beef

and chorizo), cochinita pibil (slow-cooked pork) and beef-and-mushroom tacos. Flour tortillas are available for a little extra. Don't miss the salsa bar. The dark-green jalapeño-and-cilantro salsa may be the mildest; the dried chile salsa is complex and picante. Only the most dedicated chile-heads should attempt to ingest the incendiary orange chile de árbol sauce and the rip-your-lips-off neon green serrano slurry. The food is a little cheaper and a little faster at the taco trailer, but they have the same tacos inside the air-conditioned restaurant, where you also get chips, ice water, knives and forks and an expanded menu.

Taqueria Tacambaro
2520 Airline Drive (Behind Canino's)
What to get: Tacos de mollejas and tripitas (sweetbreads and tripe) are awesome. If you don't like offal, try the spicy pork al pastor, crisped up in a frying pan and served with raw onion and cilantro, and the awesome gordita, made with a thick masa cake split in half, then stuffed with homemade refried beans and Mexican cheese. Don't miss the roasted jalapeños. Mexican nationals come from miles around to eat Maria Rojas's home-style Michoacán-style cooking.

El Ultimo
Southwest corner of Long Point and Antoine
Look for a shiny new taco truck parked in front of a car wash. The sanitary standards are exceptional. Both the man and woman behind the counter were wearing hair nets. What to get: The breakfast tacos are $1 a piece, and they're huge. They come with your choice of scrambled eggs with bacon, ham, potatoes, nopalitos, machacado (shredded beef), chorizo or roasted peppers on a corn or flour tortilla. The flour tortillas are handmade, and the chorizo is truly exceptional. The thick green salsa is pretty hot. There's no coffee, but there are fresh fruit aguas frescas available.

El Norteño
Long Point and Gessner
This is a "chain" with a couple of blue school buses and at least one blue trailer. They change locations often, but they can usually be found around the corner of Gessner and Long Point. At this

writing, there is a blue bus on Gessner north of Long Point and a blue "El Norteño" truck out in front of the shopping center at 9893 Long Point. What to get: "Pollo asado estilo Monterrey" is their specialty—$6 for half a chicken, $10 for a whole one. Both come with tortillas, a roasted onion, chiles and condiments. The chicken is good, but "costillas al carbón"—a whole slab of grilled spare ribs with onions, chiles and condiments for $15—are even better. A half slab, which goes for $7.50, is more than enough for two.

La Silla Pollos Asados
Lawndale and Highway 225
This bright-yellow bus has a giant chicken character and the saddle-shaped mountain peak called "la silla" (the saddle) painted on the side. "La silla" is a landmark of Monterrey, Mexico, which must be famous for roasted chicken, because all the pollo asado operations brag about their roots there. What to get: For six bucks, these guys give you half of a tasty charcoal-grilled pollo, a bowl of frijoles, salsa and a stack of tortillas. A whole chicken is ten bucks.

Tacos Tierra Caliente
1300 block of Montrose Boulevard in the "We Fix Flats" parking lot
Maria Samano and her flirtatious crew from the "hotlands" of Michoacán run this extremely popular taco trailer in the Montrose. What to get: barbacoa tacos with onions and cilantro. Ask Maria for the "salsita," and she'll hand you a squirt bottle full of her creamy green "hotlands hot sauce."

Sabor Venezolano
Southwest corner of Westheimer and Fondren
For a change of pace, try this Venezuelan-owned taco truck on the West side. The truck opens for business at 7 a.m. with 99-cent breakfast tacos. There's also a Mexican taco menu if you aren't interested in trying el sabor venezolano. What to get: The patacón looks like a sandwich, but instead of two slices of bread, there are green plantain slices that have been fried together into crispy rounds. A pile of shredded beef, a slice of ham, some cheese, and lettuce, tomato and mayo are layered between two of the plantain crusts. It tastes spectacular, and it's also very filling. A sauce made

of cream with a little feta and basil is served on the side. Chile-heads might consider taking their patacones home and doctoring them up with a little hot sauce. The corn cakes called arepas are split, gordita-style, and stuffed with your choice of meats.

El Mapache III
Northwest corner of Renwick and Gulfton
The parking lot of the Bestop convenience store is attractively decorated with potted palms, giving the El Mapache III dining area a festive ambiance. El Mapache means "the raccoon." It's also a nickname for a bandit. What to get: The barbacoa taco features a huge mound of hot cheek meat, nicely shredded and very moist, on your choice of flour or corn tortillas. The salsa is a thick and creamy green concoction. The truck also sells roast chickens, and the beans are free on weekends.

Taqueria Torres
4400 block of Caroline Street
The Mexican Consulate is on San Jacinto. Behind it on Caroline Street, there are two competing taco trucks, Taqueria Torres and Jesse's Taqueria. Torres has the edge for tangy al pastor, best enjoyed with lots of gooey cheese on a quesadilla. But Jesse's has a decent chicken taco. And they have a copy machine, too. What to get: quesadilla al pastor, Mexican Cokes.

Tacos El Amigo
Northwest corner of Renwick and Dashwood
What to get: "torta cubana," a Mexican twist on the Cuban sand-wich made with fajita meat, ham, a hot dog cut into lengthwise sections, cheese, lettuce, tomato and lots of guacamole, with hot sauce on the side. Doña Maria is the head chef, and her food is "todo estilo México," according to her card. The tacos are plain. The gordita is a bad joke. But Doña Maria's Mexican Cuban sand-wich is outrageous.

The World's Kitchen

The Soulful Crêpes of Brittany

by Nancy Coons
from *Saveur*

Novelist Coons lives in France's Lorraine region, which makes it easy to take a jaunt up to Brittany to discover the local art of crêpe-making. By the time she's finished, it's clear that we've never tasted anything as satisfying as a real crêpe.

I'm shivering on a windswept cliff on the coast of Brittany's Cornouaille, the spit of land that juts farther west into the Atlantic than any other point in mainland France. Waves curl and crash far below. I can't tell the spray from the mist that's seeping under my scarf and down my neck. On the heathery moors behind me, someone is practicing on a *biniou*—the local bagpipe—and the keening drone creeps into my bones. I turn tip my collar and think about food. Something warm would taste good right now. Something rib-sticking and buttery, honest, and plain. I climb back to my car and head for a crêperie.

A crêperie is not hard to find in these parts. In Celtic-souled Brittany, the humble crêpe is an art form; it's a canvas on which the region's poetic character expresses itself. Crêpes are often scoffed at elsewhere in France (a nation of natural scoffers) for the very things that make them great. They are fast ("Ah, non! Le fast food!"). They are high carb ("Hélas, my waistline!"). And they are family-friendly ("Enfants in restaurants? Take them to MacDo and leave us to dine in peace!"). Toddlers are taught to prepare them in France's *écoles maternelles*. Harried working parents whip them up as a quick fix for finicky kids. Teenagers make them instead of pizza for slumber parties. They can be gooey and generically comforting, folded across an over-easy egg or slathered with Nutella. But in western Brittany, the crêpe, known here since the Middle Ages, reaches its apogee. Whether they're served at communal events like the penitential Catholic processions called *pardons* or at everyday suppers, crêpes are the salt of the earth, and the sea.

Within 20 minutes I'm seated at a wooden table in La Crêperie l'Épok, a candlelit cottage of a restaurant in the granite-cobbled old town of Pont Croix, a village near the coast. Within another ten minutes there's a platter in front of me with a crêpe on it so wide and crisp and thin I can see the china through it. It is glistening with butter and heaped with a jammy, cider-spiked confit of onions and garnished with bacon. I set down my mug of cider and dig in. The crêpe feels light but solid, and when it crunches on my tongue I taste salt. But I can also taste something more: the malty, acid tang of buckwheat. I scrape my plate clean and order another one.

By the time I've finished a crêpe topped with whole, tender scallops in a white wine sauce, I'm ready to sit back in my chair. Then David Nahon, the chef and owner of L'Épok, comes over and offers me the menu again. I order dessert. I'm so visibly delighted with the *kouign bigouden aux pommes*—a thick, yeasty pancake, perfumed with cinnamon and topped with sautéed apples—that Nahon sticks around to watch me eat, hands on his hips. The kouign reminds me of the sourdough pancakes of my Michigan youth. I dare to say it out loud. He smiles a little. Then he brings me two more.

By now I'm showering him with questions. Raw milk? Is that yeast or a sourdough culture? A self-deprecating man with a dry sense of humor, Nahon talks about his crêpes with quiet zeal. "The reputation of crêpes has gone downhill," he says. "So many places make them badly these days—warmed-over fast food—that Brittany is making an effort to bring them back to what they were. There are only a few left who make them as they should be, with fresh ingredients, on the spot."

I'm invited into his kitchen to learn how. Nahon buys his ingredients locally: raw milk from the Centric dairy in the nearby village of Pouldergat, smoked tongue and andouille (chitterling sausage) from the Boucherie-Charcuterie Quéré around the corner, buckwheat flour from the Tremillec mill in Ploneour-Lanvern. And, in a literal extension of the French saying "*Il faut mettre la main à la pâte*" ("You've got to get your hands in the dough"), he blends his crêpe batter—a mix of eggs, flour, water, and sea salt from Brittany —with thick, strong fingers, lifting and slapping rhythmically as the tough, gluten-free buckwheat releases its starch and air inflates the doughy mass.

Nahon shows me how to puddle the batter onto the *crépière* (griddle; in the Breton language, *billig*) and spread it thin with the *rozell,* a wooden tool that resembles a squeegee. As he demonstrates the ideal crêpe-flipping technique—lifting it from one griddle and turning it onto a second one—his wife, Nathalie, fills, folds, and garnishes the finished crêpes while his 15-year-old son, Thibault, serves them to customers in the burnished-wood dining area. It's a good life for a Breton like Nahon, who bought this 15th-century building in 2004. The three Nahons live upstairs in rooms that overlook the Goyen, the tidal estuary that once carried merchant ships inland from the open sea. Back rooms look onto the church square, where a weekly farmers' market sells regional products at the foot of the Gothic church of Notre Dame du Roscudon.

One of the local products the market offers is Breton buckwheat flour—locally called *farine de blé noir* (black wheat) because of the tough, dark hull that encloses the buckwheat grain. I ask Nahon, Why buckwheat in Brittany? "Nothing else will grow here," he deadpans. Elsewhere in France, crêpes are rich, eggy, and usually sweet treats made with white flour and prepared in ways that range from simple (sprinkled with granulated sugar) to flamboyant (doused in brandy and set aflame). While those kinds of crêpes are also enjoyed in Brittany, the classic crêpe in these parts is an austere, savory one made with buckwheat and sometimes called a galette. The soil of the Cornouaille, and of almost all Brittany, is acidic and salty, a thin, gritty skin over solid granite. Buckwheat, a resilient and resistant survivor, flourishes in it. It even tastes of it.

• • •

At Nahon's recommendation, I head south across the interior toward the town of Ploneour-Lanvern. The countryside known as the Pays Bigouden flashes past in shades of khaki and beige, punctuated by dark granite villages and dour churches spiked with gargoyles. Inland pastures are snowy white with buckwheat flowers, as flat and delicate as Queen Anne's lace. Once these blossoms go to seed, they must be milled.

After passing through a forested area east of Ploneour-Lanvern, I emerge into a garden idyll, where the Moulin de Trémillec, a mill that has been in operation since before the Revolution, hums beside a stream called the Abbé. René and Odette Bilien and their energetic 40-year-old son, André, run the family business, while the waters of the Abbé turn the wheel.

Next to a tidy house with the date 1837 marked over the door, the mill shelters a Rube Goldberg–esque maze of wheels, pistons, whirring belts, and churning tumblers. The plank floors and other surfaces of the room are coated in flour; André even has some on his nose. I shout my questions over the roar.

"There used to be 16 mills on the Abbé alone," André yells back. "My grandfather René bought the place in 1932. He learned to be a miller from his father, my great-grandfather. They were always millers in this region, the Bigouden. In the old days, neighbors brought their own grain to grind. Now I buy my grain through the local coopérative."

Buckwheat has flourished here in Brittany since it was brought from Asia Minor after the Crusades, which is why it's also known as blé sarrasin, "Saracen wheat," in reference to an antiquated name for Muslims in Asia. Nowadays China exports a comparable buckwheat, but the best local crêpe makers prefer Breton buckwheat when they can get it. "Local blé noir, I can tell the difference," André says. "It's alive, volatile, reactive. There's lots of ferment in it. It transforms, it boils from within."

The Biliens treat their grain with kid gloves, passing the raw product through no fewer than seven separate stages of processing to remove the black hull without damaging the tender, almond-like kernel inside. "You must clean it well but not treat it too harshly," André explains. After the second tumbling, the mild kernel, the *amande,* is set aside, and the following five spins release the flavor from the tougher bits of the grain. The remaining robust, full-flavored reduction is mixed back with the *amandes,* to yield a final, balanced flour.

André pours the finished product into my hand, and I taste a pinch. It has a nutty sharpness. René, André's 76-year-old father, tastes a pinch too and nods, remembering. "We used to eat buck-wheat crêpes four or five times a week when I was little. More, during the war. There was nothing but buckwheat and homegrown pork available. We lived on *soupe au lard* [fatback soup]. And crêpes. Always crêpes."

Some things never change, even in more prosperous times. When I wake up in my bed-and-breakfast in Pont Croix and pad down-stairs, Corinne Sirhenry, my hostess, greets me with coffee, hot milk, croissants, and a crêpe. It's made of white flour, it's eggy and sweet, and it melts in my mouth. I heap on some of her home-made orange marmalade and ask for her recipe.

Soon, I find myself in her vanilla-scented kitchen learning first-hand how to make this kind of crêpe. Alain, Sirhenry's husband, joins us, and as the griddle heats up, their sons, Charles, ten, and Richard, eight, follow their noses into the room and watch the process hungrily. Charlotte, their 15-year-old daughter, herself an aspiring chef, pays close attention too.

Before the lesson on sweet crêpes, however, comes a batch of the savory buckwheat version. "First we will make the sarrasins ones," says Corinne, "then the sweet." There should be no dessert before the main course, after all. She lifts a tea towel from atop a mixing bowl full of gray-beige buckwheat-and-white-flour batter and ladles a scoop onto the billig. "Always at 11 o'clock!" she insists with a giggle. She shows me what she means: with her rozell cocked sideways, she deftly spreads the puddle clockwise around the griddle until it meets itself at 11 o'clock again. No holes, no thick spots. (It you're left-handed, start at one o'clock.) With a flick, she turns the browning pancake a few seconds later, slathers it with *beurre an sel de Guérande* (a sea salt butter), lays on a slice of rosy ham, sprinkles on grated gruyère, and tips on an egg yolk. As the yolk begins to harden slightly, she folds over the edges of the crêpe and slides the meal-in-a-blanket onto a plate. Richard is standing by to receive it. "This is called the complete," Corinne explains. "We Bretons eat these at least once a week." It's not only homey comfort food, Alain assures me; it is the single most ordered kind of crêpe in Breton crêperies.

After everyone gets his own complete, Corinne scrapes the griddle and, using a lightly twisted kitchen towel, smears it with butter. Now she pours on the sweet batter, made of flour (both white and buckwheat), sugar, and eggs. This crêpe, once turned and browned, is garnished with butter and a generous drizzle of Corinne's own caramel sauce, made with yet more butter. Corinne laughs and blushes. "I know. Butter and salt are my weakness. We really love our salt butter here in Bretagne." With a mother's skill, she slips the caramel crêpe to Charles and somehow has another one almost finished for Richard, waiting at her elbow with envious eyes. She offers me one, but I demur there's an evening of feasting ahead.

The *FEST NOZ*—night festival, in Breton—seems to be Brittany's revenge on winter. Held in any number of towns year-round but most frequently during the summer months, the events draw locals and visitors out of their cottages for feasting on mussels, fish stews, and, of course, crêpes. To burn off calories, the festival-goers dance, scores of them, in a ring, backs straight, feet tapping in intricate patterns in time to the rhythms of the bagpipes and drums. There are scores of variations of these spirited Breton dances, which can be traced back hundreds of years. There are *sonneurs*—players of bagpipes and a strident double-reed horn called a *bombarde*—and, as the night stretches on, a full Breton dance band with fiddle, guitar, drums, and vocalists, often singing in the Breton language.

Tonight I head for Penmarc'h, where the *sonneurs* have set up on a temporary stage at the foot of a massive old lighthouse, the Phare d'Eckmühl. As the lantern turns, casting its beam over the tidal flats of the Atlantic, the dancers trot and stomp in a circle. I queue for crêpes instead. Dozens of families press up to Monette LeCorre's kouigns bigoudens stand, waving their euros. With brisk efficiency, LeCorre, who usually works out of the bar around the corner, pours and flips four thick yeast crêpes at a time, tending to her griddles with a tympanist's grace. Two other women pass the final product, glistening with butter and jam, to customers. I buy one for a euro and feel its warmth on my palm. I nibble. Its sour-doughy bite plays counterpoint to the jam and salt. I wolf it down so hungrily I almost eat the napkin.

A drizzle has begun to fall, but it doesn't faze the dancers. They pull up the hoods on their windbreakers and keep on going. The musicians pick up the pace, drumming and droning as Breton musicians have for centuries. The beam from the lighthouse blazes through the rain and illuminates the incoming tide. I turn up my collar and order another crêpe.

―――

Crêpes de Blé Noir

(BUCKWHEAT CRÊPES)

David Nahon uses a wooden tool, called a rozell, *to spread out crêpe batter on his griddle. For our home-style version, picking up the pan and tilting and swirling it in several directions spreads out the batter just fine.*

½ cups buckwheat flour
½ tsp. sea salt
1 egg, beaten until foamy
1 cup milk
8 tbsp. salted butter, preferably sea salt butter

1. Combine flour and salt in a bowl; form a well in the center. Pour in egg. Using one hand, with fingers spread wide, mix egg into flour while pouring in 1½ cups cool water. Stir and slap batter upward with your right hand, scooping it up from the bottom. Continue with increasing speed and force, lifting and slapping the batter to make a hollow, spanking noise with the impact. Continue this process until batter is smooth and elastic, 3–4 minutes. ("The more you work it, the easier it will be to work with afterward," says Nahon.) Transfer batter to a medium bowl and pour 2 tbsp. water evenly over the top (this protects the

batter from drying out). Cover surface with plastic wrap, tucking in the edges. Cover and refrigerate overnight.

2. Stir milk and ⅔ cup water into batter. Heat a well-seasoned 10 ¼" crêpe pan over medium heat and brush with a bit of butter, wiping off any excess. Pour about ¼ cup batter onto pan, swirling quickly to spread batter out to edges. Cook until light golden and just crisp, about 2 minutes. Using a spatula, flip and cook until light golden on the second side, about 2 minutes more. Repeat with remaining batter. Spread a dab of the butter onto each crêpe and serve hot with cider-spiked onion confit or scallops in white wine cream sauce.

SERVES 8

Sauce Noix de Saint Jacques

(SCALLOPS IN WHITE WINE CREAM SAUCE)

This sauce pairs nicely with Nahon's earthy buckwheat crêpes. Melt 1 tbsp. butter in a large skillet over medium-high heat. Season 12 scallops with salt and freshly ground black pepper to taste. Cook scallops in skillet until golden brown on both sides, 5–6 minutes; transfer to plate. Add 2 cups muscadet and 2 cups fish stock to skillet; cook until thickened and reduced, 20 minutes. Pour liquid into a blender; purée with scallops and ¾ cup heavy cream. Whisk together ½ cup muscadet and 1½ tbsp. cornstarch in skillet, removed from heat. Add scallop purée; cook over medium heat, whisking constantly, until thickened, 4–5 minutes. Keep warm. Melt 1 tbsp. butter in another large skillet over medium-high heat. Working in batches, cook 24 scallops halved crosswise until golden brown on both sides, 5–6 minutes. Scatter the scallops over buckwheat cream sauce.

SERVES 8

Confit d'Oignons au Cidre

(CIDER-SPIKED ONION CONFIT)

This condiment is a version of one David Nahon serves with his buckwheat crêpes. Melt 4 tbsp. butter in a large skillet over medium-high heat. ("You need a pan that sticks a bit," says Nahon, "or the onions won't caramelize.") Add 10 thinly sliced medium yellow onions (about 4 lbs.) and cook, stirring often, until blond in color, 18–20 minutes. Add 2 cups sweet hard apple cider, 2 tsp. freshly grated nutmeg, and sea salt to taste. Stir well. Reduce heat to medium, cover skillet, and cook until onions are light brown, about 25 minutes. Uncover skillet and continue cooking until liquid has reduced and onions are a few shades darker, about 20 minutes more. Dollop spoonfuls of the onion confit over buckwheat crêpes, along with a few slices of crisp, fried bacon and a sprinkling of parsley.

MAKES ABOUT 4 CUPS

Shanghai High

by Adam Sachs
from *Bon Appetit*

As Western money and travelers flood into Shanghai—the economic capital of the "New" China—it takes a savvy travel writer like Adam Sachs to scout out its exploding restaurant scene, from the swankiest dining rooms to the most delectable street food.

The sign in the backseat was pretty straightforward: "Psychos or drunkards without guardians are prohibited to take taxis." I think my driver was trying to figure out which one he had on his hands after I'd hopped in and, with a straight face, asked to be taken to the "very tall tower with the hotel on top."

"Jin Mao Tower?" I said. "The Grand Hyatt?"

At 88 stories high, the Jin Mao Tower is one of the tallest structures in all of China. It is a spiked postmodern pagoda, with the top 30 or so floors given over to the loftiest hotel-room views in the world. I figured that might ring a bell. I figured that the fifth-highest building on the planet would be fairly easy to pick out on the skyline, but I was wrong.

"Many tall buildings," the cabbie answered.

I dug up the hotel address and as we drove deeper into the forest of glass and steel that is Shanghai's Pudong district, I started to see his point. Taxi drivers here—many of them fresh recruits from far-off rural villages—can be forgiven for not being able to distinguish one sparklingly new skyscraper from the newer one next door. Everywhere you look in Pudong there is new construction, filling out a city within a city that 15 years ago was just rice paddies and chicken farms.

We drove down a wide boulevard lined with red Chinese flags. Two canary-yellow Italian sports cars sped by the taxi as we circled the Jin Mao. I checked in at the hotel reception on the 54th floor and was shown a room at cloud level. The floor-to-ceiling window took in three iconic Shanghai views: There was the Oriental Pearl Tower, that goofy but wonderful retro-futurist rocket of a building; beyond it, the sober colonnaded colonial structures of the Bund lined the river; and directly below my feet, a vast construction site, future home of what was sure to be an even bigger skyscraper.

Shanghai is said to be rising so fast that the weight of its new buildings is causing the city to sink back into the earth. The city is a riot of contrasts, at once glittering and grimy. Within its glass towers, this is a city of new-car smells. Outside, it's exhaust fumes and the honking, foul madness of Shanghai traffic. Gracious colonial mansions survive the garish new constructions. And ambitious, freshly minted luxury restaurants compete for attention with the greatest street-stall fried dumplings imaginable. It's a high-low experience in the extreme, and I was there to eat.

Here is how I came to eat 25 soup dumplings before noon. It was my first full day in town and I figured I'd acclimate myself with a breakfast of *xiao long bao* at the famous Nan Xiang Steamed Bun Restaurant in the Yu Yuan Garden. *Xiao long bao* are little thin-skinned dumplings full of a rich, porky, intoxicatingly delicious soup.

To beat the crowds, I headed out early and had the taxi drop me off far from the new construction of Pudong on the outskirts of the Yu Yuan Bazaar, an old Chinese market complex that's now very touristy. Inside I found what I took to be Nan Xiang and lustily commandeered an empty table (they were all empty). The xiao long bao were satisfying: intense, filling, potentially fatal. To be honest, though, they weren't much better than the ones I knew from Joe's Shanghai, my local Shanghai restaurant back in New York. The dough was maybe even a bit tougher. So this was the sadness of globalization, I thought. You fly halfway around the planet and the dumplings in China aren't transcendently better than the dumplings in Chinatown.

The windows of the dumpling house opened over the koi-filled ponds and little bridges leading to the nearby Huxinting Tea House. Here I sat for an elaborate tea service that involved two kinds of black tea, three of jasmine, and one sweet brew made from the leaves of the lychee plant from southern China. From the Ming dynasty teahouse I could see a Starbucks across the pond, but I didn't notice anyone going in.

I walked back into the sunshine and noted with some satisfaction the crowd queuing up for their mid-morning xiao long bao fix. Shanghainese are not known for their orderliness, but here they were semi-patiently standing in line for seats in the restaurant and for boxes of dumplings from a take-out window I hadn't noticed before. Next to that take-out window was another dumpling restaurant that was completely empty. The deserted dumpling house looked strangely familiar. Ah, yes. I'd had my first 12 dumplings of the morning not at the famed Nan Xiang but at a sad impostor.

Humbled but determined, I took my place in line and eventually received admission and a seat at a packed communal table upstairs. Here I tasted what was undoubtedly the first real xiao long bao of my life. I don't know how to explain the difference except to say that they were at once more elegant and more richly porky than any I'd tried. The skins were thin and delicate and the soup had none of the fatty excess of the copycats next door. In the interest of sound reporting, I ordered another basket, these with crab-meat. I had turned into a kind of human xiao long bao, ready to burst, but unable to stop. I ordered one final giant dumpling, described on the menu as containing "crab ovary stuffing." It came one to an order, filling a miniature steamer and served with a large drinking straw stuck in the top through which you sucked the super-hot crabby goodness inside. And it was delicious, though by the second slurp I was more than ready to grab a taxi and head back to Jin Mao for a much-needed late-morning nap.

To appreciate Pudong you've got to get away from it. The best view of the architectural insanity is from across the river on the

Bund, the broad curving avenue that recalls Shanghai's days as a playground for foreign money and glamour back in the 1930s. I headed to Three on the Bund, the flashy restaurant and shopping complex in a stately old building. Each floor has a different design and purpose, each in its way an argument for what Shanghai is or could become.

There is an Armani boutique on the ground floor, an Evian Spa, and an outpost of chef Jean-Georges Vongerichten's restaurant empire. But it's not just an invasion of international luxury brands; there are claims here, too, to a kind of modern Chinese revolution. On the third floor, an art gallery shows the works of avant-garde Chinese artists.

And above that is a remarkable restaurant called Whampoa Club, where the chef, Jereme Leung, does for Shanghainese cuisine what architect Michael Graves did for the design of Three on the Bund: revamping it while respecting its roots. At lunch one day at Whampoa I had raw bluefin tuna marinated in X.O. sauce on a little square of silken tofu. On the same plate, clam and sweet sea urchin roe were mixed with soft egg and served in its shell. A green-onion fritter was a dressed-up, grease-free version of street food. In keeping with the city, Leung's interpretations run high (miniature Peking duck with foie gras) and low (homey fish dumplings in a bowl of curry broth).

A local put all this flashy newness in perspective for me at Jean Georges, which is probably the grandest dining room in Shanghai right now, with its eel-skin settees, long dramatic stone bar, and front-row seats for the space-age skyline of Pudong. I sat with a young Shanghainese woman, eating foie gras. "That wasn't there when I was a teenager," she said, casually dismissing the instant-city across the river, all lit up like a carnival ride. She was only in her early 20s.

The sophisticated, self-conscious swank of Jean Georges is fine, but I wanted to know what Shanghai food is really about. Eric Johnson, Jean Georges's young American chef, offered to show me around. We took a taxi out to the city's central fish market. The variety was amazing. Johnson took photos of fish he didn't recognize so that he could ask his Chinese cooks about them. At the edge of the seafood shanties was a vegetable market, and it was there that I had one of the more spectacular tastes of my trip. I put a single green Szechuan peppercorn in my mouth and bit down. An almost minty taste gave way to the slightest bit of hot, and then the tip of my tongue went totally numb. I'd never had anything like it and none of the Szechuan meals I had later came close to the immediate anesthetizing power of that one single peppercorn.

We had lunch that day in the old French Concession district at a popular spot called Bao Luo. Stinky tofu. Salted chicken. Live shrimp that were soaked in wine sauce and twitched drunkenly as you put them in your mouth. "Let's get up early tomorrow and go to Xiangyang Road," Johnson suggested when we were back at the restaurant. "There's a thing they sell on the street that I like to call a Shanghai breakfast burrito; I think you should try it."

This was my kind of four-star chef. And, I discovered the next morning, my kind of street food—basically a fried egg wrapped in a fried flat doughnut, dipped into a brown goo of unknown origin and salty sweetness.

Given my success with Johnson's local recommendations, I asked Leung at Whampoa for his. He gave me the number for Xin Guang. This was the place for hairy crabs, and I was to ask for a Mr. Fang and tell him Leung sent me.

Arriving at Xin Guang I understood why we'd called ahead. Not for special treatment, but just to make sure someone would be in the kitchen. I went with a friend who speaks the language and knows the city, but even she wasn't sure we were at the right address when the taxi pulled up to an unmarked office building on Tianjin Road. Fumbling around a bit, we found the restaurant and were shown upstairs to a room completely empty except for one of the staff members, who was hidden behind a screen, sleeping (and snoring).

In an American Chinatown you might be tempted to skip this place because it was small and uninviting. This was, however, a celebrated hideaway, where wealthy Shanghai businessmen come to spend hundreds of dollars for little crabs with hairy claws (an incredible amount for a city in which a dozen people could be fed on a quarter of that). Drunken crab, marinated in Shaoxing wine, was dark, gooey, and delicious. Another course looked to be a kind of porridge, but was actually a bowl of the roe of 30 crabs. In another arrangement the meat of only male hairy crabs was mixed with bits of rice noodles. More than 100 crabs gave their lives for that meal, and I'm guessing the person with the tiring job of picking through their meat was the one asleep in the dining room.

And there likely will be more exhausted kitchen staff throughout the city as the restaurant boom continues. One can hardly keep up: In Xintiandi, a fashionable shopping area built on the site where the Communist party was formed (you can't make this up), there is the very elegant Soahc, and hip cocktail bars like T8 and TMSK. French twin brothers Jacques and Laurent Pourcel, of the Michelin three-star restaurant Le Jardin des Sens in Montpellier, have opened the sleek and maximalist Sens & Bund. And there are other large-scale luxury developments on the way. This mind-boggling moveable feast may be rough on taxi drivers, but it's incredibly satisfying for hungry visitors.

Old School Madrid

by Anya Von Bremzen

from *Saveur*

Von Bremzen is one of those veteran travel writers whose curiosity about local fare—with an emphasis on the truly local and authentic—makes her articles invaluable to all traveling foodies.

At a swank Madrid restaurant recently, I was sampling gin and tonics rendered into pearl-like orbs with the aid of calcium chloride and a gazpacho sorbet flash-frozen in liquid nitrogen. The food was magical, but somehow it made me crave chickpeas and pigs' feet. Chronicling Spain's gastronomic revolution, as I've done for a decade now, has been an exhilarating ride on the wild side; yet during my last trip to Madrid I was overcome by an urge to say *basta* to conceptual cooking and to revisit the classics. Perhaps I'd simply OD'd on metaphysical bonbons dished out by Ferran Adrià (the reigning prince of new Spanish cooking) wannabes. Or maybe it was the sight of the Tryp Reina Victoria hotel, once a famous torero hangout, gutted and reborn as the Hard Rock Hotel.

Only a few years ago, Madrid still felt like a frenetic, oversize village—a place where fast-talking locals packed dark-tiled bars and little old ladies gleefully fanned themselves in the stands at a gory corrida. But that Madrid is vanishing faster than a *ración* of ibérico ham at a tapas bar. Thanks to Mayor Alberto Ruiz Gallardón and his relentless march toward modernization, the streets are a jumble of traffic and scaffolding. Old-order vermouth on tap is giving way to new-wave mojitos; Madrileños have gone loco for sushi. His grand construction projects nearing completion, Gallardón is close to transforming Madrid into a brash global capital. Faced with that prospect, I decided to turn back the clock by basking in the burnished atmosphere and simple, dignified cooking of the city's stalwart *tabernas* (taverns), *marisquerias* (seafood places), and *casas de comidas*. The term for the last eludes precise definition but generally refers to establishments that do most of their business at lunch, have no written menus, function like a cross between a restaurant and a private dining club, and serve homey, market-driven cuisine. In short order, I plotted a Madrid eating adventure that would involve zero foam.

Until 1561, when Spain's King Philip II moved his court to this former site of a Moorish fortress, Madrid had little serious cooking to speak of. Over time, the city experienced a vast influx of migrants from all over the country, and today its cuisine represents an amalgam of regional styles. By some accounts, one major force sprang from the central region of La Mancha, which surrounds Madrid: La Manchans, also known as *manchegos,* ran taverns where coarse valdepeñas wines were complemented by folksy regional dishes like *migas* (fried bread bits) and *gallina en pepitoria* (hen in an almond sauce). From Andalusia, in the south, came *frituras* (fried "stuffs") and gazpacho. Later, Galicians from the north popularized marisquerias, captivating Madrid's residents with pristine shellfish from the chilly Atlantic. Then, in the early 1980s, the Basques, also from the north, exported their own version of nouvelle cuisine; Catalan disciples of Ferran Adrià followed. A melting pot, yes—but Madrid cooking retains its own, slightly rugged identity, defined by a handful of specialties: *callos* (a tripe stew), croquetas, roast lamb, a profusion of egg dishes, and, above all, *cocido*, an orgy of boiled meats, vegetables, and chickpeas.

Dreaming of a perfect cocido, I cross the Puerta del Sol with its iconic Tio Pepe sign suspended above the traffic. My grail: Casa Lhardy, the grandest surviving monument to staid Madrid dining. The place is entered through its ground-floor deli–cum–tapas bar, a marbled cubbyhole squeezed behind a vintage façade of Cuban mahogany. Inside, patrician señoras in dowdy blazers help themselves to beef consommé from ornate silver samovars in a Madrid ritual that dates to the early 19th century. I ascend the tatty staircase to the main dining room and find myself inside a baroque painting—a plush chamber illuminated by Isabelline period chandeliers, with red velvet chairs, dark varnished wallpaper, and a carved cupboard filled with ornate silver bowls.

Founded in 1839 by Emilio Lhardy, a chef of Swiss origin who had previously cooked in France, Lhardy soon became the most important restaurant in Madrid, patronized by monarchs, ministers, and celebrated artistes. Political coups were plotted in its private salons, particularly the Japanese Room, still resplendent in its faded Second Empire chinoiserie. Lhardy's kitchen—credited with introducing Parisian haute cuisine to the Spanish capital—continues to turn out such relics as veal orloff and tournedos rossini. What virtually everyone orders, though, is the cocido, miraculous for its improbable combination of excess and restraint.

First comes the noodle soup—light yet so densely flavorful it feels almost solid. Next, jacketed waiters ceremoniously pile one's plate with carrots, potatoes, cabbage, and the traditional meats: blood sausage, chorizo, a chicken breast, fresh pork sausages, ham, beef shin, and a homemade sausage called a relleno. But a good cocido madrileño is ultimately all about the chickpeas; cocido specialists are sometimes called *garbanceros*. Lhardy's garbanzos—a pedigreed variety from Fuentesaúco, to the northwest—are supernally creamy and seemingly as weightless as popcorn.

Despite all the liquid nitrogen and calcium chloride being used today in Spain's kitchens, *cocina popular* isn't going the way of the dodo. Inspired by the country's newfound pride in its ingredients and cuisine, many old-school restaurants are dishing out food that's cleaner, purer, and more vital than ever before. Such reformed traditional cooking flourishes in Madrid's casas de comidas, and to go to the right casa de comidas is to feel like a true Madrid insider.

"We don't advertise; our clientele is mainly friends of the house and their friends," says Juan José López Baemar, the owner of the stupendous La Tasquita de Enfrente, an olive's toss from the florid masonry of the Gran Via boulevard. "Madrid has always been a *ciudad familiar* [a familiar, informal city]," López explains, "and casas de comidas are all about human contact." Neither classic nor cutting-edge, Tasquita's precise cooking epitomizes the culinary ethos of modern Madrid. López brings out fat little anchovies on a smear of tomato jam ringed by an aromatic puddle of olive oil, followed by an amazingly plush *revuelto* (scramble) of eggs, blood sausage, and pumpkin. Fried eggs with sautéed *angulas* (baby eels) give way to delicate white beans called *verdinas*, simmered in a broth bolstered by langoustine heads and served with sea urchins—an urbane riff on a soulful northern stew of white beans and clams. "My cooking is traditional," López declares, "but I constantly update it with better ingredients and techniques."

Another day, I search out De la Riva, a 74-year-old casa de comidas in the area around the Santiago Bernabéu soccer stadium. Weekday lunch hours, De la Riva is colonized by chain-smoking men playing *mus,* a popular Spanish card game. On weekends, when large families descend on the plain white-washed room, the feeding frenzy can recall that of a Hong Kong dim sum emporium on a Sunday morning. "You don't come here for comfort or ambience—just eat and beat it," quips proprietor José Moran Harpeaja. His menu is a litany of Madrid classics—ham and shrimp croquetas, potato tortillas, saucy meatballs, roasted sea bream, salt cod in tomato sauce, stews of braised oxtail or pigs' feet. For dessert, Moran offers the most sumptuous flan in town.

While casas de comidas are the current rage among local cognoscenti, traditionally Madrid has always been a city of taverns, so much so that a 17th-century refrain went, "*Madrid ciudad bravilla . . . tenìa tres cientas tavernas y una sola librerìa* [Madrid, a brave little city, 300 taverns and only one bookstore]." Many of the capital's early drinking and eating dens were clustered around calle Cava Baja, just south of the plaza Mayor. Madrid's restaurant row for more than three centuries, the narrow street continues to buzz with busy establishments. The most famous among them is Casa Lucio. To an outsider, Lucio might look undistinguished, but to Madrileños it is the most blue-chip *taberna* of them all. On my last visit to Lucio, I went with a Spanish TV starlet whose sultry looks helped us land a prime table. Dining at separate tables around us were the Duchess of Badajoz, the king's sister; novelist Mario Vargas Llosa; and a gentleman rumored to be Spain's richest man. Everyone was eating *huevos estrellados*, "smashed eggs," a legendary Lucio specialty of fried eggs broken up over french fries.

Reservations at Lucio are hard to come by, and the celebrity circus can be grating. But there is an alternative, called El Lando—Lucio's casual offshoot. "To be seen, you go to Lucio; to be left alone, you come here," says manager Angel Gonzalez Hernandez, who proceeds to wax rhapsodic about Woody Allen. Allen was apparently so impressed with El Lando's food that he asked for a giant doggie bag to take back to America. Tables here are set with house starters: tomato-rubbed bread, an impeccable salad of sliced tomatoes, and plates of ibérico ham handpicked by Gonzalez from a producer in Ávila, about 50 miles northwest of the city.

One of El Lando's great triumphs is callos, Madrid's emblematic tripe stew. In a days-long process, tripe from a butcher who's been supplying the restaurant for over 20 years is first cooked with veal, then rinsed in vinegar and simmered again for five hours with chorizo, jamón, and blood sausage. The final layering of flavors comes from a *refrito* of sautéed onions, garlic, tomatoes, and pimentón, Spain's dusky smoked paprika. "The trick is letting the tripe rest overnight so that the cooking liquid seeps deep into the meat and thickens the sauce," Gonzalez tells me. The result? A stew so refined that it seems almost like an abstraction of tripe. And then there is the smashed-eggs dish served at Lucio. Batons of yellow Galician potatoes are cooked in good olive oil until they're crisp but still creamy inside; fresh farm eggs are gently fried. While letting the spuds soak up the rich, improbably bright orange yolk, I wonder why anyone needs deconstructive cuisine when simply prepared potatoes and eggs can taste so amazing.

You wouldn't think that a tripe-crazy town like this would be the place to find great seafood. Well, think again. Madrid happens to be one of the world's largest dry ports, snagging the best fish before it's shipped to the rest of the country. A lot of it ends up at O'Pazo, an exclusive, Galician-style seafood mecca hidden away on a residential street and populated with regulars, mostly men at lunch, who think nothing of dropping a hundred dollars on a few stunning *cigalas* (langoustines). The 73-year-old owner, Don Evaristo García, a tall, upright grandee in a dark suit and pink tie, circles the room. García came to Madrid from León, in north-western Spain, as a boy and supported himself by hauling fish on his back to rich families.

"Nobody would let me into the elevator, because of the fish smell," he recalls. Today, García is Spain's preeminent seafood sup-plier and counts the royal palace among his clients. "The secret is choosing," García says, sniffing conspiratorially and pointing to his nose.

There's a majestic austerity to a meal at O'Pazo: ingredients distilled to their essence, unencumbered by garnishes. The restau-rant's philosophy is summed up in a discreet note on the menu: "Don't ask for lemon if you want to appreciate the taste of our seafood." And what seafood! I dig into a pile of fearsomely pricey *percebes* (Galician goose barnacles) that squirt sweet, primal juices all over my skirt when I break them apart. Next, I move on to *camarones* dotted with crunchy specks of coarse salt, then luminous clams bobbing in a parsley-flecked sauce so uncorrupted it seems a crime to dunk bread into it. Last comes a whole grilled turbot with taut, glistening flesh, washed down with the vivacious house albariño.

After lunch I make a mental checklist of old Madrid eating rituals I've yet to indulge in on this trip. Savor a slab of turrón at Casa Mira, a specialist for more than 150 years in that honey-and-almond confection from Spain's southeast. Dip crisp churros into pudding-like hot chocolate at Chocolatería San Ginés. Eat the definitive gal-lina en pepitoria at Casa Ciriaco, one of Madrid's most stately *tabernas*. My cell phone rings. It's a friend inviting me to a new restaurant run by a rising-star chef. On my next visit, perhaps.

—∞∞—

Albondigas en Salsa

(TAPAS-STYLE MEATBALLS)

These saucy meatballs from Casa Alberto figure in a wide range of dishes that make up the constellation of little snacks served in tapas bars all over Madrid. Pick them up and pop them into your mouth with toothpicks. In the past, the discarded picks were tallied up so that the bar owner could compile the bill at the end of meal.

1 ½ lbs. coarsely ground beef
1 ½ lbs. coarsely ground pork
½ cup fresh white bread crumbs
¼ cup finely chopped flat-leaf parsley
4 eggs, lightly beaten
8 cloves garlic, finely chopped
Salt and freshly ground black pepper, to taste
1 cup plus 2 tbsp. flour
1 cup Spanish olive oil
1 large yellow onion, chopped
1 large leek, white part only, chopped
1 dried bay leaf
2 ½ cups beef broth
1 ½ cups white wine

1. For the meatballs: Mix together the beef, pork, bread crumbs, parsley, eggs, 4 cloves garlic, and salt and pepper in a large bowl. Let chill for 1 hour. Put 1 cup flour into a bowl. Using wet hands, form meat mixture into 20 even-size meatballs. Roll each in flour; shake off excess; transfer to sheet pan.

2. Heat half the oil in a large skillet over medium-high heat. Brown half the meatballs in the skillet, 10–12 minutes. Transfer meatballs to a plate. Wipe out skillet and repeat with remaining oil and meatballs, leaving oil and caramelized bits in skillet.

3. For the sauce: Heat skillet (with reserved oil) over medium-low heat. Add remaining garlic, onions, leeks, and bay leaf and cook until softened, 12–15 minutes. Add

remaining flour; cook for 2 minutes. Whisk in broth and wine, raise heat to medium-high, and bring to a boil while whisking constantly. Reduce heat to medium-low; simmer until thickened, 12–14 minutes. Let cool; discard bay leaf. Purée sauce in blender in batches. Return sauce to skillet along with meatballs; bring to a boil over medium-high heat. Reduce heat to medium-low; simmer until thickened and meatballs are cooked, 16–18 minutes. Season with salt and pepper. Divide between four 6"–7" *cazuelas.*

SERVES 4

PERFECT BITES

As Madrid's historic heart falls prey to the tourist hordes, some old tapas bars are relaxing their standards, while others are being edged out by Cuban-themed cocktail joints. Hence, choreographing the perfect series of nibbles in the most appealing atmosphere can be a challenge. I start my own dance one evening near the plaza Santa Ana at La Casa del Abuelo (calle de la Victoria 12; 521-2319), a century-old haunt specializing in shrimp served *a la qabardina* (battered) or *al ajillo* (in garlic sauce). Nearby is Las Bravas (calle Álvarez Gato 3; 532-2620), dedicated to patatas bravas, a classic tapa of fried potatoes drizzled with a smooth, sharp, smoky, tomatoey sauce. The sauce is also served on potato tortillas, chicken wings, even pigs' ears—surprisingly delicious with an inexpensive glass of crisp, cool rueda white. Up next is La Venencia (calle de Echegaray 7; 429-7313), one of the last truly authentic bars left on the popular calle de Echegaray. Packed with old sherry barrels, the place is so woodsy and smoky it's like the inside of a frayed leather briefcase. Match a fino, oloroso, or palo cortado sherry with traditional Andalusian bites: stupendous fried marcona almonds, green olives that snap in your mouth, and tangy dry-cured tuna roe, all served with pointy crackers called picos. Hungry for something meaty, I continue on to Casa Alberto (calle las Huertas 18; 429-0706). Dating to 1827 and housed in a building where Cervantes once lived, it boasts a breathtaking interior that features a beautiful, oak-trimmed onyx counter and elaborate antigue taps that still dispense vermouth and soda. I try the plump meatballs and a cazuelita of oxtail stew, then move on to Casa Labra (calle Tetuán 12; 531-0081). Located off the Puerta del Sol, Labra is renowned among Madrileños as the place where Spain's Socialist Party was founded, in 1879. I order one of the bar's fried salt cod specialties—croquetas and *tejadas* (nuggets of the fish enrobed in a crisp, doughy batter)—get a glass of cheap red wine, and join the crowds on the pavement outside. The streets around Casa Labra might be a mess of construction, but some rituals live on. —*A. V.B.*

Visiting the Old City

by Madhur Jaffrey

from *Climbing the Mango Trees*

In her delightful memoir, actress–cookbook writer Jaffrey relives growing up in an extended Indian family. Her clan straddled so many food cultures, she was keenly aware of the meaning of what and how they ate—and the sensory delights of it, too.

Whenever my mother wanted to visit her own family home, she said, "Come, *beta* [child], let's go to the City." We knew what that meant: a visit to our *nana ka ghar* (maternal grandfather's house). Her father and mother had lived and died in the Old City, in a house where her eldest brother's family still resided. I think that, to her, the orchard site of her in-laws, beyond the City's walls, beyond the northern Kashmiri Gate, would always be the suburbia of the la-de-da set into which she had, by good fortune, married.

It was usually just my mother, Veena, and I on these City visits. The ritual generally began on a Saturday morning. After breakfast, my mother would remove the big silver key chain clipped to her waist and open her locked cupboard. Inside was a State Express 555 tin, from which she would fill my father's silver cigarette case, tucking a row of cigarettes behind an elasticized band. The cigarette case would be clicked shut and handed over to my father, who hovered behind her. She would also remove some cash, whatever my father needed for the day, and place that in my father's palm. The cupboard would be relocked, and the bunch of keys tucked back in her waist. My father would stride off to the car waiting to take him to his office.

Freed of household duties, which my mother took very seriously, she would pull out her *attachee* case. Yes, that is how we pronounced it. I thought it was an Indian word. I did not discover its French connection until I was fully grown. Into this rectangular leather box, this attachee case, went a fresh cotton saree, my mother's knitting or sewing, a comb, and a few gifts. Then my mother would disappear into her dressing room with its three-mirrored dressing table, and change into a printed silk saree.

I never understood this. Some odd sense of propriety had convinced her that she should travel and arrive in silk, change into crisp cotton for the day, and change back into flowing silk to return home.

By this time my father would have sent the car and driver back for us, and my mother, smelling sweetly of Hazeline Vanishing Cream, would step into the car, attachee case in one hand, her handbag in the other.

My father almost never came with us or deigned to join us later in the evening. He had been raised in the Old City, but once he left it, it gave him no joy to return. A part of him viewed it as old fashioned, germ-infested, and dangerous.

The residential section of the Old City then, as now, was a maze of such narrow lanes that a cow and a human could barely pass each other. We would have to leave the car on a wider road at a fairly distant point with instructions to the driver about the time at which he could collect us at the end of the day. Then my mother and her two youngest children would walk. We would have to walk carefully, sidestepping sleeping dogs and oncoming cycle-rickshaws. If a shopkeeper decided to empty a bucket of dirty water onto the lane, we expertly hopped out of the way as we simultaneously dodged a man carrying a hundred cardboard boxes on his head. If my mother stopped to buy sweets for her family, she knew enough to keep an eye on her handbag at all times. If we saw a street-sweeper approaching with her wild broom, we held handkerchiefs to our noses so we would not inhale the dust she raised. My mother walked at a steady pace, one hand gripping the attachee case, the other (with the handbag) holding her saree a few inches off the questionable ground.

Our journey took us through the Lane of Fried Breads (Parathe Vali Gulley), where I always urged my mother to stop for a quick *paratha* (fried puffy bread) stuffed with fenugreek greens. There were two or three open-fronted shops, all with shallow *karhais* (woks) set up almost on the street, right where passersby could be easily enticed. Inside the karhais, bobbing in a lake of hot ghee, were three or four big, fat, puffed-up parathas.

A word here about nomenclature. In our family, a small ball of whole-wheat dough, rolled into a flat round and deep-fried into a puffball, was called a *poori*. If it was stuffed with spiced split peas, it was called a *bedvi*. A paratha, on the other hand, was a flatbread, made on a *tava* (a griddle), somewhat like a pancake. Why, in this lane alone, a bedvi—or stuffed poori, if you will—was called a paratha, I do not know. And why, in this lane alone, was the karhai, however shallow, called a tava? Delhi was an ancient, idiosyncratic city. I never asked the questions, and my mother never explained. My preoccupation then was that the parathas, or whatever anyone wished to call them, came stuffed with a choice of green peas, potatoes, fenugreek greens, chickpea flour, spiced split peas, cauliflower, or grated white radish. Which one, or ones, would I choose? To make the choice even harder, combinations were also possible. All were expertly spiced, all were utterly delicious.

The peculiarity of these shops was that they charged only by the paratha. This had been the tradition since time immemorial—time immemorial, in this case, being 1875, when the first of these shops-cum-restaurants opened. The vegetables and condiments served with the parathas were free.

As my father frowned on all bazaar food, my mother at first denied my request. But she herself was tempted by the smells and, if asked enough times, capitulated with a certain relief. "Just don't drink the water," she would whisper, convincing herself that now she had dealt with my father's fears. We climbed up a few steps, went past a billboard reassuring us that only the purest "real" ghee was used on the premises (as opposed to the kind my father had churned out in his factory), and took our seats at the rough wooden tables. A young man whizzed by dropping *pattals* (plates made out of semi-dried leaves) in front of us. He came by again, ladling out the chutneys and pickles with equal speed: sweet chutney, made with dried green mango, dried pomegranate, and dried jujubes; sour chutney, made with fresh mint, green coriander, and grated white radish; and carrot pickle, made with carrots, yellow chilies, crushed mustard seeds, and tamarind. Already on the table was some salt seasoned with ground roasted cumin and crushed red chilies.

Before any real food arrived, we would start dipping our fingers in the condiments and licking them. Then came the vegetables— meats did not belong in such places—carrots stir-fried with young fenugreek greens; potatoes, and peas cooked with cumin, asafetida, and tomatoes; cauliflower with ginger and green chilies. As soon as the vegetables were on our plates, the hot, hot parathas floated in, whichever we had ordered, all puffed up, ready to be deflated and devoured even before all the steam had hissed out.

My mother never allowed us to eat too much, as we were, after all, on our way to spend the day with her family. This was just a taste to tide us over until lunchtime. But what a taste it was—vegetarian, pure Old Delhi, and exclusively Parathe Vali Gulley.

We crisscrossed a few more narrow lanes before coming to the portals of our mother's family home, our *nana ka ghar.* There was no way anyone could gauge from the outside what the inside might be like. The well-worn wooden double doors were always shut. We would knock, and a servant girl would come to unlatch them to let us in. As the doors closed again behind us, the pace of life slowed instantly, and we seemed to enter an earlier world.

My nana ka ghar was of the same basic design as other attached houses in the Old City. All the rooms, on several floors, were built around an inner courtyard that served to let in light and air. Wealthier homes had several intricately carved stone courtyards, one leading to the next, some even with gardens and trees in them. But my mother's home was modest. One courtyard, plain, undecorated, and treeless, sufficed. The rooms were simple, too, with Moghul-style arched niches for closets, and seating either on low divans covered with white sheets or on the floor, with bolsters to lean against. The office room did have a desk, but it was the short-legged kind that required the writer to sit cross-legged behind it.

I must confess I thought then that my inner-city family and I had very little in common, though their undemanding, noncompetitive nature made them unusually comfortable to be with. What attracted me there was the food, which was uncommon, and, of course, witnessing my mother's relaxed pleasure at being "home." As in Kanpur, she seemed to be in control of her own life once again, falling into the pace of her childhood days with ease. Veena and I would climb up the narrow stairs to the roof. From here we could hear the hum of the city. If we spun around, our eyes could look down on family life in hundreds of courtyards that receded into ever-smaller sizes as they stretched into the distance. If we looked straight ahead in a southeasterly direction, our gaze would meet the grand dome and minarets of Jama Masjid, the seventeenth-century mosque. We could hear all the calls to prayer. Meanwhile, my mother changed into her cottons and settled down to knit or hem or attach a border to a saree—she rarely sat idly—and to catch up with family news.

There were few servants in this household, and the cooking was done mostly by my aunt, my mother's brother's wife, though all the women and girls pitched in, scraping bitter gourds, shelling green chickpeas, and pinching off small fenugreek leaves. My sister and I were rarely allowed to join, as we were considered "guests." We hung around, unable to tear ourselves away from the aromas.

One of the specialties of the house was a sauced dish of monsoon mushrooms. I never had them as good anywhere else. These were not the common white mushrooms now sold all over Delhi, though they were white in color. Called *khumbi,* they consisted of very slight three-inch edible stems topped with elongated narrow caps that closed in on themselves so no gills were visible. These mushrooms chose to spring out of the earth only when the rains poured during the monsoon season. They were so delicate—and expensive—that they were sold in baskets, heaped into little piles. Their texture was smooth and satiny, not unlike that of the fresh straw mushrooms I have since eaten, but only in the Far East.

My aunt Mainji, with her large protruding teeth, knew how to cook them to perfection. She always said, "There is nothing to it."

There must have been something to it, because even my mother's khumbi were not quite like hers.

Mainji would take off her shoes, step into the kitchen, and squat on the floor in front of a brazier, blowing on the charcoal until it glowed to her liking. A pot would go on top of the coal, some oil next, and the cooking began. The mushrooms took but ten minutes and seemed to require only cumin, coriander, turmeric, and chili powder, but in some magical proportion that she alone had mastered. She prepared one dish after another. There was meat—all the men in her family required it, just as those in ours did—and several seasonal vegetables, each one more delicious than the last, tiny stuffed bitter gourds, okra with dried green mango, green chickpeas cooked in a pilaf, and pumpkin cooked with fennel seeds.

The pièce de résistance, for me at any rate, was the mushrooms. But would I get to eat any? Lunch was served quite late, and the men were always served first. Striped dhurries were spread out on a shady end of the courtyard, topped with a fresh white sheet. The men took off their shoes and sat down in a circle. The women served them, placing all the food in the center.

I would watch the mushrooms disappear, wondering if there would be any left for us. As the men served themselves generously, I would hold my breath. When it was our turn to eat, there were fewer mushrooms and more sauce. By that time I hardly cared. The sauce was delicious, too. I scooped it up with bits of my poori and just devoured it.

After lunch, some grown-ups napped; others sat in groups and talked. My sister and I went up and down the stairs, in and out of all the rooms, breaking off and eating a leaf of holy basil (tulsi) whenever we passed the plant near the prayer room.

For tea, Mainji sent out for some roasted white sweet potatoes (shakarkandi), some star fruit (kumruq), and some roasted water chestnuts (singfiaras). These she made into a spicy chaat to serve with our sweet, milky tea. Then it was time to leave. My mother gathered up her needlework, freshened up, and changed back into her silks. Attachee case and handbag in hand, she walked out of her family portals, and we followed. We always returned a different way, partly because of where the car could park and partly because my mother still had some unfinished business in the Tinsel Bazaar

(Kinari Bazaar) and in Dariba, the Street of Jewelers. In the first she picked up spice mixes like *chaat masala* from a specialty stall that has existed in the same spot for all of my life, and in the latter she checked on pieces of jewelry that she always seemed to have on order, bangles, rings, and necklaces. We made our last stop right at the end of Dariba, just where it met the main street, Chandni Chowk. This was at the shop that sold *jalebis,* the squiggly, pretzel-like sweets filled with syrup. We liked them hot and crisp, straight out of the wok, and freshly dunked in syrup. The jalebis would be served to us on a leaf, which we would carry to our car. Our sticky hands and sticky mouths would be quite busy throughout the journey home.

Waiting for a Cappuccino

by Carolyn Thériault

from *Gastronomica*

The study of Egyptology first brought Carolyn Theriault to North Africa, but she's now planted in Morocco, where ancient history underlies the surface of everyday life. Travel writing and photography support her curious ramblings around the region.

As I wait for my cappuccino, I subconsciously but quite mechanically begin to play with the salt and pepper shakers on the vinyl tablecloth—pairing them off as ballroom dancers across the checkerboard design, then transforming them into charging bull and lithesome matador. In its zeal, the salt delivers a deathblow to the pepper, knocking it over and spilling much of its contents. Turning my head slightly, I note that I am being watched in disbelief by the server. Embarrassed, I set the pepper shaker aright, affording it (and myself) a little dignity.

Dignity? What dignity can I offer my spilled pepper—its day is gone, the sun has set on its empire, it has paid for its commonness in a questionable currency of novelty shakers, plastic bags from bulk stores, bins, and unimaginative pressed-glass bottles. If pepper (and the same holds true for all spices) is distanced from its origins, then we are wholly ignorant of them. Do peppercorns look longingly back on an illustrious past when bloody battles were fought, queens seduced, peoples enslaved, lives lost, pirate-infested waters crossed, and worlds discovered for their sake, when their value was such that they were counted peppercorn by peppercorn? If they don't, we should, for the "discovery" of our world was founded upon the rapacious pursuit of these peppers, as well as vanilla and allspice. Our land mass stood inconveniently in the way of those ships seeking direct passage to the "wealth of the Orient," but this diversion was serendipitous if not rewarding: the bounty of the Americas proved to be equally profitable to that of the Far East. Our kitchen cupboards are a living map of trade routes: shelves and racks peppered with spices that have traveled since antiquity along their own routes or hitched a ride along the silk and amber roads of China, India, Indonesia, Africa, and Persia—their distant homelands still evocative of culinary erotica.

My cappuccino arrives, and I note that the cinnamon has burrowed deeply into the foam, leaving rabbit holes in its milky peaks; my nostrils flare at the sharp, aromatic hit of spice. The cinnamon gives me pause. Herodotus, the so-called Father of History, wrote that giant phoenixes, notably called *cinnamolgi,* used cinnamon sticks to make their nests. He goes on to say that in order to harvest the spice, men would lob chunks of meat at the nests, causing them to fall to the ground and break apart. It would be an understatement to say that such bits of arcana intrigue me. In fact, I wish I could fumble with a few mechanical knobs and not only turn back time but turn myself into a cinnamon stick so that I could travel by camel and tall ship across the ancient world to be traded in Malabar, Cathay, or Babylon, to be lauded in the courts of Kublai Khan, to be put on the "historical" map by the likes of Marco Polo. Since I cannot be that piece of bark, I must use less fantastic means to savor that spice experience and, regrettably, rely upon my memory. Sipping my coffee, I allow my mind to return to the *souks* (or markets) of North Africa in which I have not only spent a great deal of time but have become deliciously lost over and over again.

It is in Egypt that I first discover that pyramids of saffron and cardamom can surpass their limestone counterparts across the Nile in both beauty and elegance. Crushing hibiscus flowers underfoot, I meander deeply into the Khan Al-Khalili, the labyrinthine souk of medieval Cairo, where I am blinded by color: baskets piled high with spices of vermilion, saffron, ochre, and burnt tangerine. These multihued pylons appear to defy the laws of physics, but it is I who lose balance, reel at the headiness of cloves, turmeric, cumin, and pepper. Here, desiccated pods, roots, fruit pits, stems, seeds, gums, bark, berries, and petals from neighboring continents all coincide in blissful coexistence. These modern souks are the heirs of the world's first interracial marriages, gastronomic multicultural harems where Lebanese fenugreek flirted with tamarind from Delhi, where no one raised an eyebrow in horror.

The spice trade was once both a serious and a dangerous business: only a few centuries ago, the English stevedores who emptied spice ships were obliged to sew their pockets fast to discourage theft. Spices traveled thousands of kilometers of inhospitable terrain and wild seas by long camel caravans fraught with brigands and in ships plagued by piracy. Conditions at sea were so perilous that if the spice ships returned at all, they normally dropped anchor with significantly fewer crewmembers than when they had left.

But this is relatively recent history: before humans could leave historical records, they were seasoning their food with aromatic plants. Later, the ancient Egyptians used spices to flavor the lives of the living and to preserve the bodies of the dead. The Chinese were importing cloves from the Moluccas over two millennia ago, and spices were traded in Europe before Rome was founded. It was not unknown for Arab merchants to guard the identity of their sources and hide spice routes by inventing bizarre and horrifying tales to discourage other entrepreneurs. In Roman times wealthier households made a conspicuous display of using spices in their daily cuisine and thereby increased their social standing. Later, Crusaders returning from the Holy Land brought with them spices and inspired fortune seekers, merchants, and adventurers to ply the seas for spices, Christian converts, and new continents. Spices became ingrained in everyday life, and their uses far exceeded enhancing the taste of unpalatable or insalubrious fare: in many towns one could pay taxes, tolls, and rent, as well as bribe judges with just the right amount of pepper. Spices were ground into medical compounds; curative wines were enhanced with saffron; and sick rooms were liberally fumigated with spice-bearing smoke. The economic and political fortunes of vying global powers, notably Venice, Genoa, Spain, Portugal, England, and the

Netherlands, were directly linked to their ability to control trade routes and their hegemony over the Spice Islands. The colonization of the New World ultimately created a new and highly motivated merchant class that was able to successfully undercut their competitors. The markets of the world became flooded with less expensive spices, and with the increased availability of sugar, coffee, tea, and cocoa, the sun began to set on the sovereignty of the peppercorn and its kin.

The value of a man's life was once equivalent to a bag of pepper; in light of this, it seems frivolous if not obscene to consider the current price of spices. In the spice souks it seems equally disrespectful to be able to simply walk by such historical wealth with modern indifference. Nonetheless, as I do, the breeze from my passing causes a slight tremor, and a few grains of allspice hover in the air like dust motes. I freeze—how much money have I inadvertently wasted? An annoying mechanical noise jars me from my spice-guilt, and I turn to watch a man in the Khan Al-Khalili operating what looks like a wood chipper, grinding curled cinnamon bark into its more common powdered form. Connecting with my imaginary cinnamon stick persona, I wince in sympathy for my fallen comrades.

In the Nubian markets of Aswan—the southernmost point of pharaonic Egypt and the most "African" in temperament and temperature—I buy henna to color my hair. The ancient Egyptians likewise dyed their hair and tattooed their bodies with these dried plant leaves. After spending an afternoon sitting on the balcony of my hotel with malodorous goop on my head, I fear that my hair more closely resembles the garish locks of the Egyptian Museum's dehydrated mummies. In the souks of Khartoum, I buy kilograms of frankincense from Somaliland. I have no clue what I will actually do with it—my experience with frankincense is limited to the Three Magi and interminable high masses from my childhood—but know that I must have it. In a world where Catholic parishes are increasingly offering incense-free masses— *O mores! O tempores!*—I can indulge my obsession for a fragrant hit of this freakishly sinus-purging but soothing sweetness behind closed doors. In a charred brass pot from India, I set charcoal briquettes alight and sparingly add a few grains of the amber-like resin—sparingly because the smoke is so prolific that I must disconnect my smoke alarm beforehand lest I invite the entire fire department into my home.

In Fès, considered by many the largest living medieval city in the world, I visit a *khan* or *caravanserai* (from the Persian for "merchant's inn") still guarded by colossal wooden doors able to admit laden camels and still kept secure by massive iron locks so large that I cannot cover them with my two hands. These hostels served the caravans that traversed the East and North Africa and were ingeniously designed around an open concept to cater to its entire clientele, both man and beast. Spices and goods were stored under lock and key; camels were kept safe in stalls on the ground floor courtyards; and merchants were lodged in the overlooking upper galleries. Looking about this now-derelict building, I am momentarily transported to a bygone era of travel—I am certain that I hear the tinkle of camel bells. Peering out the great doorway, I see instead a white mule pass by loaded with plastic crates of clanking Coca-Cola bottles. Caravans of cantankerous camels no longer wind their way through the twisting alleyways of Fès's souks, but deliveries haven't changed much in the last nine hundred years.

Not long ago, I presented my mother with an unlikely souvenir from Africa: nutmegs from Marrakech. When I was a girl, my mother baked cookies flavored with nutmeg. Unlike my friends' mothers, she grated her own spice and stored the scraped brindled nut in the receptacle of her nutmeg grater—an aged tin coffin that was affixed to the kitchen wall. It was no wonder to me that her molasses cookies were the world's best. On a rainy afternoon in Marrakech, I sought refuge in the souk, where I forewent indigo leather slippers and Berber carpets for a clutch of nutmegs the size of robins' eggs. These formidable nutmegs made their grocery store counterparts pale in comparison; indeed, they were so large my mother's grater could not hold them. Her home on the south shore of Nova Scotia completed these nutmegs' journey, which possibly had begun in Madagascar. Thus the cycle continues. The trade route lives even if a knapsack has replaced a Portuguese sailing vessel. This ancient gift of spice still feels like a serious and somber business, and it should—execution awaited thieves who stole nutmeg trees from the Dutch.

I play with my coffee cup and watch the foam and cinnamon sprinkles swirl about the sides of the cup, leaving Rorschach patterns for my contemplation. I think about Herodotus and his giant birds. I wonder if he was the victim of a dodgy merchant hoping to protect a source or if perhaps, just maybe, cinnamon sticks once had such fabulous origins. I finish my cappuccino, now grown cold, with a quick gulp and wistfully hope that they did.

The Japanese Paradigm

by John Kessler
from *The Atlanta Journal-Constitution*

Though you might not expect it from a food editor based in Atlanta, John Kessler knows whereof he speaks when it comes to Japanese cuisine. Some writers would get lost in the details; Kessler's eye for the big picture gives his food writing extra credibility.

Sit down to a Sinatra roll at Shout restaurant, and this is what you get: a sushi roll stuffed with three kinds of fish and cream cheese, breaded and deep-fat-fried, and served up with spicy mayonnaise and a syrupy brown sauce.

My friend, I'll say it clear; I'll state my case of which I'm certain: Sushi "my way" is just so wrong.

How did it come to this? How did we Americans take an iconic Japanese dish that should be the essence of simplicity and freshness and turn it into seppuku on a plate?

Sushi is everywhere—so everywhere that it's turned into American food.

Supermarkets may no longer have butchers or bakers on site, but thousands now have chefs who spend all day pressing California rolls. There's even one at the Wal-Mart in Plano, Texas. I saw it. Two nice Burmese men prepare 300 boxes each day next to a wall of Velveeta. The franchiser, AFC Corp., hopes to be in 200 more Wal-Marts soon.

We claim to love Japanese food, but we simply don't get it. Every good thing about the Japanese diet has been lost in translation.

Granted, the Japanese way of eating, unique to the culture that produced it, does not cross cultures easily. We may be in thrall to the small part we know, but we're still blind to the big picture of the Japanese diet—both its untold pleasures and its implications for health and well-being.

Japan today has the thinnest people among 30 industrialized countries, with an obesity rate around 3 percent, as opposed to America's 31 percent. Japan also has the world's longest life expectancy. Yet the Japanese encounter the same lifestyle issues most often implicated in America's rampant obesity problem. They face the same daily stresses, the same disappearing family dinner hour, the same reliance on processed foods, and the same sedentary workplaces.

The Japanese eat more fish and vegetables and less overall fat. But the vital difference, I think, is in how they present flavors, approach meals, respond to hunger and engage all their senses at the table. Simply put, the Japanese know how to eat less and enjoy their food more.

The only way to explain this truth is to tell it.

In 1983, after graduating from college, I moved to the Kansai region of western Japan for two years to teach English. When I first arrived, each meal seemed booby-trapped. The yellow spongy tile on the sashimi platter was merely sweetened egg. But the pinkish goo in the small dish? Fermented squid innards that tasted like shark chum mixed with ammonia.

Learning to appreciate this food took patience. Some of my expat friends gave up hope and subsisted on McDonald's and care packages bearing Old El Paso taco kits.

For me, the turnaround came after I had been in the country for about a month and an American colleague who knew the ropes invited me out to dinner. The meal was unlike any Japanese meal I had eaten back home. The restaurant was in the labyrinth of Osaka's uptown entertainment district, in a dark underground bunker of a dining room. It was an *izakaya*—a kind of pub with an extended menu of snacks and other small dishes.

My friend and I knocked back draft beers as he did the ordering—crisp grilled rice balls, dressed boiled spinach, pork dumplings and a few other easy-to-like dishes.

No squid goo.

The food arrived helter-skelter, and we shared it all. We ordered more as needed, but after eight or ten plates, our diminished appetites cut us off.

This one meal encapsulated everything I would come to learn about Japanese food over the next two years.

For starters, it offered a far greater variety of foods than any I had eaten before. Variety, above all, is key to the Japanese diet.

At restaurants, at home, in packed lunches, Japanese meals do not seem complete without constant contrasts. A boneless chicken breast with rice and one vegetable? This kind of "wholesome American meal" would never pass muster in Japan.

Tokyo-based author Elizabeth Andoh attributes this deeply ingrained Japanese impulse to a 1,200-year-old set of dietary guidelines. In her new cookbook, *Washoku* (Ten Speed Press, $35), she notes that washoku, a derivation of Buddhist practice, suggests that each meal should contain five different colors, primary tastes (sweet, salty, etc.), textures and cooking preparations. These principles are not something most modern Japanese think about, but, as Andoh maintains, they are second nature.

"You could follow a girl who's been up all night in a club into a *konbini* [convenience store], and the assortment of junk food she puts into her *kaato* [shopping cart] will follow washoku, " says Andoh.

The Japanese Health Ministry published a more contemporary set of nutrition guidelines in 1985 with the slogan "ichi nichi sanju hinmoku tabeyo, " or "eat 30 different foods each day." (Japan's Martha Stewart, popular cookbook author Harumi Kurihara, still recommends this.) Compare this to the original USDA Food Guide Pyramid from 1992, with its suggested 15 to 26 servings of the various food groups, and the message is telling: Americans quantify what they eat, the Japanese qualify.

With such variety on the table, no one dish can predominate. Granted, my izakaya meal was similar to a tapas spread (albeit with more, smaller dishes), but in Japan this kind of decentralized approach is the norm, whether at a formal dinner, in a quick-service restaurant or sitting around the family dinner table.

"There's no main dish, but many small dishes, " says Shinobu

Kitayama, a University of Michigan psychologist who studies group dynamics. At a typical home dinner, he says, each member of the family gets a bowl of miso soup and rice, while the group shares a variety of *sozai*, or side dishes.

But these are not really sides in the American sense. They may be seasoned vegetables, meat or fish. Most often, sozai combine vegetables with small amounts of animal protein; any given meal might feature fish, beef and pork.

"Basically, Japanese are meat-eating vegetarians," says Kitayama. "You'd never see a 500-gram steak like you would in America."

Sozai may be homemade but will just as likely come from the freezer case, a supermarket, a convenience store or from the vast food halls in the basements of department stores. Everything is portioned and individually packaged—hundreds of small dishes for the taking. Compare this deli experience to, say, Whole Foods Market, where the hot bar, salads and cheesy casseroles come by the pound.

Again, it's quality vs. quantity.

With so many small dishes on the table, the vessels themselves matter. Any Japanese meal presents a tableau of artfully mismatched dishware. Home pantries brim with small plates and bowls.

On a formal level, the art of Japanese food arranging is as codified as flower arranging; in daily practice, people cook from a huge repertoire of dishes, each of which has an accepted "look." Embedded in the aesthetic lie constant visual clues to portion size.

Bear in mind this describes the sushi experience in Japan. Diners sit at the bar and order sushi by the piece or pair directly from the chef or, in an inexpensive kaitenzushi shop, taking plates off a conveyor belt. Most small neighborhood restaurants operate in a similar fashion. The moment a bite of food is ready, the cook hands it to you.

The Japanese approach to satiety is a parabolic curve with an infinite endpoint. "Stuffed" is never the desirable conclusion.

Kitayama believes this is why Japanese food favors subtle seasoning. "Strong tastes can stimulate your appetite, like in Chinese food." Japan may have the only national cuisine with no traditional use for garlic.

If an incremental, small-plates meal leaves someone with a big appetite hungry two hours later, there's a time-honored tradition called shime—"closing" the evening at a soup noodle stand. The broth will be dashi—the ubiquitous stock made from dried skipjack tuna and sea kelp—and it will be filled with umami.

This Japanese notion of a fifth primary taste (in addition to sweet, sour, bitter and salty) was proven by researchers at the University of Miami in 2000, who isolated receptors on the tongue for the amino acids naturally abundant in dashi and many other foods.

In the West, we associate the satisfaction of umami with meats, cheeses and other caloric sources of animal protein. Because the Japanese didn't eat meat until the Meiji Restoration of 1868, the cuisine found ways to extract umami from sea vegetables, fish and plants. The food is low in fat but richer in sources of umami. On the most basic neurochemical level, it tastes meatier that actual meat.

That izakaya meal was for me the beginning of a lifelong passion for Japanese food. When I returned home after two years, I remember thinking how unnecessarily large the portions were here and how the food sat in my stomach after meals. Sadly, the feeling didn't last.

Fried anything—even sushi—is easy enough to eat.

The Insidious Rise of Cosmo-Cuisine

by Salma Abdelnour
from *Food & Wine*

So many articles about international restaurants have crossed *F&W* travel editor Abdelnour's desk—it's no wonder she's begun to spot a few patterns in them. Herewith, her plea for a return to home-grown flavor.

Normally, I cut chefs a lot of slack in the way they write their menus. If they want to give too much information about certain ingredients (where the baby octopus on your plate took its first swim) and nothing about other key details (what exactly are *brovada* and *scorzonera?*), that's their choice. But I've been feeling increasingly frustrated with the labels chefs are using to describe their cooking—and my patience reached its limit recently at a certain Boston restaurant. The talented young chef there (I'm not naming names yet) calls his cuisine "modern European." What's on his menu? Barbecued pork ribs with Thai green chile sauce and sticky rice.

Wishy-washy terms like "modern European" and "modern American" have insinuated themselves into the restaurant lexicon more and more over the past few years—and the more common they become, the less they mean anything at all. The labels have become shorthand for a hodgepodge of ingredients, techniques and cultural references from pretty much anywhere on earth. What those terms really mean is, "Whatever the chef feels like doing."

Restaurants claiming to specialize in modern American and

modern European cuisine aren't the only culprits. Terms like modern Mediterranean, modern Australian, modern South African, modern Mexican, modern Caribbean, modern Chinese and modern Japanese can be just as hard to pin down. Guess what type of restaurants these dishes come from: sweetbread roulade with cauliflower mousse; terrine of chicken and foie gras with pear-apple-raisin chutney; green risotto with zucchini and fava beans. They're examples from restaurants in Cape Town, Dublin and Mexico City, respectively, each claiming to serve a modern or eclectic version of the local cuisine. Modern European and its friends are even wigglier than last decade's trendy hybrid, Asian fusion. At least you can usually pick out Asian fusion in a lineup.

This is not just an issue of semantics. The fact that it's getting harder to come up with useful labels for menus might be a pain in the neck for chefs, food writers and restaurant publicists, but it points to a more dire situation: The cuisines of the world are merging into one giant, amorphous mass. In theory, it's exciting to find chefs everywhere opening up their kitchens to influences from around the planet, discovering obscure international ingredients and creating cosmopolitan, border-crossing menus. And the dishes they come up with can be absolutely delicious. Why wouldn't I want to eat caramelized pork hocks with chile vinegar or coconut-braised short ribs with parsnip dumplings, fennel and lemongrass? The problem is, too many chefs worldwide are creating menus that flit across so many borders and reference so many traditions that they—and we—lose any sense of place.

In most cities with a vibrant food scene, you could take some of this year's hottest new restaurants—the ones with the most ambitious chefs, the best real estate, the most stunning design— and plop them down in another city, another country, another continent, and no one would notice. The irony that the more worldly menus get, the more alike they sound will be familiar to anyone who has stayed in a boutique hotel or shopped in a trendy clothing store lately. It's the increasing—and depressing— homogeneity of what passes for sophisticated international taste. In his 2006 book *The Naked Tourist,* Lawrence Osborne coins a word for the sense that cultural experiences are becoming interchangeable all over the world: "whereverness." There is an upside to whereverness: You can feel well-traveled without going anywhere. The downside? Traveling starts to seem a lot like staying home.

A few months ago, at star Puerto Rico chef Wilo Benet's San Juan restaurant Pikayo, I was confronted with a menu that read like this: spicy tuna tartare with peanut sauce; crab cake with apple-ginger remoulade; beef tenderloin with sautéed spinach; foie gras with black truffle honey; wild mushroom risotto with truffle oil. The few references to Puerto Rican or Latin American food were relegated mostly to the "fritters and hors d'oeuvres" section, which listed a few items like beef *alcapurrias* (fried dumplings) with aioli. How does Benet describe his cooking? He says he has "redefined" Puerto Rican food and calls his style "global mix cuisine . . . combining traditional Puerto Rican ingredients with Japanese, Chinese, Thai, Spanish, Italian, French and Arab influences." But if I wanted crab cakes, tuna tartare, risotto and foie gras, I could just as easily get those in New York City, Paris or London . . . or Sydney or Hong Kong.

When I travel, I love eating local foods at holes-in-the-wall and street-food stands; I don't need a white tablecloth or a glittering chandelier. But I do wish more chefs and restaurateurs around the world with Benet's talent and training, and a beautiful dining room like Pikayo's, would be eager to embrace, elevate and show off their local cuisine without disguising it behind so many fusion fads. By no means should chefs feel hog-tied to their national traditions—or be unswervingly faithful to indigenous ingredients—but it would be nice if their menus showed a little more loyalty.

In a way, just about every cuisine in the world is already a fusion cuisine: Wars, invasions, colonialism and changing population and immigration patterns have played key roles in the evolution of most food cultures around the globe. The culinary heritage of the United States is a perfect example; the same is true of Latin America, Australia, most of Africa—virtually everywhere. But every country or region has a unique constellation of influences and its own brand effusion. It would be a shame if now—thanks to jet-setting chefs and menu trends that whip around the planet faster than Brangelina—the cuisines of the world end up evolving in the same generically cosmopolitan direction. I may love braised short ribs and squid-ink risotto and pork belly confit, but I don't want to see them everywhere I go.

In some countries, the cosmo trend isn't the only problem. In many places with phenomenal local foods, like Morocco, Lebanon, India and Pakistan, the most glamorous and ambitious restaurants serve a high-prestige foreign cuisine instead. You're much more likely to eat an incredible tagine or couscous in a private house or *riad* in Morocco than in a restaurant. This is partly because cooking Moroccan food is considered a female domain, while most of the country's restaurants are owned and staffed by men. In Tangier recently, I had a hard time finding locals who would strongly vouch for one of the city's Moroccan spots. Several recommended a tiny old place called Saveurs de Poisson, where I had simple but spectacular northern Moroccan seafood dishes like smoky, charcoal-grilled sole served on skewers with generous slices of lemon, and buttery pan-fried whitefish with spinach, onions and garlic. The restaurant is cozy—tucked into an alley off one of the town's bazaars—but seems too small and modest a space for what many consider the city's best Moroccan restaurant. For more see-and-be-seen outings, Tangier's well-heeled residents, expats and tourists trickling back to the city after a 30-year slump frequent French spots like the crowded bistro Relais de Paris and the luxurious hilltop Villa Joséphine, and Italian restaurants like San Remo and Casa d'Italia. The Interzone days before Morocco's independence in 1956—when Tangier was run by an international coalition that included eight European powers—may be long gone, but European cultural clout lives on.

In Pakistan, too, I've found that while the fiery and addictive local cuisine plays a starring role in people's homes—in spicy curries and juicy kebabs with Indian, Afghan and Iranian influences—it's not a major player in the restaurant scene. In Karachi, there are some good, casual, meat-centric Pakistani spots, like Bar B Q Tonight, but they can't compete with the prestige of restaurants like Okra, which has a rustic-chic design that would be equally at home in Berkeley or Barcelona and a menu of vaguely Euro-American dishes, like roasted chicken with cream sauce. The same is true in India. Mumbai's prominent food writer Rashmi Uday Singh explains that "There aren't many great Indian restaurants in

Mumbai, simply because the best food is still in our home kitchens." In my hometown of Beirut, Lebanon—which has, in my biased opinion, one of the world's best cuisines—the hottest restaurants, like Hussein Hadid's Kitchen and Yabani, are usually French, Italian, Japanese or cosmo.

In some European cities too, like Amsterdam and Berlin, good restaurants specializing in the local cuisine are hard to find, though the situation has been improving slightly. Maybe in cases like these, the national cuisine itself is to blame. (I'm sure I'll get some hate mail for saying that.) I do like a hearty Dutch meat-and-potato stew, and I love bratwurst and sauerkraut and spaetzle, but I don't blame chefs like Marije Vogelzang of Amsterdam's Proef for getting more inspired by her country's produce than its somewhat limited culinary repertoire.

The countries that most proudly show off their cuisine in restaurants tend to be the ones least insecure about their cultural status in general. The restaurants in France with the most swagger and status are almost always French at their core; their technique and foundation and most of their ingredients are French, even while they incorporate cosmo influences. The same goes for Italy—although, perhaps sniffing danger ahead, Italy has taken out a sort of insurance policy in case its traditions erode and someday vanish from public view: The Home Food organization anoints home cooks around the country who are skilled at reproducing classic regional dishes, then sends tourists to their houses for a private dinner. What a fantastic idea. Every country needs one of those.

There are other signs that culinary diversity isn't dead yet. Some ambitious, prestigious restaurants worldwide—if not as many as we'd like—are offering brilliant, refined and truly original versions of national cuisines. They're coming up with menus that are identifiably regional and at the same time wildly creative—menus you won't see anywhere else (well, not yet). In the United States, chefs like Gabrielle Hamilton of Manhattan's Prune, Scott Dolich of Portland, Oregon's Park Kitchen and Colby Garrelts of Kansas City, Missouri's Bluestem are revitalizing regional American traditions with painstakingly sourced local ingredients and innovative but not schizophrenic riffs. A few chefs in Scandinavia are showing that it's possible to introduce global, 21st-century influences while still maintaining a strong regional allegiance. Other chefs, like Peru's Gastón Acurio (of Astrid y Gastón in Lima and its numerous spin-offs) and Istanbul's Musa Dagdeviren of Ciya come to mind, too. And Ferran Adrià is a one-in-a-million example of a chef who managed to invent a technique and style that's radically new and shockingly different from what anyone else was doing—a style both worldly and deeply rooted in Catalan traditions. Granted, not every chef can be as extraordinarily innovative as Adrià—though his many imitators are certainly trying. China's cuisine is enjoying a healthy self-image, too. Some of the hottest new restaurants in Beijing, Shanghai and Hong Kong—besides the inevitable outposts of global superchefs like Jean-Georges Vongerichten and Alain Ducasse—are resolutely Chinese.

Another good sign is that some national cuisines are finding their way to parts of the world where they weren't as prevalent before. In the Midwestern U.S., in Canada, even in hard-to-crack European markets like Rome, greater numbers of immigrants from all over Asia, Africa, Latin America, and parts of Europe like Greece and the Balkans are opening both casual and upscale restaurants that show off their native dishes. Soon it might be easier to find great Moroccan restaurants in Paris or Madrid than in Marrakech or Tangier, and easier to find a great Pakistani spot in Queens than in Karachi or Lahore. And some chefs are adopting another country's cuisine, making it their own, and introducing new audiences to it, like Lachlan Mackinnon-Patterson of Boulder, Colorado's, Frasca, who is obsessed with the food of Italy's Friuli region.

These examples are reassuring, but it remains to be seen whether the world's regional food traditions will ultimately survive in an age of cosmo-cuisine, cosmo-design, cosmo-culture, cosmo-everything. In a January 2007 interview in the French magazine *Paris Match,* celebrity chef Paul Bocuse said. "People are traveling an enormous amount, and they tend to want to find the dishes and tastes they're used to wherever they go." I'm hoping he'll turn out to be wrong.

The Meat of the Matter

Meat

by James Sturz

from www.leitesculinaria.com

New York–based novelist/travel writer/ journalist James Sturz counts food writing among his many specialties. As contributing editor for this award-winning Web site, he approaches food as a cultural historian might—then gives it a novelistic spin.

A man in Wyoming calls his lover in New York. It's been 11 days since he has seen her, and it feels long and terrible because their relationship is new. "It's midnight here," he says, "so I know I must be waking you. But I have to tell you about my dinner. Are you there? This is important." He cradles the receiver to his cheek, sitting on the hotel bed with his socked feet rubbing against carpet. "We went to dinner, and I need you to know about the prime rib I ate. It was swimming in a gully of juice. I mean, sopping and red, and . . ." He catches his breath now, recalling the bites and the texture, the moments of flesh. "It could only make me think of you," he tells her. "I was the only one at the table without boots or a cowboy hat," he starts laughing. "I was supposed to be talking about raising capital, and about getting it into Cheyenne fast. But I was thinking of you between each swallow, and all I could think of was your body."

The woman in New York says, "God, I miss you lots. Hurry here; hurry home. It's two o'clock in the morning, and now I'm not going to be able to sleep."

"Then I shouldn't have told you."

"I'm glad you did."

He says into the receiver: "You make me hungry. I'm hungry now." He's wide-awake.

"Say more," she says to him, suddenly.

He has a handful of bedspread drawn into his fist. "I want to hunt you. Inside your clothes."

There is the smell: steak, grilled over charcoal, colluding with a breeze, while dribbles of sizzle impregnate the air. And there is the taste: the seared, tender flesh, trickling mouthfuls of juice at each bite. Like monkeys, we are omnivores. We have been eating meat since we first discovered we could—since the first Homo erectus realized that killing for food made the stomach feel good. In the days when there were many gods, and many of them were wild and choleric, we sacrificed animals to them, and sometimes we even sacrificed ourselves.

Meat is about celebration. It's alimentary sex. Tristan Tzara, the great Dada poet, said in 1920 after a performance: "For the first time in the history of the world, people threw at us not only eggs, vegetables and pennies, but beefsteaks as well. It was a very huge success." The fiction and food writer Bob Shacochis recalls an anecdote about his girlfriend, the formerly vegetarian Miss F., whose doctor diagnosed her as severely anemic and prescribed liver pills with enough iron to turn her into an I-beam. "She left his office and made a beeline for Safeway, where she purchased two pounds of the antidote in its nonpharmaceutical form," Shacochis writes.

It's only an observation that people in health food stores often look sick. It is an indisputable truth that kissing a woman after a meal of steak and red wine is different from kissing her after you eat tofu. It is better.

The man in Wyoming, on the twelfth day of his trip, says to his lover, "Grow your stomach big for me. Make it round and full. We'll age you nine months." He gets off the phone, and then calls her back immediately. "I have this fantasy of you as a milk cow." She says, "I like that."

The humanivorous shark swimming off the Florida coast has the right idea: Don't waste time with herring or carp. Follow the scent of sirloin in salt water.

A woman on a second date surprises her companion by kissing him back with twice the ferocity. She is ravishing. She says, ravenously: "If I bite off your tongue, I'm not going to return it."

I am a flesh-eater. I have eaten Bambi, Chicken Little, Fernando el Feroz. I have watched slabs of steers hang in New York's Meatpacking District, dripping their essences down to the brick street. I have read the story of cannibals (human flesh is one of the finest sources of protein, experts tell us), devouring their prey with ritualized table manners and special wood forks. A half-century before Dahmer, the essayist M. F. K. Fisher suggested that the best human beef would come from adolescents raised in the countryside on apples and creamy milk. For well-behaved cannibals, including Micronesian princes and kings, fillets from the ball of the thumb were once considered unparalleled delicacies.

A friend says that the reason people eat Gummi Bears is they have the same consistency as earlobes. I believe him.

I have left marks with my teeth on others' bodies and I have felt teeth biting down on my own skin, and I have liked it. Sometimes, I have craved it.

The mother looks at her four-year-old son, still bundled in layers of baby fat. She presses a finger into the soft flesh of his tummy, and watches it spring back into shape. "I could eat you alive!" she coos, and the boy breaks into giggles. He's nine years away from his first junior high school hickey.

Who dares tell me the rump is a cheap cut of meat? Filet mignon is what you do with a lover. Hamburgers are for something lustful and quick, when you're short on patience and badly needing relief. I am ready for vegetarians to send hate mail, to tell me that you can't justifiably martyr an animal in the name of passion. But I am ready to tell them I can live comfortably with the guilt. It's a guilt I want.

"Full-bloodedness is the raison d'être of steak," argues the French semiotician Roland Barthes. In his country, if you want your steak rare, you order it saignant or bleu. You ask for it wounded and bloody. To make steak tartare, you double its animality: You take raw meat, and then you beat in a raw egg.

The diner at Smith & Wollensky looks at his dish, points to the tenderloin on his plate, and says savagely, "Hey, it was either him or me."

At a Fourth of July barbecue, an analyst wipes sauce from his chin, and says, innocently, "Yeah, it may have been a steer, but how do I know it was a nice steer, a simpatico steer?"

I asked the woman I was seeing, "Do you want to join me for eating meat?" (The syntax was awkward, but it was exactly what I meant.) My brother-in-law, the chef, offered a recipe. I bought the best piece of beef I could find. It was all tied up, bound by cotton strings. First, I seasoned with salt and pepper. Then I seared the edges of the filet mignon in a pan. I put it into the oven at 375°F, just a half-inch from the bottom, and we waited for a half-hour to pass. When we pulled it out, steam eased from the surface. Black peppers were nestled there like freckles or birthmarks. Dimples in the meat had flooded with juice. "What do you think?" I asked. "It looks luscious. I want to eat it," my own Miss K. said, not mincing words. She cut into the loin delicately, then stabbed with the prongs. Once inside her mouth, she chewed the flesh like a lioness.

I want vegetarians to explain to me how I didn't enjoy this.

Three days later, the lover returns from Wyoming. He goes to her apartment, with two weeks' worth of fantasies about her body. They sit, cross-legged in the living room, on the shag rug. He kisses her and their teeth clink. She has a freckle on her lip that he wants to chew off. She says, nervously, "I used to bite my nails and eat my cuticles. I wonder how many pounds of my skin I've swallowed since I was a little girl—because I don't think I ever spit it out."

He's looking right at her, almost laughing. He sighs, "I've really missed you."

She has a scar on her calf that he traces back and forth with his fingers. The skin is stretched smooth like a sail.

He tells her, "You're the good cholesterol inside my arteries."

She says, with her head leaning against his chest, "And now I'm making your heart work twice as fast."

If you saw the way her neck poured into her shoulders, you wouldn't need to ask why he bites.

What's at Stake at the Butcher Shop

by Pete Wells
from *Food & Wine*

The *New York Times*'s new Dining section editor, Pete Wells has long been charming *Food & Wine* readers with his witty, insightful, wide-ranging food articles. Here he hones our appreciation for the endangered art of the butcher.

Let me see if I can put the steer back together.

Spread out on my kitchen counter are 33 pounds of prime aged beef wrapped in brown paper. The biggest package holds eight huge rib steaks, each tapering into a jutting prow of bone. The steaks weigh in at just over 13 pounds. Then, in descending order of mass: a seven-pound standing rib roast, a four-pound pile of meaty bones for stock, thick and enticing short ribs to the tune of three pounds, a slightly smaller quantity of stew meat in one-inch cubes, and, finally, 30 ounces or so of hamburger. Flashing forward to later this evening, six friends will show up for dinner, and when they stagger to their feet a few hours later, the steaks will be gone. The rest of my bounty I will somehow contrive to cook over the next two weeks. But right now I'm trying to run the film in reverse, backing up to three o'clock this afternoon, when these heaps of flesh and bone made up a single colossal hunk of beef.

My original plan was to cut all this meat myself. One day I had realized with creeping horror that I was breathtakingly ignorant about meat for a guy who eats some part of an animal at nearly every meal. I didn't know what a steak was, really, or the difference between short ribs and spareribs, or why I had such trouble slicing a ham.

Apprenticing myself to a butcher seemed like the fastest route to knowledge. If a veteran of New York's meat trade taught me to cut beef into shapes that I recognized from the dinner table, meat would become no more mysterious to me than potatoes or apples. That was the plan, at least. The stupidity of that plan became obvious the minute Pino Cinquemani pulled out his hacksaw.

Pino is the proprietor of Pino's Prime Meats, a butcher shop on Sullivan Street in lower Manhattan. Pino's establishment, with its hand-lettered signs and 19th-century fixtures, is a little piece of old New York, and sometimes it feels like a little piece of the Old World, too, as friends passing by the door sing out "Ciao, Pino!" (More Italian is spoken at Pino's than in certain quarters of Florence or Venice.) Pino has been carving up sheep, pigs and cattle since he was a teenager in the Sicilian town of Castrofilippo, and you might say that meat is in his blood. When I asked him about his family, this was his answer: "My grandfather was a butcher. My father was a butcher. My brothers are butchers. My brother-in-law. My sister-in-law. My nephew and my other nephew—butchers. My son is a butcher." And I, fool that I am, thought I could spend an afternoon at Pino's side and learn how to take apart a steer. I might as well have tried to master rocket science by watching an episode of *Lost in Space*.

To watch Pino in action is to see an uncanny blend of brute strength and magic. With an unerring pass of his knife, he separates a thick layer of fat from the ribs as easily as if he were cutting a deck of cards. Moments earlier, though, when he took a hacksaw to those ribs, he leaned into it with a force that made me understand why he'd spent the morning in physical therapy. His shoulder has been bothering him since December, when night after night he stayed up late, sawing through bones to meet 182 orders for Christmas roasts.

Cutting up meat is no job for a slacker, and this is one reason butcher shops have nearly vanished from the American landscape. Stanley Lobel recalls a time in the middle of the last century when there was a butcher on every block of Broadway in Manhattan from 100th Street down to the 60s. His family's business, Lobel's

Prime Meats, is one of the few shops from that era surviving today. "The other generations didn't want to be in the meat business," Lobel explains. "They're all doctors and lawyers and rabbis and architects—anything but butchers. In those days, butchers really had to work hard. My dad would ring my doorbell at three in the morning, and my wife would push me out of bed. I'd come down late the first five or six years. I'd make it nonetheless, with one eye open and one eye closed. Then we'd go to the market, choosing what was good and what wasn't. Five days a week we used to do that. We'd pack the sides of beef in big, heavy plastic bags and put them in the trunk of the car and bring them up to the store." A side of beef weighs about 300 pounds; driving away, the Lobels' car sagged as if it had two flat back tires.

The Lobels still break down sides of beef, but Pino stopped some time ago. When he drives to his wholesaler each weekday, he picks up mostly primals, the nine sections into which each half of the carcass is traditionally subdivided. The primal I am buying today is called the rib. I imagine it will resemble a roast. Instead, Pino emerges from his wood-paneled walk-in refrigerator straining to keep his grip on a piece of meat the size of a television. Swaying precariously, he somehow brings it in for a landing on his scale: 53 pounds.

"Uh, Pino," I call out. "How much did you say all this meat is going to cost me?"

Pino had promised that if I bought a whole rib primal—more beef than I'd normally eat in a year—I'd save a pile of money. The big-ticket item on this cut is the prime rib, which can be carved into roasts, rib steaks or both. Pino normally charges $18 a pound for this luxuriously marbled meat. I'm paying $5.99 a pound, but I need to take the whole primal. According to Pino, I will come out ahead. I'm not so sure.

Pino's first move is to saw across the ribs about six inches from where they meet the backbone, dividing the 53-pound mass in two. The smaller piece contains the short ribs; he slaps this down on a battered butcher block for later, then returns to the big round piece, the prime rib. First he uses his hacksaw to loosen the chine bone from the ribs. Then he pries it completely off using his cleaver as a wedge. Finally he switches on his electric band saw to separate the chine into nine blocks. "You can use this to make a stock or gravy," Pino says. Nothing on his butcher block looks like dinner yet, but Pino has gotten more exercise in 10 minutes than I have in the past year.

I can see why a young man who had a choice of dismantling steers or filing briefs might turn to law school. Mere aversion to heavy lifting, though, can't take all the blame for killing off independent butcher shops. The chief culprits are the grocery stores and the meat packers. In the early days of supermarkets, the meat department was a real butcher shop, staffed by men in white aprons who broke down carcasses and cut your brisket to order. Faced with this competition, independent butcher shops across the country closed. Then the supermarket butchers began to work behind the scenes, laying the brisket on Styrofoam trays and wrapping it in cellophane. Old-timers still sometimes asked to see the meat man for a special order, but most customers simply made do with what they found in the refrigerated cases.

Today, bold changes in the industry are making it easier for supermarkets to dispense with butchers entirely. The biggest packing companies sell what they call case-ready meat, which means that they, and not the store, cut up and package the shopper's steaks, roasts and so on. Until recently, this system would have failed, because exposed surfaces of red meat start to look pretty dismal after just a few days. But American ingenuity found an amazing high-tech solution: sealing meat inside plastic with some combination of oxygen and carbon monoxide. (Often carbon dioxide and nitrogen are added, too.) The gas keeps meat looking rosy for six weeks or longer—even after it's begun to rot.

Case-ready meat, which now accounts for more than 60 percent of the stock in supermarket cases, was in the news this winter when critics began questioning the safety of gassing. The real scandal, though, may be the way it is putting butchers out of work. "The butchers used to be the highest-paid guys in the store," says Bruce Aidells, who wrote *The Complete Meat Cookbook*. "Now clerks put the meat on the shelves and they get the same low wage as everybody else." It might seem that the butchers have simply moved from the stores to the slaughterhouses, but in fact meat packers have perfected an assembly-line system in which unskilled workers repeat a single cutting motion all day long. According to Eric Schlosser in his well-researched book *Fast Food Nation,* most of the employees are poorly paid, have no health insurance, and stay on the job less than a year. Schlosser called work in a meat-packing plant "the most dangerous job in the United States" because of the high rate of injuries.

Pino locates a thick seam of creamy fat an inch or two below the surface on the top end of the prime rib. He runs his knife through it and the beef falls open like a book.

One side of the book will become, after some more fat and the leathery outside edges are removed, my steaks and the roast. The other side is a layered slab of fat and lean that is sometimes called "lifter meat." Pino can extract six or seven pounds of useful beef from this section, but first I have a choice to make: Would I like stew meat, ground beef or flat slices for braciola? I ask for a couple pounds of hamburger for my toddler and the rest cut into cubes that will go into a ragù for me and my wife.

Thomas Keller, the chef at Manhattan's Per Se and the French Laundry in Napa Valley, serves a steak of grilled wagyu beef that is, in fact, lifter meat. Ordinary lifter meat can be tough, but wagyu is so richly marbled that Keller's oddball steak is quite tender, and it's a good buy, too (at least for him). A smart butcher examines a steer and sees a gold mine of these bargain cuts. Alongside $18 rib eyes, Pino sells Newport steaks for as little as $5.99 a pound. The cut comes from the sirloin primal and is known outside New York City as the bottom butt triangle. A butcher Pino worked for in New York renamed it the Newport—a marketing triumph that puts great prime steak within reach of almost everybody. My wife and I served Newport steaks at our wedding without going broke.

Taking apart animal carcasses is a craft, but selling them is an art. Profit margins in meat retailing are slender. To stay afloat, men like Pino have to find paying customers for every inch of the cow. A great butcher is a meat psychiatrist: He can read your mind. At times, he may refuse to give you what you ordered because he's figured out what you really need. Lobel's sells a very tender steak that has too much gristle for grilling. Who wants gristly steak? You do, after Stanley Lobel gives you a recipe for using it in a rich stew that's done in less than 30 minutes.

"Most people know the easy cuts—rib eye, filet mignon, porterhouse, T-bone," Pino tells me. "But there are so many different cuts. I have a lot of customers say, 'Pino, what am I gonna eat tonight?' And I suggest."

Once, this strategic salesmanship made butchers key players in supermarkets. "In the old days, the obligation to sell the whole side of beef fell on the grocery stores," Aidells explains. "It was worthwhile for them to pay a butcher because he knew how to market all those cuts. Now that it's all case-ready, you don't need a butcher. You don't even need a saw."

The modern supermarket refrigerator case is a medley of greatest hits, the cuts that sell themselves. The rest simply don't get sold. This explains why pork legs, prized around the world for their versatility, fetch a rock-bottom price in this country. And it is a big part of the reason that about half the beef in America—the best in the world, ranchers will tell you—gets run through a grinder. For an old-school butcher, turning a delicious cut into hamburger might mean charging less for it and, worse, admitting defeat. With butchers muscled out of the food chain, customers have narrower options and, in many parts of the country, classic recipes calling for old-school cuts already seem as fanciful and as useless as an alchemist's manual.

"The steaks, you want 'em seasoned?" Pino asks me. Go ahead, I say. He dusts the steaks with black pepper and then reaches for a plastic jug with a faded label that says Cheese Balls. Inside are not cheese balls but rosemary leaves that Pino picked in his mother's backyard in Sicily last year. He mashes some with minced garlic and smears a bit of the paste on each steak. Preheat the broiler for at least 15 minutes, he says, but don't let the pan get too close to the flame.

Finally he shows me the thickest, most alluring piece of meat. "That one is yours," he says, scoring the outer layer of fat so that I'll recognize it tonight at the table.

With service like this, it's no surprise that customers drop in to Pino's all day long to ask what they should eat tonight. Not everybody wants artificially rosy beef; some people even want meat that tastes good. Fortunately for them, America is now seeing a small renaissance in butchering. Lobel's has a thriving

Web store for carnivores outside New York City. High-end super-markets like Whole Foods employ butchers and supply them with excellent meat. The chef Barbara Lynch opened a wine bar with a working butcher counter in Boston three years ago, and Thomas Keller will be opening his own butcher shop in Napa Valley this summer.

Now it is time for some math. Pino taps his calculator and informs me that my whole rib primal will cost $315. In return, I get two bags so heavy I start to worry that I'll contract butcher's shoulder, too. They would be even heavier but 20 pounds of fat and bones that I've paid for aren't worth keeping, in Pino's opinion (although, he says with a shrug, "some restaurants would take it"). The steaks and the standing rib roast together, at $18 a pound, would have worked out to $364. Already I've made money, and we haven't even factored in the stew meat and ground beef and short ribs and soup bones. Pino's advice, of course, was right. I thought that by spending an afternoon with him, I would learn to cut up meat. Instead I learned the value of the man who does it for me.

The Best Burger

by Raymond Sokolov

from *The Wall Street Journal*

> In his 40-plus years of restaurant-reviewing and international gourmandizing, Sokolov—author of *The Cook's Canon* and *The Saucier's Apprentice*—has earned an almost magisterial authority on matters of the table. When he says something's the best, folks tend to take his word for it.

Patties of ground beef weighing from 1 ounce to 15 pounds, often not seasoned and cooked until gray, then served as a sandwich, usually between two halves of a compressible, flavorless untoasted bun, are this nation's leading contribution to world cuisine. In their fast-food form, burgers provide quantitative evidence for the charge, more widespread than ever, that Americans are a bunch of insensitive louts.

But all across the country there are places, almost all of them locally owned operations, that cook and sell my idea of a first-rate burger. And I've been on a hunt to find the best of them. After braving aortic clogging in several dozen of the nation's most highly touted burger joints and burger temples, I found burger perfection—in the form of a simple bacon-topped double patty dusted with cayenne—in the heart of a big city, but along the way tasted everything from fast-food's big names to haute-cuisine burgers with foie gras.

After a certain amount of time spent wallowing in burgers, you inevitably begin to see complexity where most people just see a simple dish. But a fellow who is about to announce his choice for the WGB (World's Greatest Burger) should have an aesthetic, a set of standards that guide his judgments in burger court. So here is mine.

First, the burger is more than the sum of its parts. You take a bite of all of it at once—the meat, the bun, the condiments and any other additions such as raw tomato, lettuce, fruit, nuts. At the hallowed Primanti's on Pittsburgh's gritty 18th Street, they put the fries inside the burger. And it's pretty good.

If you are any good at burger degustation, you should be able to add all those sensations up in your debauched little sensorium and then, and only then, try to sort out what went into it. It should start with beef, the humble ground chuck—not the pricier ground sirloin or any other variant. Chuck has the Goldilocks amount of fat, not too lean nor too much like hand cream. Chuck also has the right mouth feel; it gives the teeth something to do. You also want a patty thick enough so that it can be charred yet remain moist within. I like mine medium rare, because I want the fat in the meat to get hot enough to melt and spread its flavor. The patty should be seasoned with salt and pepper, at the very least.

The bun is a crucial component of the dish. Toasted bread is not bad for a change-up, but a bun is better, gives better grip and more al dente contrast to the meat. The best bun is a sesame bun, lightly toasted and warm. There is nothing wrong with the braided pretzel bun at the Rosebud in Chicago, but the raised pattern is an eccentric distraction and the bun too doughy, in my view.

From there on, individual preference rules. The eminent burgerologist Jimmy Buffett disclosed his recipe for a "Cheeseburger in Paradise" thus:

> *I like mine with lettuce and tomato, Heinz Fifty-Seven and french-fried potatoes.*
> *Big kosher pickle and a cold draft beer.*

I applaud all this but see no reason why the great man doesn't go for a couple slices of bacon, very crisp, and a sunburst of melted cheddar.

One other thing: If it's too big to fit in your mouth or hold easily in your hand, so big that you have to use a knife and fork, well, I'm not coming back.

I can't pretend I have sampled every good burger in every Hamburger hamlet and town. Nor was it humanly possible to follow up every recommendation. So this is a necessarily subjective report on a vast territory, an assessment by one person of one dish and the obsessive passion it provokes.

No one knows just how the first American burger chef took the ground-beef patty that came over with German immigrants in the early 19th century and turned it into a sandwich. The hamburger steak (no bun) appeared on a New York restaurant menu as early as 1834, but the evolution from the naked patty that Eastern European cooks like my grandmother from Lithuania called a cotelette or kutlett is a mystery. At least three traditions champion different men as the culture hero who turned a chopped beef patty into a sandwich. The most vehement keepers of the flame congregate at Louis' Lunch in New Haven, Conn., where the faithful insist that a certain Louis Lassen put what we would call a burger patty between two pieces of bread in 1895. You can still buy a descendant of this ur-burger there, but don't you dare ask for a bun.

Another contender for the burger-birther title is a Texan, Fletcher Davis, who may have served a hamburger at a stand at the 1904 Louisiana Purchase Exposition in St. Louis. Out of respect for this Lone Star claim, we flew into Austin, where we remembered with awe the burger we ate at a stand known as Dirty's in 1971. Local legend has it the grill had finally been cleaned after years of ritual neglect. I doubt this explained the impressive lack of flavor in this thin and lackluster sandwich. (One did much better at an antiseptic retro drive-around place not far away called P. Terry's.)

At the other end of the hamburger spectrum, highflying chefs have taken our classic burger, given it a makeover with luxury materials and the culinary equivalent of bling. I do not love these "gourmet" burgers made by men who wear toques blanches instead of T-shirts. Their fan-cyburgers are as awkward and condescending as pop songs recorded by opera stars. I don't cotton to funky meats, ostrich or the buffalo burgers Ted Turner sells in a chain that, with characteristic humility, he calls Ted's Montana Grill. Like many good chefs trying to survive in a business-casual world, Daniel Boulud has tried to put his stamp on popular comfort food by adding foie gras to a burger at his Manhattan DB Bistro Moderne. The talented Laurent Tourondel has lost his way at BLT Burger in Greenwich Village with a menu of overwrought burgers with too much class for their own good. Other chefs around the country grind up precious Kobe beef for burgers that just ooze fat and melt weirdly in your mouth. I don't want truffles either. I want the slightly chewy mouth feel of chuck in my burger. The best compromise I found between these $50-plus concoctions and the humble drive-in sandwich is Danny Meyer's open-air Shake Shack, near his much grander Eleven Madison Park.

Shake Shack, which will awake from hibernation March 21, draws crowds because, despite its finesse, it does not highhat. The burger concept—the most successful food idea since mother's milk—does not need to be improved with culinary finesse and luxury ingredients. If you're not content to eat a great burger made from average beef on a normal bun, you've missed the point. Are you French?

I love a good hamburger. But I loathe bad hamburgers, especially the most famous fast-food burger. The only Big Mac attack I ever get is a headache after eating one. For this caper, I did not hang out at the big burger chains, stuffing myself with thin, dried patties and Kleenex buns in cookie-cutter stores with all the atmosphere that regimented teenagers glum about their coolie wages can provide. I'm an equal-rejection consumer, choosing to have things my way not at McDonald's, Burger King or other places of their ilk where I am sure to be gravely under-whopped.

I confess that I did make the pilgrimage to the oldest operating McDonald's, in Downey, Calif., outside Los Angeles. The attached museum was a hoot with its vintage McDonald's stuff and pictures of old stores, but the Downey store itself lived up to the company standard of predictability: All burgers were mediocre, dry and tasteless. The decor was as tacky as anywhere else in the McEmpire.

The only exception to the curse of the chain that I know is In-N-Out Burger, which achieves a friendly, immaculate atmosphere with its red and white tiles and teenagers out of a Spielberg film of suburban life. The burgers are unspectacular—fairly thin, cautiously seasoned—but they do pass the char and juice test, barely. For its spoiled Hollywood mogul fans, In-N-Out must fulfill some yen to escape from high-pressure lunches at Spago.

Am I immune from this Rousseauian urge to retreat to the simple life through burgers? Not at all. As I ate burgers from coast to coast, I realized that my passion in this area is a simple, id-driven lust. I love a burger just like the burger that I got from dear old Dad. Or with him, in a "bar and grille." This led me to little, intimate places, distinctive and unpretentious diners and taverns like the bar in Cheers but with better burgers: thicker, charred, seasoned.

In Detroit, where I consumed my first hamburger in 1944, the returning native can motor from one end of a metropolitan area devastated by urban renewal and economic implosion to the other, tasting excellent burgers in settings that preserve or recreate the ambiance of better days. Miller's Bar serves handmade hefty, grilled-to-order burgers—nicely charred, with optional slices of raw onion, on waxed paper without plates—to capacity lunch crowds in a cheerful, low-key bar-restaurant near the once-world-beating Ford Rouge Plant in downriver Dearborn.

Ford's, as older locals call it, is, to put it politely, on the wane, but inside Miller's, it's easy to feel like it's the day the place opened in 1950 and the Tigers still are playing in Briggs Stadium at the downtown end of Michigan Avenue. An eight-point buck's head is etched in the mirror behind the bar, and the bartender reminisces with a regular about the most burgers eaten at Miller's in one sitting: "I've seen 11."

The portions are much smaller at The Hunter House in the posh northern suburb of Birmingham. Just a mouthful, really, but a mouthful topped with fried onions, the same way they did them here back when the Red Crown gas pump in the corner of the little diner was still filling 'em up.

By the time it took to drive the 15 miles downtown to Slow's Bar BQ, I was ready for a burger with a forward-looking attitude. The people who opened this temple of eclectic barbecue two years ago this St. Patrick's Day had to be optimists. Slow's is at the bleak edge of Detroit's Corktown, the Irish enclave where Briggs (later Tiger) Stadium now stands derelict and the most prominent competition for Slow's is a bar called O'Blivion's; across the way is another monumental hulk, Michigan Central Station, where we once caught the Wolverine to Chicago and no trains chug any more. Inside Slow's, customers start arriving around 11 a.m. Premium beer flows. Pulled pork is pulled. And I get my best sandwich of the day. The beef is charred. The cheese is Gouda with a nice snap. The bun doesn't ooze away under finger pressure.

This is an important point, practical and historical. Burgers are finger food. The bun, among its other virtues, keeps your hands dry, or should, and lets you pick up the meat without making you wish for a finger bowl.

This principle made me wary of the one-pound burger at Nick's Tavern in Lemont, Ill., a Rust Belt backwater some 20 miles south of Chicago's Midway airport. Indeed, Nick's is more successful as a shrine to the Chicago Bears than as a burger Shangri-La. A fellow in a billed cap cooks your giant burger to order, steaming it, in effect, under a metal cloche. No detectable salt perks up this slab of meat.

You'd be much better off spending your cab money on a loop from Boston out to Cambridge, Mass., for a textbook well-charred burger at Mr. Bartley's Burger Cottage in Harvard Square. At seven ounces, it's a hair shy of the ideal, but perfectly cooked and nicely enveloped in a sesame-seed bun.

I found another classic burger in Seattle at the unpretentious Red Mill Burgers in the quiet Phinney Ridge neighborhood near the zoo. Following Northwest Coast custom, even the basic burger has lettuce.

But wait. I can hear a million Angelenos wondering, "When will he get to L.A.?" Yes, there are great burgers in Los Angeles. I love the Apple Pan. The burgers are cooked to order, flavorful, just big enough for lunch. Nevertheless I think the best burgers in America are three time zones away . . . in Atlanta.

The Vortex, a pseudo-biker joint that you enter through a human mouth, serves an estimable burger, as good as any in Tinseltown. Even better is the well-charred number with beautifully crisped thick-cut bacon at the Earl, in East Atlanta.

But the outstanding hamburger experience I found in an odyssey of several months and thousands of miles was at Ann's Snack Bar, a justifiably renowned little diner on a broken-down industrial stretch of highway.

Miss Ann, as habitués call her, is a woman of commanding style and ready banter. She works alone at her grill, patting each ample patty lightly as she sets it down. Her masterpiece, the "ghetto burger," is a two-patty cheeseburger tricked out with bacon that she tends closely in a fryolator.

Observing Miss Ann in action would be enough of a show, one perfected over many decades. But while she demonstrates the extreme economy of motion of a superb short-order cook, she simultaneously carries on a running dialogue of lightly sassy repartee with customers she knows.

Then Miss Ann dusts your almost-ready patties with "seasoned salt" tinged red from cayenne pepper. It looks like a mistake, too much, over the top. But when you get your ghetto burger in its handsomely toasted bun envelope, you regret doubting the lady for one second. The big burgers stand up fine to the spice. This is the next level in burgerhood. And it just barely fits in your mouth.

Steak, Well Done

by Colman Andrews
from *Gourmet*

> Having moved on from *Saveur*—the food magazine he founded 13 years ago—Colman Andrews brought his urbane, well-traveled palate to *Gourmet*, where he continues to deconstruct high-end dining as a restaurant reviewer and contributing editor.

S teak houses have saved my life—well, okay, saved me from bad dinners—more times than I can count. Back in the latter half of the last century, every large or medium-size town in the nation seemed to have at least one or two of these establishments, and some, like Chicago or New York, had considerably more. Occasionally, these were well-known destination restaurants: Peter Luger, in Brooklyn; Bern's, in Tampa; the Pacific Dining Car, in Los Angeles; the original Morton's, in Chicago. More often, though, they were just local favorites, comfortable and friendly, where you could be fairly sure of getting a decent martini, a wedge of crisp iceberg with creamy blue cheese, a big hunk of charred rare beef with an oversize plate of fried potatoes on the side, and a bottle of credible Cabernet. The menu might have been predictable; the salad dressing might have come from a food-service canister; the meat might have been a bit chewy—but the meal was still likely to be miles better than a take-your-chance dinner at some red-sauce-and-plastic-mozzarella joint with "Mamma" in its name, or the "Continental" fare at the local version of (as Calvin Trillin puts it) La Maison de la Casa House.

In the 1990s, though, the culinary landscape changed dramatically for American meat eaters: We became increasingly concerned with health issues and with animal welfare, and we began to learn from other cuisines, principally Asian, that animal flesh could be used as an accent or minor ingredient rather than a centerpiece. As a result, steak houses, those veritable temples of meat worship, all but disappeared.

Oh. Wait. What am I talking about? Exactly the opposite happened. Yes, we talked about cutting down on our red-meat consumption; yes, we recoiled in horror at tales of slaughterhouse abuses; yes, we admired stir-fries and noodle dishes flavored with no more than a few shreds of beef or pork. Then we went out and ordered a 16-ounce prime rib eye, charred rare, with a side of hash browns— which became ever more convenient to do as steak houses began stampeding through the land. Individual restaurants like Shula's, in Miami Lakes, Florida, and Smith & Wollensky, in Manhattan, launched nationwide expansion programs; existing chains like Morton's of Chicago, The Palm, and Ruth's Chris started opening outposts right and left, in competition with newcomers like Fleming's Prime, Sullivan's, and the Capital Grille. And then big-name chefs started getting into the act. Today, chef-conscious carnivores can order up their steak-and-fries (and plenty of other stuff) not only at Emeril Lagasse's Delmonico Steakhouse, in Las Vegas; Tom Colicchio's Craftsteak, in Las Vegas and New York City; David Burke's Primehouse, in Chicago; and Charlie Palmer's Charlie Palmer Steak, in Washington, D.C.; but also at Jean-Georges Vongerichten's Prime, in Las Vegas (though no longer at his short-lived V in Manhattan's Time-Warner Center, which never recovered from lukewarm opening reviews and a bordello-look décor); Wolfgang Puck's Cut, in Beverly Hills; Bobby Flay's Bobby Flay Steak, in Atlantic City; Michael Lomonaco's Porter House, in New York; Michael Mina's StripSteak, in Las Vegas; Laurent Tourondel's BLT Steak, in New York City and Washington, D.C. (with San Juan, Puerto Rico, soon to come); and probably a few other places I'm forgetting. Can Alain Ducasse be far behind?

What sparked the vigorous growth in what restaurant-industry magazines call the steak-house segment? Some observers have proposed that as we eat less beef (American beef consumption has indeed declined over the past decade or so, though not dramatically), we want the beef we do eat to be special—steak-house cuts, professionally cooked. Maybe. To me, the question isn't what has caused the proliferation of steak houses over the past 12 or 15 years, but why it didn't happen earlier. We've always been a nation of meat eaters. Beef is practically our heraldic emblem. Remember cattle drives? Remember cowboys? Remember the home where the buffalo roam? (Okay, buffalo meat isn't exactly beef, but as Ted Turner will tell you, it makes great steaks.) Beef is America—and if beef is America, steak houses are our national shrines.

The pioneering celebrity chefs in the steak-house field were Larry Forgione and Joachim Splichal. Forgione, one of the first generation of "new American" chefs—and now the proprietor of An American Place, in St. Louis—opened the Grill Room Chop House in lower Manhattan's World Financial Center in 1997, describing it as "a modern steak house melded with an oyster bar," and then launched an unmelded steak house called Manhattan Prime in 2000, in the nearby Embassy Suites Hotel in Battery Park City. (Both are now defunct, victims first of business disputes and then of 9/11.) In 1999, meanwhile, the talented German-born, French-trained Splichal, who owned several topflight restaurants in Los Angeles before opening his enduring Patina in 1989, created a steak house called Nick & Stef's—named after his twin sons—near the city's new Staples Center sports arena. (A Manhattan version of the restaurant opened in 2001 at Madison Square Garden.) Forgione, who is considering opening a steak house in St. Louis, believes that celebrity chefs' involvement has "automatically upgraded steak houses."

At first glance, the celebrity-chef steak house is a curious phenomenon. Why would culinary personalities known for the originality and complexity of their cooking (Vongerichten has three *Michelin* stars, for heaven's sake) embrace an established, old-fashioned restaurant style that would appear to offer so little opportunity for creativity? Most of the chefs who have done so say that it was primarily a business decision, and that it was somebody else's idea: They were approached by a real-estate developer, a hotel, or a casino (steak is apparently the definitive high-roller food) and asked to open a steak house, and they thought it might be fun (and, of course, profitable). It might also be pointed out, though, that a lot of chefs just plain like steak, to eat and to serve.

But once a chef opens a steak house, how can he make it his own? If you run a steak house, you've got to deliver a steak. Where the fancy stuff—the cheffing—comes in is usually in the appetizers and side dishes. Thus at Charlie Palmer Steak in Washington, the oysters on the half shell come with green onion, fennel, and red *verjus* mignonette, and the shrimp cocktail includes heirloom-tomato salad, celery sorbet, and gazpacho coulis. At Michael Lomonaco's Porter House (which occupies the site of Von-gerichten's vanished V), alongside the lobster bisque, clams casino, and chile-rubbed rib eye, you'll find lobster cocktail with black radishes and kohlrabi, and wild Alaskan salmon with Pinot Noir sauce and lobster risotto.

"A steak house should be a steak house," says Bobby Flay. "With a few surprises." His surprises are mostly crustacean in nature: "I spent a lot of summers in Spring Lake, on the Jersey Shore, when I was growing up," he says, "and I think of Bobby Flay Steak not as a casino restaurant but as a South Jersey restaurant. Even though this is labeled a steak house, I want to serve all the foods South Jersey is known for—lobster, clams, corn, tomatoes. In fact, I'm trying to get as much lobster and steak on the table at the same time as possible." To that end, he offers lobster by the pound—broiled, steamed, or Fra Diavolo style (in a hot-pepper-and-herb-infused tomato sauce)—and what he dubs "strip and shore," an American Kobe beef strip steak sharing a plate with a lobster tail.

With so many new steak houses, chef-driven and otherwise, opening around the country, you'd think sourcing good meat might be a challenge. Not a single chef I spoke to, however, would admit to having any problems finding the best possible beef. Most of them have longstanding relationships with good meat purveyors already—and while some may seek out small quantities from specialized producers (Michael Lomonaco, for example, buys some hormone- and antibiotic-free cuts from California's Brandt Beef), most chefs seem to depend on conventional top-graded meat, from various sources, bearing the Certified Angus Beef (CAB) label. (More than half a billion pounds of CAB products are sold annually in the U.S. and abroad.) One exception is David Burke, former vice president of culinary development for the Smith & Wollensky Restaurant Group. Last year Burke spent $250,000 on a prize black Angus bull, named Prime 207L, in order to be able to breed his own beef for his Primehouse.

I doubt, however, that any steak-house-owning chef spends more time thinking about beef than Tom Colicchio. The menu at his Craftsteak in Manhattan lists not only more than half a dozen different cuts of meat but also offers steaks dry-aged for 28, 42, or 56 days, meat from cattle both grass- and corn-fed, and Wagyu steaks from Idaho, Australia, and Japan. (The Las Vegas menu is only slightly less diverse.) "My feeling," says Colicchio, "is that beef is probably one of the most misunderstood foods out there." Reviewing the restaurant for the *New York Times,* Frank Bruni took it to task for compounding this misunderstanding with its plurality of choice—"forget the omnivore's dilemma; this was more like the carnivore's discombobulation"—and for the fact that the steaks were all roasted, not grilled or broiled. At first, after the review, says Colicchio, "I kind of backed away from what we were doing with the menu, but now I've decided to go full bore, and I'm giving people as much information and as much choice as possible." As for the cooking method: "I'm not a huge fan of the grill," the chef explains. "I don't like it. It dries everything out." So when Craft-steak first opened, he tried searing his steaks on a griddle, then finishing them in a high-temperature oven. By his own admission, it didn't work as well as he'd hoped. "The griddle just didn't get hot enough," he says. So now he pan-sears both sides of the steaks and then finishes them on . . . a grill.

Michael Mina, best known for his seafood dishes at Aqua, in San Francisco, developed a new technique for cooking his meat at Strip-Steak: he slow-poaches it, for as long as eight hours, in butter and herbs in pans set into large bins of temperature-controlled circulating water—then flash-sears it on a wood-burning grill. Whatever works, I guess. As Colicchio says, "Having a steak house is ultimately about putting the best meat possible on the table, period."

Wolfgang Puck opened his steak house, Cut (for "cutting edge"), because the venerable Beverly Wilshire hotel approached him about installing a restaurant there, and, he says, "I thought about what would fit into this grand old place, and something too young and hip didn't seem right. I thought that if we were to do a steak house with different things on the menu, it might be interesting and challenge us a bit."

The result is a steak house, I suppose, by virtue of its large, Craftsteak-like selection of meats—in this case including not only numerous cuts, but aged corn-fed beef from both Nebraska and Illinois, and American and Japanese Wagyu (at $120 per six ounces)—but it is also just an extraordinarily good restaurant. The dining room, designed by famed architect Richard Meier, is elegantly spare and contemporary, and the food is superb, from the slabs of silky foie gras sandwiched between Tunisian-spiced *tuiles* and the bone-marrow flan with mushroom marmalade to the slow-cooked Kobe beef short ribs with Indian spices, the braised oxtail and sweetbread pot-pie, and the delicious potato *tarte Tatin*. And the steaks? Perfect.

Personal Tastes

A Memorable Fruit

by Shuna Fish Lydon
from *Edible San Francisco*

An accomplished pastry chef as well as a cooking instructor, food blogger, and writer, Shuna Fish Lydon has worked at such star restaurants as the Gramercy Tavern and the French Laundry and is currently based in the Bay Area.

Spring. Barely perceptible lime-green leaves push out of naked tree limbs, blossoms explode, rain comes in blasts, tiny pale petals glide, sticking to surfaces like light snow, releasing their subtle but oily perfume into the air. Light shifts from winter white to pale yellow.

As soon as I see these changes, smudges of visual trickery, I think about fruit I've been missing since it was last warm. I day-dream about strawberries, what I would make with them, how I would savor them, how happy they'd make me. I let myself be filled with strawberry stories.

Two years ago this spring my mother stood in the kitchen doorway, a wide smile across her beaming face, and asked me an existential question about some small red berries in her refrigerator.

"How could it be that you've just brought me the best strawberries I've ever had in my life? How could that be?"

Admittedly, she had well-earned fruit eating credentials, having eaten lots of strawberries in her sixty plus years. But today she was ebullient about this particular brown paper bag full of Swanton berries I'd given her. The answer, silent, almost visible, trembled in the air between us, unspoken. Her taste buds had recently been indelibly affected by innumerable rounds of chemotherapy and radiation treatments. My mother and I knew she was at the end of her life. The sensual relationship she had with fruit was changing rapidly and inexorably, but in that one moment, she was as happy as the taste sensation itself.

Although my mother's question was one without answer, it's the very one people asked the first time they crouched down in the woods, whether on European soil or in the Americas, to eat strawberries, these small, seedy, pale pink and white fruits.

The berry we eat today is an amalgamation, like many other cultivated edible plants, of the fruit's characteristics we've embraced and discarded over time. The strawberry's flavor, and scent is a multidimensional idea, concrete and philosophical, historical and sexual, manufactured and inherent.

In *Fruit: A Connoisseur's Guide and Cookbook* (Mitchell Beazley Publishers, 1991), Alan Davidson and Charlotte Knox illuminate a fact known by few when they state, "The strawberry, the fruit of the plants of the genus *Fregaria,* has a peculiar and unique structure. It is technically known as a false or accessory fruit. The seeds which, unlike those of any other fruit, are on the outside, are the true fruits of the plant."

And David Karp, America's famous fruit detective, elaborates in the article "Berried Treasure" at Smithsonian.com in the Science and Technology section. "The hormones produced by fertile seeds, are needed for proper development of the strawberry."

Mr. Karp's article is about horticulturalist Jan Swartz "attempting to breed a strawberry unlike any tasted in the United States for more than a century . . . *Fragaria moschata,* the musk strawberry, the most aromatic strawberry of all."

Although the strawberry we're eating today is the product of crossbreeding that's been going on since the sixteenth century, he goes on to say,

> What's missing most from commercial berries is fragrance, the original quality that gave the strawberry

genus its name, *Fragaria*. Only in 1926 did scientists discover why the different species are not readily compatible: the wild and musk species have fewer sets of chromosomes than modern strawberries.

Alas, no other fruit has been so radically transformed by industrial agriculture. Breeders over the decades have selected varieties for large size, high production, firmness, attractive color, and resistance to pests and diseases; flavor has been secondary.

Because strawberry plants grow so close to the ground, they are particularly susceptible to soil related illnesses, making for heavy reliance by some commercial growers on the soil fumigant methyl bromide. It's no secret that a berry grown without this chemical tastes better than one grown with it, simply because the red fleshy berry is basically a sponge, becoming fatter with water and poison if that's all the farmer is feeding it.

While working at the French Laundry I got to know the owners of Middleton Gardens, Malcolm and Nancy Skall, city dwellers turned organic farmers. Malcolm commanded attention, both for his contrastingly patterned outfits of stripes and checks—all held together by his signature red suspenders—and his warm, straightforward personality.

He took to calling me Sweet Pea and when I met Nancy one evening as they came in for dinner, she presented me with a bouquet of the sugar scented flowers and an open invitation to come to the farm. Middleton Gardens, a compact, eight-acre plot, is like the secret garden, a hidden nook and cranny in Sonoma's more rural wine grape growing region.

Nancy's produce was expensive, even by the standards of the specialty goods we were buying at the French Laundry. But what produce we did manage to buy and use produced hushed reverence from even the most skeptical palate. Shallots so tiny, sweet and rosy, that I begged Thomas Keller to let me make an ice cream from their caramelized husks. Raspberries with enough technicolor-flavor saturation to explain away the exorbitant price tag. Strawberries still warm from the morning's teasing valley heat, exuding a sweet red scent—a perfume as floral as roses, powerful as the deepest musk.

My pastry chef, Stephen Durfee, and I made sure to keep them from being refrigerated, trying to preserve their utter strawberriness.

When Thomas promoted me to pastry chef at Bouchon he told me, in no uncertain terms, that I would not be allowed to buy berries from the Skalls. For the volume and level of desserts I was expected to create at his new restaurant, the produce from Middleton Gardens was far too dear. It was an emotional talk, because he knew that I had become close with the couple and had fallen in love with their fruit.

One day, well into spring the following year, Malcolm showed up. Cutting a large grandfatherly figure, in his hands he held one small pint of Nancy's perfect strawberries. A gift.

"These are for you," he said softly. I took them carefully, wordlessly. Malcolm gave me a familiar look. I realized Thomas had not told him of our conversation. My voice was small, uneven. "I can't buy from you and Nancy anymore, Thomas has forbade me. He says I can't afford them."

To which Malcolm, in his unforgettable mischievous, wily way, leaned down to my ear and whispered, as if Thomas could hear his conspiratorial tone half a mile away, "I'll give you a better price."

Needless to say the favoritism Malcolm was showering me with didn't go over so well with my boss up the street. I was caught in the crossfire of a strawberry coup.

And so, an equally passionate and iconic dessert with these recruits became immediately necessary. Middleton Gardens Strawberry Soup was born; the first dessert special I created for which I had a following, fans.

When strawberries are perfect one need not interfere much. Stephen Durfee, now an instructor at the Culinary Institute of America's St. Helena campus, says if you must wash strawberries, do so in Champagne. Strawberries develop spots and mold soon after they've come into contact with water. The pastry chef trick for keeping fresh berries longer is laying them out, not touching, on a cloth towel lined pan. This is especially important when handling and refrigerating ripe berries.

Except for making jam, I'm not a fan of introducing a heat source to strawberries. Like refrigeration, extreme temperature will steal any aromatics the fruit has inherited.

Craig Stoll, chef/owner of Delfina Restaurant, is responsible for introducing me to the only cooked strawberry I've liked. Whole roasted, vanilla-sugar-specked strawberries garnish his wildly popular carnaroli rice pudding. But he admits, "It's a bit of a waste for insanely good strawberries." The roasting packs a deep, warm, intense strawberry punch. It's a simple dessert; the traditional strawberries and cream pairing, but with a frisky texture and taste sensation.

Because a strawberry is a balance of texture, flavor, and scent, ripeness is of utmost importance. The factors involve weather, soil, breed, growing practices, and the taste memory you're chasing. "Certain growers grow certain kinds of strawberries better," Craig Stoll states when I ask him from whom he most likes to buy his berries.

I am looking for strawberries in hopes of conjuring memories, attempting to track down an elusive old world scent, for a specific dish, or to eat them as I did in my grandmother's kitchen: with side-by-side dishes of sour cream and sugar for assembly line dipping. I am tasting strawberries at every market, every week in every sunny day, to feel what my mother experienced that memorable spring day almost two years ago.

I am a fruit inspired pastry chef for these reasons. When fruit tastes as it should, when its unique characteristic is indisputable, when I can keep my ego from interfering too much, when my hands are barely noticeable, the desserts I create are an ode to the farmer, the soil, the relationship between all of these romances.

Middleton Gardens Strawberry Soup

If you can't get a hold of Middleton Gardens strawberries, just use the reddest, most aromatic, and pliable specimens you can. For the elixir, in which the strawberries are pureed, I recommend Groth's aromatic chardonnay, but many other wines will work; you may even want to try an ice wine or a rosé for added complexity. And, if you're game for more adventurous garnishes, here's some inspiration from the Bay Area's doyenne of fruit preserving, June Taylor "Strawberries for me stand alone, but they also love to be kissed by flowers and herbs. A little satin jacket to go out at night in; maybe rosemary or lemon verbena, and they always love rose geranium and Provençal lavender."

1 (750-ml) bottle chardonnay, preferably Groth
2 generous cups cold water
4 cups sugar
Juice of 1 lemon
6 pints organic strawberries

In a large, stainless steel pot, bring the wine to a boil over high heat. Add the water and the sugar. Lower the heat to medium-high and bring to boil again. Remove from the heat and stir in the lemon juice. Set aside and let cool to room temperature.

If the strawberries are overly dirty, wash with a brief blast of cold water. Set aside 16 to 20 of the best-looking berries for use as a garnish. Using your thumb and forefinger, stem the remaining berries. (You'll lose less fruit using your fingers rather than a knife.)

Using a blender, puree the stemmed strawberries in small batches with ½ cup of the chardonnay elixir and ¼ cup filtered water. Taste as you go; depending on the sweetness of the strawberries, you may want to instead use more water than elixir. Pass the puree through a fine-meshed sieve. Stir in more elixir or more water, ½ cup at a time, as necessary until a coulis-like consistency is reached.

Cover and chill the soup for one hour in the refrigerator before serving. Garnish with the reserved strawberries.

Strawberry soup will keep for one week refrigerated in a nonreactive, tightly covered container.

SERVES 6

A Sugar Binge

by Charles Ferruzza

from *The Pitch*

Charles Ferruzza's column for this Kansas City alternative weekly is aptly titled "My Big Fat Mouth"; his restaurant reviews are invariably funny, discursive, and entertaining. No wonder he's also the host of "Anything Goes," a weekly radio show on KKFI-FM.

A brief season of cheap, mass-produced, bulk-packaged candy has just ended. October always brings flashbacks of my Halloween forays as a kid. I'm not talking about my own trick-or-treating in those flimsy five-and-dime costumes that tied in the back like a hospital gown. I'm thinking back to my days as a conniving teenager, when I agreed to escort my youngest brother only if he compensated me with a hefty percentage of his candy.

Back then, we'd get big, full-sized candy bars, not the pathetic "miniatures" of today. I remember Caravelle bars, candy lipstick and candy cigarettes, even something called a Chicken Dinner—a nut-covered chocolate roll made by the Sperry Candy Company until the 1960s. I'm part of the baby boomer generation that still took home apples on Halloween (before that whole razor-blade scare), though I threw them out of my bag faster than you could say Granny Smith. They only weighed down my haul and were repulsively healthy. When you're craving pink El Bubble bubblegum cigars and boxes of Boston Baked Beans, a crisp Red Delicious just takes up valuable space.

That kind of obsessive thinking is the reason that I have to be careful about what I buy to give out on Halloween night. If it's stuff that I like, such as those enticing little Kit Kat bars, I'll plow through an entire bag before the first kid rings my doorbell.

Thus, I do my best to find something unattractive—say, the milky orange-and-cream lollipops that I discovered at the Dollar Store (or any other hard candy). I had four giant bags of that stuff last year but ran out before 8 P.M. Just like the voracious zombies in *Night of the Living Dead*, the treaters who had descended on Brookside kept knocking on the door until, in a state of desperation, I ran to the kitchen and grabbed a handful of square ramen-noodle packages and threw them into the bags.

A couple of kids tossed them back at me, but most of the greedy brats just assumed that ramen was Japanese for *big candy* and thanked me so profusely that I was overcome with guilt. At the next lull in the begging action, I locked my storm door, turned out the lights and crawled under the blankets.

Though one season of candy has ended, another is just beginning —this one even more dangerous for those of us who seem constitutionally incapable of abstaining from sweets.

And so this week is devoted to sugary self-indulgence. With Halloween just past and visions of sugar plums already dancing in my head, it's as good a time as any to out myself as a longtime candy junkie. Confession is good for the soul, right?

My love affair with the sweet stuff started early, back in the days when there was still such a thing as penny candy. It seems like a million years ago, but in the late 1960s there was still one of those dark, dusty, family-owned corner groceries in my father's hometown of Lockport, New York, and it still had an ancient, rounded-glass display case loaded with penny candy, including weird stuff that I haven't seen since: tiny ice cream cones topped with a dollop of sugar-dipped marshmallow, little wax bottles containing colored sugary liquid, Fizzie tablets. Kids would point at the pieces they wanted, and the chubby Italian woman behind the counter would pluck it up with her fingers—this was before modern hygiene required plastic gloves—and toss it into a paper bag. You could indulge a major sugar binge for less than a quarter.

I still have dreams about the stuff in that candy case, but the old grocery store was gutted decades ago. I assumed that the confections I saw in there had passed into history. Recently, I stumbled across the Web site oldtimecandy.com, an Ohio-based company from which I could still buy Turkish Taffy, root beer Fizzies, Mexican hats and marshmallow cones. Don't tell my dentist, but I ordered some.

Crate & Barrel in Leawood was giving away candy samples on its opening day last week, but I missed out. A store spokeswoman assured me that the sweets selection in the new store was comparable, if not better, than the array in the Chicago-based retailer's holiday catalog. I leafed longingly through those color pages, staring at the old-fashioned peppermint bark, chocolate-covered marshmallows and English toffee.

It was all seductively nostalgic, but plenty of old-time candy is made right here in Kansas City, too.

Steve Almond, the author of 2004's *Candy Freak* (who opens his book with the admission that he's eaten a piece of candy every day of his life), devotes an entire chapter to Kansas City–based Sifers' Valomilk. The chocolate candy bar filled with runny vanilla cream has its passionate devotees—the company sells well over a million bars a year—but I'm not one of them, only because it's too messy and sticky.

The Sifers family has made candy bars since 1903, but it long ago discontinued the confections that sound most interesting to me, such as the Old King Tut and Subway Sadie bars. What happened to them?

Russell Sifers, who now runs the candy company started by his great-grandfather Samuel more than a century ago, tells me that his grandfather Harry often came up with the name for a new candy bar before his chief candymaker created the recipe to go along with it.

"My grandfather loved current events," Sifers says, "so when the tomb of the Egyptian pharaoh Tutankhamen was uncovered on November 4, 1922, it was such a big news story that everything Egyptian was hot. My grandfather decided to sell a candy bar named after King Tut."

The Old King Tut was a nut roll (not unlike the Chicken Dinner, which was introduced in Milwaukee about the same time), though Russell Sifers says he never tasted one. He didn't get to sample a Subway Sadie, either, which Harry Sifers named after a popular 1926 silent movie of the same name. But Russell says he did find a roll of old paper wrappers for the defunct candies when he was a teenager sweeping up the fourth floor of the old Sifers building at 20th Street and Main (where the Hereford House restaurant's parking lot is today). "Those nickel candy bars didn't have a long life span," Sifers says. "A big flash, then they were gone."

On the Valomilk Web site, Russell graciously includes links to other sites that sell vintage candy, including California's Annabelle Candy Company, which still manufactures the hard-to-find Rocky Road candy bars and the suggestively named Big Hunk ("A long-lasting mouthful of chewy, honey-sweetened nougat," the company boasts) bars.

Not that I need to go online for a fix. All kinds of head-spinning sweets can be had right here in town, including the chocolate-enrobed Double Stuff Oreo cookies and chocolate-covered butter caramels at Panache Chocolatier and just about anything in the display cases at Andre's Confiserie Suisse. Nothing costs a penny, alas.

My snobbier friends are dismissive about the more pedestrian selections at Russell Stover stores, but I have great fondness for this 83-year-old local candy company (which purchased the iconic 94-year-old Whitman's Sampler brand in 1993) and its hefty boxes of old-fashioned dipped candies. Of the half-dozen Russell Stover retail shops in town, my favorite is the Candy Kitchen operation at 51st Street and Oak that stays open until the civilized hour of 10 P.M. on weekends during the summer (but only until 6 P.M. from September until April). This venue sells cookies, ice cream and caramel apples in addition to candy. Candy-craving cheap-skates can buy generous boxes of "factory seconds," too. I practi-cally went into a depression when the Russell Stover stores stopped giving out free samples of the boxed chocolates in favor of the wrapped miniatures. One of the employees told me, "It's more sanitary this way."

Don't tell them, but that chubby Italian lady behind the counter in my father's hometown, the one who threw penny candy into a bag with her bare fingers? In her other hand was a cigarette.

The Centerpiece

by Rita Williams

from *Saveur*

Author of *If the Creek Don't Rise: My Life Out West with the Last Black Widow of the Civil War*, Williams pays tribute in this piece to a very unusual home cook: her reprobate uncle Ernest, turkey-breeder extraordinaire.

For most Americans, the word *turkey* might bring to mind an image of the golden roasted centerpiece of a traditional Thanksgiving table surrounded by an attractive couple, their well-behaved children, assorted grandparents, aunts, uncles, and cousins, and, from a discreet distance, the adoring but vigilant family dog. My associations with the word *turkey* are quite different.

It was the '50s, and I was living out in the country, a ways from Steamboat Springs, Colorado, with my aunt, Daisy. Her brother, Ernest, was heading to the pen—and not the turkey pen, either. He was heading to the Colorado State Penitentiary.

In a region famous for its vast cattle ranches, we had a very small farm. In a valley valued for its Hereford cattle, we produced poultry. And in a state where both the land and its people were blizzard white, my aunt and I were a family of color. Though I found his middle-of-the-night visits via bus unnerving, Ernest, with his penchant for velvet-fringed sombreros, was the most colorful of all.

I was fascinated by this tall man whose skin was the color of the

Bronze turkeys he insisted we raise. "Them broad-breast whites ain't got a bit of taste," he would say. Ernest once worked as a chef in Denver, and he introduced me to the word *cuisine*. When he wanted to make a point, you could see his eyes squinting through the blue smoke from the Pall Mall at the corner of his mouth as he rasped, "You dig?" Maybe it was the way of the West, or maybe it was the tradition of the South, where my aunt and uncle were from, but I can't recall Ernest's ever telling me a single personal thing about himself. Daisy and her taciturn brother, born in the early 1900s, spoke to each other in a code I never did decipher. In fact, I knew more about him from the casual rumors that made their way to me from school friends.

According to one, he had been hired on to muck out sheds at a poultry farm when an 18-wheeler arrived to transport a rafter of turkeys to the Denver stockyard. Ernest introduced himself as the farm's owner and rode with the driver to the Mile High City, where he sold the birds and pocketed the dough for himself. He then hightailed it to the dog track, only to lose every penny. Whether or not this tale is true, I do know that Ernest did do time for rustling livestock.

One summer when my uncle happened to be staying with us, a woman from Steamboat Springs came out to our place. Noticing Ernest's enormous turkeys, she asked him, "Why don't you present something at the Routt County Fair?" That moment changed my uncle's life. He took her advice and went on to win countless prizes. He tacked his ribbons onto a piece of plywood. And though he remained a gambler till the day he died, I don't think he ever stole anything again.

Ernest's devotion to raising perfect poults bordered on the obsessive, but I have never tasted juicer turkeys than the ones he brought up and prepared on our little farm high in the Colorado Rockies. After I left the farm, what a delight it was for me to come home for the holidays in November and see the once downy poults, goslings, and chicks we had picked up at the train station in April now in full feather.

Ernest and Aunt Daisy carefully provided new straw bedding and grain for the birds each day. After being released from the pen in the morning, they foraged much as they might have in the wild, albeit with clipped wings. After breakfast, they turned their attention to grooming. With their beaks, the turkeys preened and lofted each feather meticulously. Despite the fact that Ernest and Daisy would lead the animals to the butcher block come fall, my aunt and uncle lavished affection on these creatures as they raised them. "All right, you little choo-choos!" Daisy would call when she took them fresh feed in the afternoon. They responded by loping up to her like puppies eager for their treats.

I grieved through the whole slaughter process, yet my uncle and aunt thought nothing of it. "Happy birds taste best," Ernest once declared, as he tilted his sombrero back.

Thanksgiving prep always started with a shopping list. Because we grew nearly everything we needed on the farm, we went to town only once a month, for lard, flour, coffee, and beans. But for the holidays, Ernest insisted that we replace our old spices. He even went so far as to search the cupboards, to make sure Daisy hadn't tried to stash the old ones away. "Nothing but the finest, now," he would say, as he unpacked the bright red cans of pepper, thyme, rosemary, and, most important, brand-new sage.

While Daisy rinsed her stone crock, Ernest brought out the special pie tin that he used expressly for toasting sage. "You take just a pinch and drop it in the hot pan and shake it back and forth until it starts smokin'," he explained. "Then put it in soaking water to season the meat. Just a dab, now—don't overdo it." After lightly piercing the interior cavity of the turkey, being careful not to push through to the skin, he would immerse the entire bird in a heavy crock of salted water, and it would soak all night in the back of the refrigerator, where it was the coldest.

The next morning, I would stay in bed, tucked under my grandmother's heavy quilt. My aunt and uncle's banging of the kitchen irons would announce the arrival of the holiday. From my bed in the back room, I could tell exactly what was cooking by the parade of smells that wafted by. The first note was the smoke of the pine kindling as it flared; then came the ruddiness of percolating coffee and roasting chestnuts. It was always the freshly cut onions that would bring me fully awake, though.

The day would pass in leisurely fashion. Once the savory aroma of sage filled the kitchen, Ernest would diligently baste the turkey every half hour. Daisy, an avid competitor, would insist that we play a game of Chinese checkers before our guests arrived.

"How did you learn to cook?" I ventured shyly to Ernest, as he lifted the golden turkey out of the roaster.

"It ain't the cookin' that's the point," he said. "It's the whole deal. Raisin' him right from the start. You dig?" I did.

A Grandchild of Italy Cracks the Spaghetti Code

by Kim Severson

from *The New York Times*

One of the best food reporters around, Severson is a tireless interviewer and researcher when analyzing food trends and issues. On this story, though, the culinary detective sets off on the trail of her own family's kitchen heritage.

My Italian is so bad I have a hard time pronouncing gnocchi, but I grew up hearing enough of it to know when I'm being yelled at. And that's definitely what was happening at a table in a small roadside restaurant in Abruzzi.

I had driven through the Italian mountains with an interpreter to find Ateleta, the village where my grandmother Floriana Ranallo Zappa grew up. I had come in search of a recipe. Or more precisely, the evolution of a recipe.

For reasons I couldn't put together until recently, I had been obsessed with tracking a path that began in my grandmother's village and ended with the pot of red sauce that simmers on my stove on Sunday afternoons.

I ended up on the red sauce trail largely because I don't have a hometown. My parents were dutiful players in the great corporate migrations of the 1960s and '70s. My dad worked for the Uniroyal Tire Company. His rise through the ranks of midlevel management required a series of moves, which were always euphemistically presented to the children as "transfers."

The company sent us from Wisconsin to California to

Michigan to Texas and then back to Michigan, where I finally got off the family train and went to college.

Through all that moving, the one constant was my mother's spaghetti sauce. As soon as we got the kitchen shelf paper laid and she figured out where the grocery store was, she made the sauce. It meant this was home, and that first plate of spaghetti and meatballs made us all feel as if everything was going to be O.K.

Now, with several more states' worth of my own transfers behind me, the first thing I cook in a new kitchen is a big pot of sauce. When my siblings and I visit each other, spaghetti is on the menu.

I wanted to know where the recipe came from. And in a way, where I came from. So I became a culinary detective.

But back in the Italian village where it all supposedly began, things weren't going so great. I was sitting with the closest relative I could find, Filomena Sciullo Ranallo, my grandmother's sister-in-law. We were at a table at La Bottega dell'Arte Salata, the small rosticceria my distant cousins run. They were thrilled each time one of the American relatives came to visit, explaining with great pride how Madonna had tried to find her relatives at a nearby village a few years ago and failed. But not you, they told me. You are luckier than Madonna.

I was trying to write down recipes when the old woman grabbed my arm, shaking it hard. Why didn't I speak any Italian? And even worse, why did I think oregano had any place in tomato sauce?

Well, because my mother put oregano in her sauce. But oregano, like the meatballs I add to the pot, was only one of the twists and turns the recipe had taken during nearly a century in America.

In fact, it turns out that there is no single iconic red sauce in my grandmother's village. There are sauces with lamb, an animal the village organizes an entire festival around. There are sauces with only tomato and basil, sauces just for the lasagna and sauces just for grilled meats. Small meatballs might go in a broth, but never in sauce for pasta.

In fact, only two things in the village reminded me of anything I grew up with. The fat pork sausages were cooked and served the same way, and my Italian cousins looked just like my brothers.

To understand why I made my sauce the way I did, I needed to start closer to home, with my mother. She has been making spaghetti sauce for almost 60 years, from a recipe she learned from her mother, who had been making it with American ingredients since the early 1900s.

My grandmother had been shipped to America, literally and largely against her will, to marry an Italian named John Zappa. He ran a dairy farm in a little town called Cumberland in northwest Wisconsin. She was still a teenager, illiterate even in Italian. To the day she died, Grandma Zap spoke only enough English to communicate the most basic things to her bored American grandchildren, of which I was one.

In between, she raised 11 children. My mother, Anne Marie, was the second-youngest.

Among my four siblings, how mom makes her sauce has been a constant source of discussion. We're all decent cooks, but none of us can get it just right. When does she put in the paste? Is a little bit of roasted pepper essential? Do you need to use oregano in the meatballs?

This is a problem my cousins have, too. Sharon Herman still lives in Cumberland, not far from the Zappa family dairy farm. Her mother (my aunt and godmother, the late Philomena DeGidio) was one of the oldest of the Zappa girls and was considered the best sauce maker. My cousin has lived for years under the cloud of never having mastered the master's sauce.

"I could never figure it out," Cousin Sharon told me. "I even took her little hand once and made her measure out all the spices like she did and put them in measuring spoons to try to get the exact amounts. It still didn't taste right."

The master's secret, perhaps, was that she ran a can of carrots, a couple of celery stalks and the onion and garlic through a blender and then put the mixture in the sauce. My mother doesn't do this. The master also put in the tomato paste at the end. My mother prefers to brown the meatballs and ribs first and then deglaze the pan with the paste.

Getting a recipe out of my mother is like trying to get a 4-year-old to explain what happened at day care. She's not one of those annoying and cagey matrons of the kitchen who build their power by dangling the promise of a secret ingredient that will never be revealed. She just cooks by hand, so she's never really able to articulate every step.

She can tell you to make sure the meatballs are well browned. ("Don't put those white meatballs into that sauce!" she'll warn.) And she can give you tips on the all-important step called "fixing the sauce"—tasting it toward the end and adding a little red wine vinegar or maybe, in a pinch, a handful of Parmesan cheese to smooth out the flavor.

But an exact recipe? Not so much. For example, thin-skinned Italian peppers were always around the farmhouse she grew up in, so she likes to use some kind of pepper to give the sauce what she calls "homemade flavor." She often just uses pickled peperoncini from a jar, which I do, too. Once, when I was out of them, I called to see if she had a substitute. She suggested green bell peppers.

"But I never put in green peppers," I told her.

"Well, if you had one you would," she said. "But don't go out of your way. It doesn't make that much difference."

O.K., Mom. Let's focus.

"When do you put the chicken thighs in?" I asked another time.

"Oh, honey, I never use chicken thighs."

"But last time I was home, the sauce had chicken thighs."

"Huh—that's funny," she said. "I guess I must have had some in the freezer."

These are maddening conversations, but I think they will go on until the day she makes her last pot.

If anything, her sauce, like her mother's sauce, and the sauces from the home village of Ateleta, are about making do. Well-browned meat is the key, but you use the meat you have.

Once my grandmother made it to America, there was plenty of meat around. So her sauce became an American version of three-meat ragù, a dish not uncommon in parts of Abruzzi. They would butcher their own hogs and fatten up a few of the dairy cows, so the sauce often simmered with a piece of neck bone or tail or even a steak from a shoulder blade.

My mother, who lived through elementary school without a refrigerator, was often dispatched to the cellar to scrape two inches of sealing grease off the top of a crock and return to the kitchen with preserved sausages and pork ribs for the sauce.

Mom happily left the farm and married Jim Severson, whose roots are in Norway. My father will never turn down a piece of lefse, the flat bread of his people, but he can still catalog the distinct tastes of almost every Zappa sister's sauce.

As he moved my mom around the country, she fell in love with convenience foods and the big, clean supermarkets of the suburbs. She no longer had to can tomatoes or dry basil and parsley on cookie sheets. And all the meat came on those nice, clean plastic trays.

Mom even took to using something food manufacturers call "Italian seasoning." But she'll also use a mix of about three parts dried basil to one part dried oregano. My grandmother never used oregano; just lots of parsley and basil. But all the Zappa daughters did.

I was stumped about why the family sauce ended up heavy with oregano and meat. So I called Lidia Bastianich, the New York chef who has written much about the transfer of Italian food to America.

"This is a cuisine of adaptation, of nostalgia, of comfort," she said. By overemphasizing some of the seasonings Italian immigrants brought from home, they could more easily conjure it up. And sometimes the adaptations were simply practical. Using tomato paste, for example, was a way to make the watery tomatoes in the United States taste more like the thick-fleshed kind that grew in Italy.

My family's serving style is to pile the pork and beef and meatballs onto a big platter of spaghetti, sometimes with sausage. That mountain of meat might be a homage to my grandmother, who found such abundance when she arrived. Or maybe she was just overwhelmed: on a farm with no refrigerator, not a lot of money and 11 children, she didn't have time for a separate meat and pasta course.

As hard as my mother tried to get off the farm, I am trying just as hard to get back. Like her, I use spareribs and a nice, fatty piece of beef. I try to buy them from local farmers who raise their animals outdoors for prices that make my mother shake her head. I would give anything to have a crock of sausage under a layer of pork fat in the cellar.

I use fresh basil and fresh bread crumbs instead of Progresso in my meatballs, but I still stick to dried basil and oregano in the sauce. My canned tomatoes come from Italy, even though my mother thinks Contadina or Hunt's is just fine.

It never tastes just like hers, but I keep trying. And maybe that's the problem. Perhaps I'm too fixated on my fancy-pants ingredients. Or perhaps it's just a psychological quirk of the kitchen. The one that makes you think nothing ever tastes as good as your mother's.

Around Thanksgiving, my parents moved into a small condominium and were going to sell the family dining table. Instead, I arranged to have it shipped from Colorado, where they live now. It's a little too big for my Brooklyn brownstone, and it's not an antique or even an heirloom. My mother bought it during one of our many transfers simply because she needed a bigger table.

But it is the table I grew up with. I have eaten hundreds of plates of spaghetti on it. I feel the need to keep it, to pass it on to one of my nieces or nephews. I want to say, "This was your grandmother's table."

And then I will make them sit down and eat spaghetti, and tell them the story of the red sauce trail.

Zappa Family Spaghetti Sauce

Salt and pepper
1 pound pork spareribs, neck bones or pork chops
1 pound beef chuck roast, blade steak or brisket
3 tablespoons olive oil
¾ cup chopped onions
2 cloves garlic, minced
1 6-ounce can tomato paste
1 teaspoon dried oregano
1 tablespoon dried basil

1 teaspoon dried red pepper flakes
1 ½ teaspoons kosher salt
1 bay leaf
1 28-ounce can crushed tomatoes, preferably Italian
1 28-ounce can tomato sauce
½ teaspoon sugar
2 tablespoons fresh parsley, roughly chopped
4 small or 2 large pickled peperoncini
Cooked meatballs (see recipe)
1 pound dried spaghetti for serving
Grated Parmesan for serving.

1. Sprinkle salt and pepper all over pork and beef. Place large pot over medium-high heat; when hot, add olive oil and brown meat. (Or cook meat in same pot used for meatballs, browning in the leftover fat.) Remove meat to a platter. Turning heat under pot to medium, add onions, and cook 3 minutes, stirring. Add garlic, and cook 2 minutes longer. Add tomato paste, and stir: cook until it absorbs fat in pan. Add oregano, basil, red pepper flakes, kosher salt and bay leaf, stirring to combine.

2. Add cans of tomatoes and tomato sauce, then 4 cups water. Stir in sugar, parsley and peperoncini. Return meats to pot with their juices. Bring sauce to a gentle boil. Turn heat down to a simmer, partly cover and leave sauce to simmer 2 ½ hours or more, stirring regularly.

3. About 20 minutes before serving, add meatballs to pot (recipe follows). Boil spaghetti according to package directions. Drain, return spaghetti to pan and add 3 cups sauce. Toss pasta in pan for a minute to coat with sauce, and place on a large platter. Pour 2 more cups sauce over pasta. Place meat and meatballs on pasta, slicing large pieces. Serve with bowls of remaining sauce and Parmesan.

SERVES 6–8

Italian Meatballs

2 pounds ground beef
1 cup fresh bread crumbs
½ cup finely grated Parmesan
1 heaping tablespoon chopped fresh basil
1 heaping tablespoon chopped fresh parsley
1 teaspoon kosher salt
½ teaspoon black pepper
⅛ teaspoon ground cayenne pepper
2 cloves garlic, minced
2 eggs
3 tablespoons olive oil

1. In a large bowl, mix all ingredients except olive oil by hand, using a light touch. Take a portion of meat in hand, and roll between palms to form a ball that is firmly packed but not compressed. Repeat, making each meatball about 2 inches in diameter.

2. In a large, heavy pot heat olive oil over medium-high heat. When it shimmers, add meatballs in batches. Do not crowd. Brown well on bottoms before turning, or meatballs will break apart. Continue cooking until browned all over. Remove meatballs to a plate as each batch is finished. Let meatballs cool slightly; cover and refrigerate until needed.

MAKES ABOUT 16 MEATBALLS

Why I Cook

The Frying of Latke 49

by Steven Shaw

from *The Daily Gullet*

Presiding over the food Web site www.egullet.com, Steven Shaw injects his own larger-than-life personality into the lively on-line discussions. Here he takes the stage as a cook—with very funny results.

S omewhere between an email from a lonely coed who wanted me to check out her webcam and a plea for assistance from the family of a displaced African dictator, I came upon an invitation from the James Beard House in New York City to participate in a latke-making competition.

There were to be three professional chefs and three "amateur chefs" (that would be my category) competing, and former *New York Times* restaurant reviewer Mimi Sheraton, among others, judging. I typed, "sure," and pressed send.

Then I panicked.

Matt Seeber, my best chef (professional category) friend and then chef at the wonderful but destined-to-fail restaurant Bid (owned by the Sotheby's auction house), was on the phone counseling me within moments. "A what competition?" (He's a gentile.) "Okay, well come over to the restaurant and we'll practice making those things." Returning the courtesy with one of my own, I inquired as to which night might be best.

"A slow night," he said. "That would be any night we're open." (Matt's now the chef at the phenomenally successful Craftsteak in Las Vegas.)

My first idea was to serve the latkes with bacon, it being axiomatic that everything tastes better with bacon. But research revealed that someone had tried that in a previous year and not been judged well. The preparation sounded great. The latkes— potato pancakes, traditionally served on Hanukah—had a hole stamped out of the middle, into which was nestled a quail egg and some bacon. The Beard House isn't kosher, but I guess when it comes to disrespecting tradition there's only so far you can go. I decided I wasn't going to do anything blatantly un-kosher. But boy, I thought, wouldn't the latkes taste good if they were cooked in . . . bacon grease? I mean, that's got to be better than canola oil, right?

Then it hit me: there is one substance in the universe that's as good as bacon grease, and that substance is duck fat. A Google search revealed plenty of purveyors of kosher ducks, so no theoretical problem there. It's not that far from chicken fat (schmaltz), which is a widely accepted European Jewish food product. Why didn't anybody think of this before, I wondered?

I got myself a seven-ounce container of D'Artagnan duck fat (don't ask me why they sell it in increments of seven ounces), made up a standard latke batter of shredded potatoes, diced onions, eggs, matzoh meal and salt and pepper, fried up a few latkes and plated them up with the standard condiments of apple sauce and sour cream on a red plate. The white sour cream looked great against the red plate.

Shit. That's why nobody cooks latkes in duck fat: in kosher cooking you can't mix meat and dairy, so duck fat and sour cream together is out of the question. Another problem: the latkes were awful. They were limp, undercooked on the inside and burnt on the outside, and they tasted like all fat and no duck.

Still, I believed—I was too emotionally invested in duck fat to give up. Did Thomas Edison stop trying to invent the light bulb after his first few experiments failed? Did Christopher Columbus turn his ships back at the first hint of poor weather? Did Evel Knievel stop at jumping only a dozen Pepsi delivery trucks? Visionaries don't just quit. I left a voicemail for Matt: "I'm going to need you to order me like five pounds of duck fat, okay? Do they even measure it in pounds?"

While I waited to hear back, I considered the sour cream

problem. Nowhere in the Beard House competition rules—or the Talmud—is it written that you have to serve your latkes with sour cream, so I figured I'd just substitute something else. I'd already been thinking about how apple sauce was sort of one-dimensional, and had decided to replace it with something along the lines of a fruit compote. I hijacked a family Passover recipe for Sephardic stewed dried fruit haroset—on Passover, the haroset symbolizes the mortar for the bricks the Hebrew slaves built with in Egypt. It usually tastes that way too, but this recipe is quite tasty. I'd grown attached to my red plate idea, and really wanted the whiteness of sour cream as part of the composition.

I made a list of white foods. Nothing. I wandered the aisles of a supermarket looking for white foods that could form the basis of a good latke condiment. Nothing. On the way home, defeated, I stopped at Falafel Express for a snack. The cook assembled my falafel platter: first the falafel balls, then a small green salad, then a lemon wedge.

And finally, a beautiful white sesame tehina sauce. I had my white condiment, courtesy of a Middle Eastern street food.

From there on, everything I ate triggered thoughts of the latke contest. One night, at dinner, I looked at the caramelized onions on my plate and my mind raced: onions are an ingredient in latkes . . . wouldn't latkes taste even better made with caramelized onions?

I got my four cast-iron skillets and two deep-frying ther-mometers through security at Sotheby's, walked through the Bid dining room—populated by maybe eleven people—to the kitchen, where my tub of duck fat awaited. I caramelized several pounds of onions and made four batters. The variations were: caramelized onions versus raw onions; and grated potatoes versus shredded potatoes. I heated up a quarter-inch of cooking fat in two pans—one duck fat, one vegetable oil—and cooked one of each of the four types of latkes in each, then repeated the exercise until everybody on the Bid kitchen team had tasted all variants.

The only conclusive findings from this first experiment were that grated potatoes make better latkes than shredded potatoes (a long-standing belief validated at last by a team of culinary profes-sionals). There were, however, divergent opinions and much inde-cision about the other permutations. Latkes cooked in duck fat were too much of a good thing—and I just couldn't find a good frying temperature. The ones in vegetable oil fried up as golden brown as a food stylist's wet dream, but were flavorless by comparison. The caramelized onions were too sweet, but they did have a great taste that the raw ones lacked.

I appealed to Matt, demanding that he rule between duck fat and vegetable oil.

"Both."

Caramelized onions or raw?

"Both."

It was Solomonic: there was no need to choose. Each element had favorable components—I could combine them. The neutral vegetable oil would lend its properties to the flavorful duck fat; the caramelized onions would enhance the raw. The only remaining question was ratio. After hours of tasting that brought the Bid kitchen team to a state of exhaustion and gastrointestinal distress, the winning ratio was 50-50, for both fats and onions.

I was glad to be keeping oil in the recipe; part of the Hanukah tradition is to eat foods fried in oil, symbolizing the one-day supply of oil in the lamps in the Temple that burned for eight days—the miracle of Hanukah (I later learned that European Jews had fried latkes in goose fat for centuries before I thought of it. Dang). Chika Tillman, the Bid pastry chef who now owns the Chikalicious dessert bar in Manhattan, helped me tweak the condiments (ground dried ginger in the haroset and rosemary in the tehina) and sketch out a plating composition kind of like a yin and yang centered around a latke. We also came up with a few other minor innovations, like sprinkling a little coarse salt on each latke after cooking. And so I had my latke and condiment recipes, ready for competition.

The Beard House advertising went out, introducing the contestants. It was said of me that, "With tastes that tend more toward France than the Lower East Side, you can bet he will prepare something creative and delicious for his latke entry." This worried me. Such big talk would not only raise expectations, but also turn the anti-snobs against me. Besides, if I have such French tastes how come I don't know why duck fat comes in seven-ounce containers?

I arrived at the Beard House with my equipment, my latke batter, my condiments and eighty red plates.

Things fell apart almost immediately. The Beard House kitchen is an embarrassment: most visiting chefs do as much of their cooking as possible in nearby restaurant kitchens and bring the nearly finished food over for final heating. You can't do that with latkes, which degrade logarithmically from the moment they're removed from the oil. Visiting chefs also have the kitchen to themselves; I had to share it with five other competitors: a woman from Long Island who hosts a large annual latke party, a young Jewish woman from Mexico who used to be an intern at the Beard House, Alex Porter (from the restaurant Norma's in the Parker Meridien hotel), Christine Kelly (from Avenue restaurant) and Chris Broberg (then pastry chef of Petrossian, now at Cafe Gray).

I had half a stovetop to work with; Broberg had the other half. The restaurant ranges were so hot they interfered with my thermometer readings, so I had to judge the oil/duck fat temperature by telepathy. The warming oven was too far from my station, which created a traffic jam, but I was actually able to produce my latkes on schedule. The same could not be said for the professionals, though, so my latkes had to sit, while they finished theirs late.

When it came time to plate the latkes, we were informed—surprise!—that we had to share presentation plates: there would be one of each type of latke on a large white plate. My red plate idea went out the window—as did any hope of a special composition, when two helpful volunteers grabbed the condiments and started spooning them willy-nilly.

We served about eighty guests this way. In the end, the panel of professional judges voted, as did the entire assembled audience of mostly Beard House members. The professional judges ranked the professional and amateur contestants separately. The audience voted for a single best latke specimen.

I had never before participated in a cooking competition, nor have I since. The professional judges didn't regard mine as the best, even among the amateurs. The audience, however, chose mine as the top overall latkes. Maybe that makes me a winner, or maybe not. But it felt good.

Caramelized-Onion Latkes with Sephardic Haroset and Tehina-Rosemary Dressing

For the caramelized-onion latkes
6 medium Idaho russett potatoes
2 medium Spanish onions
3 large eggs
¼ cup matzoh meal
½ cup duck fat
½ cup canola oil
2 tablespoons olive oil
Coarse salt and freshly ground white pepper
Fleur-de-sel

Finely dice one of the onions and place it in a skillet over low heat with the 2 tablespoons olive oil and a generous amount of salt (approximately 1 teaspoon) and pepper (10 or more grinds). Cook for approximately 20 minutes. Keep the heat low in order to get the onions thoroughly translucent and only very slightly caramelized. If you let the heat get too high, the onions will get too brown, which will cause the onions to burn when you fry the latkes, adversely affecting their appearance and flavor. When done, set aside to cool to room temperature.

Finely dice the other onion and place it in a mixing bowl.

Peel and grate all the potatoes by hand on a box grater or mandoline. Do not use a food processor or grate the potatoes into water. Just hand-grate them into the bowl that contains the raw onion. After each potato is grated, toss the mixture together with a spoon. The onion will help keep the potato from discoloring too much. There will be some discoloration, but mostly it will be reversed by the cooking.

Drain the potato/raw-onion mixture in a colander. Press down thoroughly on the mixture in order to squeeze out as much water as possible.

Return mixture to bowl. Add the eggs, matzoh meal, caramelized onions, and approximately 1 teaspoon salt.

Combine thoroughly with a fork.

Heat the canola oil and duck fat together in a heavy (preferably cast-iron) skillet until they reach 300 degrees as measured by a candy thermometer. (This is an intentionally low frying temperature, but works well for latkes.)

Take a small handful (approximately ⅛ cup) of the latke batter and, holding it over an empty bowl or sink to catch excess liquid, flatten it into a rough oval with your hands. Slide the latke carefully into the hot cooking fat. You should be able to fit five latkes at a time comfortably in a standard 10.5 inch cast-iron skillet. By the time the fifth latke is formed and in the fat, it should be time to turn the first one (an average-sized spoon, like you would use to eat a bowl of soup, works better than tongs or a spatula). Peek underneath to see if it is a nice light golden brown; if it is, turn it. Wait a few seconds and turn the next, and continue for all the latkes. When the latkes are light golden brown on both sides, remove to paper towels. Blot both sides thoroughly then sprinkle each side with a few grains of fleur-de-sel.

For the Sephardic haroset
2 large apples of a variety suitable for cooking (e.g., Rome)
2 cups assorted dried fruits (as a rough guide, my recipe
    included dried apples, California figs & dates, Turkish
    apricots, Angelino red dried plums & black prunes, and
    Monukah black raisins)
½ cup walnuts
½ cup sweet kosher red wine (such as Manischewitz
    Extra-Heavy Malaga)
½ teaspoon freshly ground dried ginger

Peel and core the fresh apples and cut into rough chunks (the size is not particularly important).

Combine the fresh apple chunks with the dried fruits and sweet wine in a saucepan sufficiently large to accommodate some expansion (a 2-3 quart saucepan should suffice). Add cold water just shy of covering.

Bring to a boil then lower the heat and simmer for

½ hour. Allow to cool to room temperature.

Put the cooked fruit-and-wine mixture and the ground ginger into the bowl of a food processor fitted with the metal chopping blade. The mixture should not be watery. If it is, pour off the excess liquid (this liquid is very flavorful and can be reduced and added back to the mixture if desired). Process for about 10 seconds until you have a roughly chopped mixture. Add the walnuts and process for about 2 seconds more. Refrigerate until needed.

Serve at room temperature with the latkes.

For the tehina-rosemary dressing
1 cup sesame tehina
2 sprigs fresh rosemary, picked and cleaned (plus extra for garnish)
¼ cup fresh-squeezed lime juice
2 tablespoons olive oil
salt

Put the tehina, rosemary, lime juice, olive oil, about ½ teaspoon salt, and 1 cup cold water in a blender or food processor bowl fitted with the metal chopping blade.

Mix until thoroughly combined—at least 30 seconds.

Refrigerate until needed.

Serve at room temperature with the latkes.

Garnish the tehina-rosemary dressing with cut-up sprigs of fresh rosemary.

FEEDS A DOZEN JEWS, OR ABOUT 20 GENTILES

Around the World to Our Kitchen Table

by Ame Gilbert

from *Gastronomica*

The premise of *Gastronomica* is that food and culture are inextricably intertwined. In this memoir by Ame Gilbert—a visual artist who's gravitated into food writing—that connection became crucial at a certain life turning point.

W hen a good friend got divorced, her dinners shifted from Asian-esque to dishes made from her mother's old-fashioned New England recipes that she'd long ago rejected. It was, I suspect, an impulse toward comfort and familiarity during a strained period of her life, as well as a manifestation of a deep-seated notion that if she'd listened to her mother in the first place, she wouldn't be single-parenting three kids, one still in diapers.

I've asked other women, too, about how their cooking had changed during divorce. One mother explained to me how to make *paneer,* which was her solution to the problem of reduced milk consumption in her household owing to custody arrangements. That last inch or two from a half-gallon carton could be curdled with vinegar, strained through cheese cloth, and transformed into the South Asian farmer's cheese. Sautéed with slow-cooked spinach and curry spices, it could be served over rice on the nights when she wasn't cooking for her finicky kids.

Another mother I met on the sidelines at a Little League game salivated through an eloquent description of shrimp-stuffed avocados lavishly dressed with mayonnaise—all ingredients previously disallowed by her ex. I loved this idea of relishing once-forbidden pleasures and embraced it as one of the surprising positives revealed in the midst of divorce. My ex-husband had, or rather has, an allergic reaction to mustard, which is insidiously prevalent in dishes you'd never suspect. For years, hoping to shield and protect my man, I scrutinized food labels for obscure mustard mentions and cajoled waiters to inquire if their chefs had used any dijonnaise finesse in their savory secret sauces. And so, wouldn't you know, my first post-separation outing was to drive an hour from my Milwaukee home to the Mount Horeb Mustard Museum to participate in an afternoon's tasting of three hundred different mustards competing for blue-ribbon recognition.

When my husband left, I gathered my boys and embarked on a culinary quest. We were intrepid travelers exploring reconfigured life. Creating a new family ritual, we'd congregate in the kitchen before a world map tacked to the wall and shuffle a deck of cards purchased at the Map Store. Each card's face, besides the usual suit symbol and number, sported a country's name and map. One son would pick a card at random, and the other would pin it ceremoniously to its corresponding place on the wall. Then I'd spend the week researching recipes and tidbits of geopolitical trivia from that chosen locale, wistfully wishing I could transport us there, away from our stress.

This map-dinner concept wasn't out of character for me, as I'd embarked on cooking projects in the past. I love to cook and am something of a food fanatic, thinking of the next meal before I've cleared the first. Between meals, I often read about food, but what interests me most isn't the recipes. What I'm searching for is a way to give meaning to what I personally, and we all collectively, spend a better part of our lives engaged in. In cooking I seek a way to communicate and share this knowledge so that food becomes meaningful beyond its consumption.

Not all my cooking projects were ideal, though. In the months before my separation, I'd hid in the kitchen, concocting culinary extravaganzas through drawn-out evenings steeped in the fog of garlic and herbs. Wine quelled my rage. I turned out deliciously complex dishes that fed evergrowing circles of dinner guests at parties meant to cheer the household dirge. But there is no recipe that mends a marriage. The eroticized dialogue of dinner that had sustained us as a couple, even as everything else shut down, evolved into ranting soliloquy.

During the earliest phase of separation, the menu changed again. I cooked endless pots of undifferentiated stew made with too much, or too little, of one ingredient or another. Unadjusted and manic, I'd make the wrong choices at the grocery store or cook dishes my husband had liked, but not the boys, or else ones that no one liked, as if I thought our tastes had suddenly changed along with everything else. Perhaps not surprisingly, I overate, while the kids picked. Our meals reflected emptiness; loss was flavored by despair.

Our map dinners were a stab at levity, a way to chart an escape route and to amuse ourselves by gambling with cards. And for me the dinners helped to mark the passage of time. We picked Sundays because weeknights were always too crowded with school projects and sports. Besides, the boys stayed with their father Thursdays and Fridays, eating overpriced french fries (while he sipped chocolate-flavored martinis) or microwavable fast food (while watching inappropriate late-night TV). On Saturday when they were back home with me, I'd rush us off to some event or invite friends for dinner, attempting to live as if everything had not just upended. But this resulted in overtired, overextended moodiness for us all. And so it was relatively relaxed Sunday that became the day we'd shop for unusual ingredients, deal with the frustration of not always finding what we wanted, and then, toward evening, cook and eat the dishes from wherever on the map we'd "gone."

The three of clubs. Mongolia. "Hot pot" with steamed millet, a grain we'd never tasted before. I dug out my mother's flame-red aluminum fondue pot and an old can of Sterno from the basement. We felt terribly exotic plunging skewered bits of lamb loin and cabbage into a gingery, simmering broth.

The four of hearts. Sweden. We served an appetizer of thinly sliced raw salmon home cured in a marinade of salt, sugar, and herbs—*gravlax*—on black bread with sweetened mustard-dill sauce before eating our main course of meatballs in cream, along with potato pancakes and lingonberry jam.

The nine of clubs. Senegal. Plantain chips and peanut chicken were accompanied by *fufu* balls made from the dried instant cassava we'd found in a dark corner of the downtown Asia Mart in a sticky package coated with dust. Bad marriages have been likened to indentured servitude, and perhaps, any relationship has elements of this, both perceived and real. Partners treat each other in ways they'd never get away with treating anyone else. Maybe they stop seeing each other as whole.

Some divorces occur when the husband (more often than not), usually in midlife, abandons his family and moves to another vanquishable consort, touting her as proffered bounty even though others inevitably judge her for being a knave's bimbo. That's what happened to my friend who began to cook her mother's recipes. When her husband left her for a woman half her age, she sought solace in the tastes of her ancestral clan.

On rare occasions a divorce can be a triumphant uprising, a revolution during which the colonized prevails over the colonizer. That was the case with the baseball mom who celebrated by expanding her culinary repertoire with fatty avocado salad.

But most divorces, mine included, are neither abandonment nor emancipation. Instead, they are a complex combination of cause and effect.

And what about the children, the circumstantial victims in these domestic wars? Life goes on. Chores are jumbled with bubble baths and bedtime stories. Pedagogical inculcation continues to be dished out along with the meat and potatoes. The custodial parent strives to maintain the household and create a new sense of family, mitigating the prevailing sense of loss. And in all of this, one universal prevails: each of us seeks to find some kind of comfort.

My little guy, whom I'll call "Pax," absolutely beamed as he snuggled under his soft blue blanket on his way to sleep. Lava light on, incense aflame, the ritual nightly kiss being pressed to his cheek—this scenario was for him the essence of bliss. Food, by contrast, was fraught with choice, presenting him with conflict.

What Pax needed to believe was that, despite our upheaval, his life had remained stable. From his perspective, then, the challenge of the map dinners was to find familiarity (meaning, exotic tastes were not for him). What he sought were the foods that offered a taste of commonality and safety, like rice or bread, or the sweetness of almost any fruit. And although a kind of cultural appropriation was involved in achieving a culinary universality that was politically questionable (meaning, many ethnic distinctions were blurred so that Pax would eat), if that gave him a sense of rootedness and knowledge, it was worth the compromise.

My older son, "Victor," required a different culinary paradigm. At thirteen, half boy, half man, commonality was the last thing on his mind. Eager to rake in so-called cultural capital, he achieved at least some of his status, I'm happy to report, from food adventuring rather than, say, drug experimentation, or worse. Chinatown congee (leftover, eaten for breakfast). Duck confit with roasted turnips. Cheese and jalapeño tamales. Or profane White Castle burgers (when the opportunity presented itself). Victor sought worldliness by tasting the Other, gaining authority through food.

As for me, heroicizing dinner for one, mythologizing it for the other, I was, I dare say, Supermom in spades, so to speak. I even fantasized about capitalizing on it, literally, by imagining myself writing a kid-friendly multicultural cookbook, cleverly packaged to include a plastic-coated, spongeable map, fifty-two enameled map pins, and brightly colored, nested measuring spoons, along with a deck of map-faced playing cards. Maybe we'd snag a TV cooking show contract, as well, so that, aside from nourishing my broken-home boys, I'd reverse the downward economic spiral so common to divorcing moms.

Besides all the other things, divorce, when children are involved, leaves you wracked with guilt. Clearly, even as you rationalize the situation to see the separation as a victory, it is a failure, and the emptiness fills you with recrimination and doubt. He was not a good husband, to be sure, but perhaps you were not always a good wife. And so on. By and by, it isn't productive, this retrospective exercise. The truly gnawing questions remain the ones about the kids.

As our marriage ended, and my husband was less and less frequently home, the boys and I took to eating in the living room while watching TV. In essence the TV replaced the missing father, and as if to disguise this reality, we abandoned the kitchen table and held our plates on our laps. With our map dinners we tried to reestablish familial formality. We not only shopped and cooked together but returned to the table to eat our meal. Food shapes familial and cultural affiliation, and eating nourishes the ego. Conflating family and food, the push and pull of the family meal is not only conformative but progressive.

Nonetheless, it was not a surprise when, after a while, the complaining began. Pax said he would rather play than cook. Victor thought whatever we made tasted "inauthentic," "ordinary," "boring." And I felt pressured not by the labor of cooking new foods nor by single-handedly juggling two children's conflicting needs but by the effort I was making to heal our wounds by the act of cooking dinner. Still, I resisted abandoning the project. For isn't emotional tumult also a part of the family meal? If while eating home-baked pita dipped into *baba ganoush* or steamed Uzbek dumplings drizzled with minted yogurt we learn how to negotiate familial conflict, then aren't we, more than ever and despite everything, still a family intact?

My Romanian mother passed through Ellis Island at age three and within a decade became more fluent and probably better educated than her Yiddish-speaking, kosher-keeping parents. At twenty she married my father, a debonair rabbinical student from Philadelphia by way of Russia and England who, like his bride, had surpassed his Orthodox parents' wildest dreams. For my parents breaking the laws of kashruth was a significant part of their journey.

In our eat-in kitchen on Manhattan's Upper West Side, my mother's meals combined history lessons with stories about her and my father's struggles to assimilate. On special occasions for breakfast, we had bagels and lox or french toast made with challah—and bacon. For dinner we might have chopped chicken liver on black bread—or Brie with crackers, followed by long-simmered brisket and iceberg salad with "Russian" dressing. Weekday meals were quicker, simpler, and less ethnically defined. Spaghetti with sauce from a jar. Honeyed, soy-sauced chicken with Rice-a-Roni and frozen peas.

My mother, herself divorced after a dozen years of marriage, worked full time. My memories of our time spent together in the kitchen, with me on a step stool by the stove pouring canned ingredients into a skillet to make chicken a la king or helping to make pudding from a mix, have stayed with me more than my memories of the tastes of the meals.

Around the time I lost my virginity, Nixon resigned, Roe challenged Wade, Alice Waters started foraging, and I, like my son now and my mother before me, discovered the pleasures of other people's foods. Dim sum. Italian beyond red sauce. Vindaloo. Fried plantains, washed down with *cafe con leche*. I experienced a sense of freedom zipping around the city exploring neighborhoods, but the activity served a deeper purpose, too. We were eating to come of age. Sharing food made connections with people outside of our families, and by picking some foods and rejecting others, we took a stand against corrupt, corporate pabulum. Eating became a politicized act, and the kitchen was our wellspring. Knives, fire, spice— these were tools to explore the self and our place in the world. Eating was an act of communication; cooking was discovery.

Each of us brings to a marriage, along with our dreams, preconceived, often dated and misguided, ideas about gender relations and family economy. Husbands should be one way, wives another, and it's remarkably difficult, yet deeply useful, for couples to sort these things out. When I married, the act of cooking shifted from identity-defining idealism to a currency for negotiating domestic terrain. The order and rhythm of the meals I prepared changed along with their ingredients. Large cuts of meat replaced whole grains and vegetables, and my mother's recipes began to dominate the exotically spiced foreign ones I'd flirted with. Even more significant, the whole emotional tenor of the cooking chore changed.

First as a mostly home-based freelancer and then as a stay-at-home mom, I found my sense of worldliness narrowed. Whereas once I'd judged myself by my interactions with others, later, in the confines of home, in the company of toddlers, I viewed the kitchen as my seat of power. Cooking became a lure used to attract community, and the food became an aspect of my longing for recognition. This isn't too hard to figure out. When your day is mostly diapers and *Sesame Street* and you need to ask for grocery money because you're no longer earning a salary and your husband comes home full of stories and you have none but he seems to enjoy your roasted chicken and mashed potatoes, you hang onto that.

Later, when the kids were older but before they had any real independence and the marital drift had begun, the kitchen became a battlefield. Unappreciated labors, especially labors of love, can cause profound and astonishing resentment.

And so the kids and I went to potlucks in other people's homes. We were a mother and children bearing covered dishes to other mothers with children, and coming home with us on soggy paper plates or in mismatched Tupperware were the leftovers that my husband reheated long after the kids and I had gone to bed.

And then, too, there's the piece about aging and getting fatter and worrying about cholesterol. . . .

With the map dinners I found myself reaching back to an earlier, more hopeful cooking self. In the kitchens of my past, I'd sought an alternative world. Now the children and I were eco-touring gastronomes. Either way the food was invested not with a longing for power but with a desire for peace. When I cooked with my kids our hands reached through time. We made connections across the globe. We ate together and shared a love for food. Our lives were rich. In those moments of cooking and eating, the incessant chattering insecurity of a divorced mother abated.

As it turned out, what ended our map dinners had little to do with anything profound and mostly to do with gamesmanship. What happened was that we drew the six of spades. Iceland, fair and square. But in Iceland they eat ptarmigan, puffins, singed sheep's heads, and dried flaked fish on dense rye loaf. Dessert is cardamom schnapps and salt-licorice dipped into chocolate. We would have none of this, so what could we do?

Everyone knows that when things don't go your way, it's important at least to try being a good sport. You may feel angry and disappointed—what has happened isn't what you thought would be in the cards—but name calling and other destructive behaviors are unacceptable. Brothers should exhibit kindness. A mother should hold her tongue about the father of her children.

For several weeks, we could only stand and stare at our map, aghast. We talked about the idea of finding one dish we could stomach. There was *kartoflustappa,* for example, which is boiled potatoes mashed with sugar and milk. But potatoes alone aren't a proper meal. We talked about slipping Iceland back into the deck, as if it hadn't been chosen, as if we could turn back the clock. Perhaps, we could fly in the face of the luck of the draw after all. Instead, we remembered that when the menu changes, it isn't necessary to reinvent the meal. Menus change all the time. In the big, wide world, pictured on the map in our kitchen, borders change, seasons change, and ingredients come and go.

Now, dinner at our house is only occasionally an adventure of exotic foods. More often, it's quicker, simpler, like the meals of my youth. The important thing is that we sit at the table and eat our meal together. Perhaps, we've assimilated enough to our changed life to abandon ritualized behaviors with decks of cards. Perhaps even though we never tasted ptarmigan but because we congregated by the kitchen map engaged in moral discourse, we found our pathway home.

Give Me Credit

by Hugh Fearnley-Whittingstall
from *Hugh Fearlessly Eats It All*

> Known for his adventurous eating and brash opinions, English food critic Hugh Fearnley-Whittingstall is never one to shy away from a food controversy—not even in his own kitchen.

I've never liked the word "foodie"—perhaps because if I accept that it is genuinely descriptive of a certain type of person, then I may have to face the fact that I probably am one. And then I might have to confront some questions that those of us "involved" with food, either professionally or as passionate amateurs, would probably rather avoid. Questions like, at what point does our interest/passion/obsession become a bore? To what extent do we let that "food thing" eat into (you see!) other areas of our lives? Is it sane to care as much as we do about what we choose to put in our mouths?

Battling with these questions is pretty futile because if one *is* a foodie (gulp!), one simply doesn't have the option to backtrack. "I think I'll stop bothering with nice food and just stoke up on rubbish, so I can concentrate on more important things in life" is not a sentence I ever expect to either speak or hear.

Nor can we prevent food from permeating pretty much all our relationships. If I'm honest, I must admit that I use my cooking skills to manipulate almost everyone I know. I love cooking for my friends, especially on their birthdays, because I believe it will earn me their undying love and loyalty. And I may be able to get away with another whole year of being petulant and self-absorbed in their presence.

Of course the closer the relationship, the bigger the role of food in mediating it. And in foodie love and marriage, even when abilities are matched, there is never equality in the taking of responsibility— or indeed credit—for the cooking. It isn't just restaurants that have tyrannical head chefs. It's any household in the land where both people in the relationship think food matters.

So in our kitchen (which I struggle not to call *my* kitchen), guess who's the tyrant? Who generously offers his partner a "choice" of what he could cook her for dinner, but in a manner transparently loaded in favour of what he has actually planned to cook all along? Who "accidentally" puts the leftovers of the rata-touille that his partner cooked for lunch into the pig bucket, in case she suggests revisiting it at supper, for which he has other plans? And who adjusts every single ingredient in his partner's salad dressing the moment she leaves the kitchen to answer the phone. Me, me, and me. In our kitchen, it's all about me.

I've noted that partners of other kitchen tyrants learn to handle the outrageous balance of power in different ways. Some become falsely modest and acquiescent: "Me? I can't boil an egg. But luckily Tom is just a genius in the kitchen. And of course he spoils me rotten. . . ." Others play the "swings and roundabouts" card, hinting at mighty victories in other domestic arenas: "She does what she wants in the kitchen, but when it comes to choosing the soft furnishings, I am the undisputed king."

But my wife, Marie, to my shame and embarrassment, just tells it how it is: "I can't do anything without him interfering. I can see the physical pain it causes him when I'm slicing courgettes to the wrong thickness, or frying onions too fast. So basically, I've pretty much given up cooking."

But I believe (because I have to), that there is an upside for my partner in my annexing the kitchen. For example, every now and again, usually when we have just come to the end of what seemed to me a perfectly robust and satisfying supper at home, she will say: "Mmm. That was delicious. But I think maybe I could just about manage a little chocolate soufflé now."

Don't be misled by the flattery and the mollycoddling choice of words. This isn't a request, it's an order. There is hard-wired female biology underpinning it, and there's no reasoning with such urges. I could try persuading her that a) the appropriate moment for pudding preparation passed some hours ago, when the offer of just such a soufflé was generously made, and declined; or that b) a few squares of untreated Green and Black's finest 70 percent will surely quell the burgeoning pheromonal desire. And she might even say "Fine. It's okay,"—in that special way which makes it so clear that the two things it most emphatically isn't are "fine" and "okay."

The urge may be biological, but my obligation to fulfil it is clearly contractual. Like that rather amusing ad on the telly at the moment, it's all in the relationship small print. I am only allowed to be a kitchen tyrant, if I can show that I can be a *lovable* kitchen tyrant. The price I pay for exercising obsessive control at the hob is soufflés on demand. He who lives by the stove dies by the stove.

Of course, I have a counter-clause, which insists: "Hugh will receive effusive praise for every soufflé, even if, owing to fatigue and the cavalier measurement of ingredients, it has collapsed like a punctured chocolate zeppelin. In fact, Hugh will be allowed to pretend it was meant to do that, so as to make it extra gooey and chocolatey."

But then she gets me back with this nasty little rider: "At no time is Hugh to claim that cooking for his family is anything other than a pleasure and a privilege; it may never be offered in lieu of his fair share of cleaning the kitchen and loading and unloading the dishwasher."

How did I ever agree to that? I mean, whenever I cook for my *other* family (the ones that begat me), the contract is all in my favour: "Hugh is a complete angel for taking over the kitchen and cooking yet another wonderful meal. He is therefore entitled to relax in front of the telly while Mum and Dad do all the washing up."

My son Oscar (three-and-a-half) is beginning to show a flair for making almost as much mess in the kitchen as his father. To my astonishment I find I am already offering him the same terms. . . .

Cooking for a Crowd

by Matthew Amster-Burton

from *Pacific Northwest Magazine*

As cooks, we all have our idiosyncracies— but few will confess to them as honestly as Amster-Burton, a Seattle-based food writer with a refreshing first-person approach to restaurant reviewing and cooking.

A chef acquaintance from Vancouver, B.C., was in town, and we met for lunch at Matt's in the Market. Over fried–catfish sandwiches he asked whether I'd ever considered becoming a chef.

"Are you *crazy*?" I said, then backpedaled hastily, explaining that I feel about chefs the same way I feel about surgeons and special-ed teachers: My admiration for what they do is exceeded only by my gratitude that *I* don't have to do it.

Chefs work insane hours in hot kitchens for little pay, and few of them will ever become celebrities or even be known outside a cadre of friends and regulars. Not for me, thanks. There's a reason chefs have a reputation as hot-tempered control freaks: They have to be. Few other jobs require that it be done immediately and perfectly or not at all.

I suspect there's another reason that chefs are grumpy: They're constantly being held responsible for things that aren't techni-cally their fault. The only thing worse than being blamed for something you *did* do is being blamed for something you *didn't*. If your line cook burns a pork chop, you can't go out into the dining room and say, "Sorry about that, I'm a great cook, but my kitchen help is incompetent." That's "the dog ate my homework" all over again.

My apartment kitchen is small but open. I love the open kitchen because I can chat with people while cooking without actually having them *in* the kitchen. People stepping into my kitchen make me go from zero to jerk in five seconds. When I'm in the zone, I don't care if you're coming to present me with a pile of gold doubloons. *Get out of my way! I'm cooking here!*

I've often wondered whether I would be less of a kitchen sociopath if I had a larger space to work in, big enough for people to help me without getting underfoot. Then, one day, I got my chance.

A couple of summers ago, my wife, Laurie, and I went to a friend's wedding in British Columbia, and we rented a vacation house on Vancouver Island for a week with 12 other guests.

Vancouver Island is home to beautiful beaches, serene forests and miles (oops, kilometers) of hiking trails. Our rental house was not near any of those things. It was in Langford, a Victoria suburb. People who live in Langford probably come to Seattle on vacation. The house, however, made it all worthwhile. Billed as the Mountaintop Retreat, the place was an extravagant maze with a view, a view that got even better when combined with beer at lunch. It was also nowhere near an actual mountain, but the beer helped us get over that, too.

I was used to cooking for two, so cooking for 14 was a bit daunting. Fortunately, I had minions. "I need a minion here," I would say, and then I would send Emily or Liza or one of the two Dans off to find a blender. It was like getting to bark "scalpel, stat!" without all the boring med school.

We did our shopping at a warehouse store called The Great Canadian Superstore. This was during the Canadian Mad Cow scare, and the Superstore posted big signs declaring, "We support the Canadian beef industry!" So did we, carting off huge packages of ground beef. We also supported the Canadian pork industry by buying kilos of bacon.

Later, next to the cart-return area, a woman said to me, I swear, "Can I use your buggy? I don't have a loonie."

I decided to make phad thai, so I found myself back at the

Mountaintop Retreat, soaking tamarind paste, measuring fish sauce and putting my minions to work.

Dan agreed to chop a head of garlic, and he did a fine job, but he left the garlic-encrusted knife and cutting board on the counter.

"Dan," I said, "the job's not done until you clean up."

You know what the best thing about the demise of the vinyl LP is? It's that when somebody makes an ill-advised comment like that, the music doesn't suddenly stop with the sound of a needle scraping across the grooves. To his credit, Dan did clean up the cutting board, possibly because I was still holding my chef's knife.

When I was a kid, I had this toy called Tipovers, which was a box of black and white dominoes aerodynamically designed to be perfect for setting up and knocking down. I still have all my Tipovers in an old two-gallon ice cream tub, and I am patiently awaiting the day when I can present them to my daughter and she will say, "Dad, what the hell is this?" Then, together, we will spend an hour setting up dominoes until one of us knocks them over prematurely and we share a heartwarming father-daughter tantrum.

Cooking for a crowd is like a successful Tipover knockdown. Getting all your ingredients ready before you cook becomes critical, and if dirty dishes are piling up, you call a minion to clear them out. When I cook at home, there's this awkward transition from cooking to eating, where I have to figure out how much quick cleanup to do before I sit down at the table. At the Mountaintop Retreat, there was none of that. I was the chef! When it was time for me to eat, the minions were well-fed and ready to take on cleanup duties, plus I got one Dan to carry each end of my sedan chair.

Not even a cabinet of minions, a kitchen with a view or free-flowing microbrews could cure my authentic chef-style grumpiness, but I made it through a week at the Mountaintop Retreat without murdering a single minion.

Dan, if you're reading this, sorry about the garlic incident, and could you fetch me the palm sugar? No, the *other* palm sugar. Dammit.

Simple Cooking, Then and Now

by John Thorne
from *Simple Cooking*

When we get all worked up over trends and fussy foods, there's always John Thorne to get us grounded again with his quarterly newsletter *Simple Cooking*. In one of this year's issues, he took time to reflect on why the essentials of food still matter to him.

It was a hot day, summer, the late sixties. I was sitting at a kitchen table across from a friend and fellow faculty member at the small independent school where I was then teaching English. He was about to show me how to make mayonnaise . . . on a plate . . . with a fork.

I later was to find out that making it this way was considered a tricky business. But in his hands it was astonishingly simple. He used the fork first to mix a little splash of vinegar into an egg yolk, seasoning this with salt and pepper. Next, stirring briskly all the while with the tines of the fork, he began to whisk in olive oil.

He covered the bottle's mouth with his thumb and lifted it high enough so that he could keep his eyes focused on the egg yolk. He shifted his thumb slightly, releasing the oil, at first drop by drop, then in a steady golden stream, as slender as a thread.

For the first few minutes, the egg yolk simply absorbed the oil, which gave it a bright yellow greasy sheen, neither appetizing nor very promising. But the fork went on squeaking across the plate, the oil kept dripping down, and the collation began to thicken, lighten, mount up.

The result was initially flabby-looking, like a scoop of vanilla pudding. But in another minute or two, the tines began leaving a distinct trail. It didn't last for long, but it was there. By now the golden thread of falling oil had become a thin stream.

"How much will it absorb?" I asked.

"A lot more than I'm going to pour in," he answered. "A cup, at least. I'm still adding it because I want to tone down the taste of the egg yolk."

"Here," he said, finally, holding out the fork to me, a clot of the mayonnaise roosting at the end.

I tasted. The experience wasn't rapturous, but it was, in its way, illuminatory. This was mayonnaise with attitude—all the more so after a childhood where, whether one opted for Cain's or Hellmann's (almost as big a decision as deciding between Coke and Pepsi), what one tasted was a certain bland unctuousness, perked up by a sharpness that, depending on the brand, might be vinegar or might be lemon.

This mayonnaise asked you not to choose but to decide if you were ready to move on, the way you might from Coca Cola to wine. The real thing, it turned out, didn't even pretend to be everybody's pal. It was what it was, and you were either up to that or you weren't. So, no, I wasn't swoony with delight. I was busy recalibrating my palate to make sense of a forthright mouthful of creamy olive oil and egg, with all the flavor notes lingeringly plangent.

This, I discovered, is what mayonnaise is all about—the emulsifying of oil into egg yolk. In her own lesson on preparing it,* Elizabeth David forbids the addition of mustard, frowns on the use of salt and pepper, and allows only a whisper of wine vinegar or lemon juice. Everything else only gets in the way.

That experience—and my subsequent success at replicating it— is what comes to mind whenever I'm asked what "simple cooking" means, and why I chose it to name this publication. Making mayonnaise this way may not be effortless—the synonym many people associate with "simple"—but it is "fundamental and straightforward," which is to say the greatest effect conjured out of the fewest

---

* *Masterclass: Expert Lessons in Kitchen Skills*, edited by Jill Norman (London: Jill Norman & Hobhouse. 1982).

possible means—a plate, a fork, an egg yolk, some olive oil, a touch of wine vinegar, and (apologies, Elizabeth) a pinch of salt.

In this sense, the phrase became the motivating force of my adventures in the kitchen. Without really noticing it, I lost interest in complicatedly impressive dishes (the hallmark of my earlier efforts at "considered" cooking) and turned my attention to the often unremarkable-seeming foods that have, ever since, been the ones to capture my heart.

The reason I'm telling you this, however, isn't to pat myself on the back. Instead, what impresses me most, looking back from a perspective of twenty-five years, is how much this aesthetic, so important to me and my writing, turns out to be, almost entirely, the product of its time and place, its particularity shaped by my idiosyncratic personal history.

As some readers will remember, I grew up as an army brat, and thus was completely sheltered from the economic forces—and resulting stresses—that shape most American lives. No one we knew risked losing their job because of a downturn in the economy or the whim of a new boss, or possessed conspicuous wealth or even an enviably higher standard of living. Medical treatment and (quite decent) housing were free. Those who made the army their career felt they were motivated by duty, a sense of patriotism, even if, like my father, they were drawn to military life because it offered someone without many prospects a way into a respected profession.

Certainly, the ethos of the armed forces is fired by idealism, and although, even as a child, I resisted the rah-rah aspect of this, I was still indelibly affected by its pervasiveness. I have always had a hard time grasping why people want to make lots of money and, once they have it (or even before), why they buy many of the things they do.

This isn't a moral position. I don't *care* that people do these things; I just don't get it. And this, by itself, has left me woefully unprepared to grasp the changes that have swept through the food world in recent decades. These, I don't think anyone would deny, have been determined largely by money—and I mean the desire both to make it and to impetuously spend it.

Spending real money on everyday food was a novel idea when I started cooking. It wasn't that people weren't interested in good food, but their perception of its possibilities was still largely determined by the Depression and the world war that followed. A roast chicken or a plateful of flapjacks was plenty enough for most people, whose image of "fancy" eating was the groaning board laid out each time a holiday rolled around—turkey at Thanksgiving, ham at Easter—or when company came to dinner.

Those who think that we Americans knew nothing of imaginative cooking before the sixties haven't read their history. It's just that our appetite was waking up then from a long slumber, and had forgotten much of what it once knew. An extended period of denial may whet the appetite, but it withers imagination, until what is longed for has calcified into an emblem of itself. Dry-aged steaks were mythic, if you had heard of them at all; quality chocolates were known by the liqueur in their centers; butter was butter, salted, please, to keep it from spoiling the long time it sat waiting in the refrigerator, while margarine was passed around the family table.

True, you could find things then that you can't now, like beef tongue or fresh goose or small, crimson strawberries brought up from the Carolinas in the late spring that were full of flavor and juice. But these were happy exceptions. Mushrooms came in cans, garlic existed as a powder, and if you wanted any fresh herb apart from curly-leaf parsley, you had to grow it yourself.

If a recipe called for anything faintly exotic, your best bet (and by no means a sure one) was to search for it at the gourmet store, or, if you happened to live near one, the local Italian market. These, as I remember them, were often nothing special—most likely a repository of Italian-American canned goods, *salumi,* and pastas, with maybe some whole, string-wrapped, dusty balls of provolone hanging from the ceiling.

If you were lucky, they might also have rounds of crusty bread sprinkled with sesame seeds, and a butcher, who could provide you with a stuffed veal roast or a whole rabbit. My own prize find was the tins of murky, green-gold olive oil. That it was imported from Sicily was imprimatur enough—the term "extra-virgin" was almost completely unknown in this country until well into the seventies.

In fact, the maps available at the time for anyone setting off on their first voyage into the world of food were covered with empty spaces marked "terra incognita"—how much so it would take me decades to discover.

However, two good consequences sprang from this, the first being that—unless you were a member of the small coterie of epicures—a tight budget was not at all incompatible with pursuing an interest in food. In those days, even the top food writers were often pressed for cash, and several wrote books on how to eat well without much money (a genre that has now pretty much disappeared).* Others, like Elizabeth David, wrote about foreign cuisines where cooks knew all manner of ways to make *cucina povera* good enough for a king, and certainly for a hungry private-school teacher.

Secondly, because culinary discoveries were then so isolated and unique, they tended to resonate in the imagination for a long time. My first bunch of fresh basil is fixed in memory partly because of its resinous intensity, partly because a whole year passed before I got my hands on another. Other gemlike memories include my first encounter with fresh brown mushrooms, authentic Parmigiano-Reggiano, just-made mozzarella dripping with whey, Kalamata olives, and applewood-smoked duck.

Today, of course, it's another world. The local supermarket sells fresh basil the year round and offers several sizes of fresh mozzarella floating in little tubs. Its deli offers genuine Italian prosciutto; the cheese department, A.O.C. sheep cheeses from French Basque country, the grocery section a whole shelf of extra-virgin olive oil, including some bottled under the store's own label. The list goes on and on—indeed, it may be endless, since items are constantly being added to it. And this in a form of generalized food retailing that may soon become passé.

Now we have large markets that specialize in natural and organic foods, others that feature high-end foodstuffs, and still others that offer carefully selected quality foods at bargain prices. Farm stands no longer have to promote themselves as tourist traps to stay in business (although it still helps if they make their own ice cream). And, in many places, farmers' markets have made a strong comeback.

---

* Including M. F. K. Fisher's *How To Feed A Wolf* (1942): James Beard's *How To Eat Better for Less Money* (1954): Sylvia Vaughn Thompson's *Economy Gastronomy* (1963) and *The Budget Gourmet* (1975): and Ann Rogers's *A Cookbook for Poor Poets and Others* (1966).

In other words, we (middle-class Americans) inhabit a world where culinary pleasure knows no boundaries. Choosing has become a lost art; you can heap your plate with anything you fancy. This, of course, isn't the absolute truth, but it's true enough—certainly to the extent that the culinary aesthetic that shaped me as a cook is of little use at all to anyone launching their little barque today. And whereas searching cooks of my generation and the one that followed it turned to food writers for inspiration, today's cooks seek it among the chefs.

Many years ago, it occurred to me that the popularity of spy thrillers with white-collar readers derived from the fact that spies also worked in offices and dealt with unimaginative, even willfully obstructive superiors. But spies also got to go on missions where they could break the law, bribe and steal, and, best of all, kill people. They got to be the cops and the robbers.

In today's information-centered corporate world, chefs have it all over spies. Chefs churn out one brilliant idea after another, thrilling their clientele while cranking out big bucks for their backers (and taking a prime cut for themselves). Their names can become household words (at least in the households that count). Chefs also work long hours, but in a testosterone-charged, genuinely dangerous workspace, crowded with guys wielding razor-sharp knives and intentionally bumping into each other. To many, this appears to be the very ideal of a job. And, don't forget, there's the food, too.

It's no accident that the center of today's culinary ethos is the chef. Being a chef is as much about money as it is about food, if not more so. As Mark Ruhlman noted recently in the *New York Times* (6 June 2006):

> Fewer and fewer chefs, it seems, strive to be the single-restaurant artist-monk. "I don't want to just stay in one kitchen," [Geoffrey] Zakarian said on the opening day of Country, dressed in street clothes while tasting dishes brought to him by a sous-chef. "I have way more interests than just cooking." He continued, "There are so many ways to enjoy this métier"—everything from

multiple books [money] to opening a boutique cooking school [money] to developing kitchen products [money] to designing kitchens for other chefs and operators [money].

More than anyone else, chefs know that there's so much good food around these days that only a fool takes any of it seriously for longer than a moment. One's eyes must always be fixed on the horizon for the appearance of the next best thing. Their recipes are a restless amalgam of many ingredients, looking for a combination potent enough to seize the eater's fickle attention. In such a milieu, simplicity only commands respect when it exudes its own particular extravagance—impressively costly ingredients, infinite preparation time.

Admittedly, my gut reaction to the nation's current obsession with chef-oriented cooking has been far from positive. In fact, I out and out hated its intrusion into the home kitchen. From my own perspective, it turned quiet but pleasurable experiences into overly competitive and embarrassingly egocentric ones.

Recently, however, a sobering realization set in. Suppose (I thought) I was in the position of, say, John Sebastian of the Lovin' Spoonful,* looking down the decades at Eminem, Yung Joe, The Pussycat Dolls, and wondering "What *happened?*" The thing is, Sebastian, even though he's been off the charts for eons, is still around, still recording albums, and still into jug band music—which is, speaking analogically, just what you could say about me.

Pushing this train of thought still further, I had to admit that even if what I believe about chefs is true, that doesn't mean it is *all* the truth. On the contrary, as chef culture continues to spread, my attitude toward it has turned me more and more into an outsider, uninterested in and out of touch with important changes in America's culinary life. In other words, without really noticing it, I've become an old fossil. Maybe the time had come to stop staring, mouth agape, at the antics of Bobby Flay, Mario Batali,

---

* Their hits included "Daydream," "Do You Believe in Magic?" "You Didn't Have To Be So Kind," and, my own fave, "Summer in the City"—especially as covered by Joe Cocker in *Have a Little Faith,* 1994.

Emeril Lagasse, Anthony Bourdain, and company—and try to comprehend what my cooking aesthetic would be like if I found them a source of inspiration.

This was hard to do, and it wasn't accomplished in a day, or a week, or even a month. I'm an old dog and I was being asked not to learn a new trick but to imagine myself as a puppy again. But the more I thought about chefs and their ways the more I found to like—and the more I found myself transferring my previous negative feelings about them to the universe of cookbooks and those who mostly write them.

When I started cooking, the food writers I admired were, essentially, literary—in the sense that they held popular culture at arm's length, while attempting to hold to a culinary aesthetic that embraced authenticity, respect for ingredients, clarity of flavor, and mastery of craft. Like serious reading, this sort of cooking was something that you did alone, in private, in engrossed communion with the writer who was inspiring you.

Writing like this was never mass-marketable, and the books written by the writers who practiced it—Elizabeth David, Madeleine Kamman, Richard Olney, Patience Gray, Mary Taylor Simeti—sold accordingly. But then Julia Child came along and showed that the right personality could make serious cooking a form of entertainment, draw an audience, make money.

Consequently, she brought into being an endless number of cookbooks written by virtuoso instructors whose natural stage was not the printed page but the dais of the cooking school. It was only a matter of time before these, in turn, were increasingly supplanted by chefs—whose performances were all the more virtuosic because they knew much more about what they were doing.

This has meant the kiss of death for a certain kind of food writing—wholeheartedly into cooking but exemplary and meditative rather than determinedly helpful and instructive. What passes for "literary food writing" (always a dangerous term) has become a subset of autobiography—my life with recipes. This sea change has been profitable and successful, and has drawn many people into the kitchen. But it has been terrible for anyone who wants to think seriously about cooking. What a lively personality may bring to life in face-to-face instruction almost always translates on the page as a monotonous, cheerily hectoring tone, a refusal to believe that no recipe is too familiar to not be enthused about and no culinary platitude too fatigued to not be worth repeating—over and over and over again.

For example, the notion that we ought to "eat with the seasons" has been with us now for decades. Yet it's still feverishly preached as if it were something just this moment discovered—despite the fact that, for the most part, the adjuration is meaningless. What, for example, is the "season" for carrots or bananas or eggplant or celery or parsley or . . . the list goes on and on. Conversely, are there any benighted souls left who have yet to learn that sweet corn, tomatoes, green peas, and asparagus are best when just picked—ideally from one's own garden?

Then there's food writing's nonstop stream of well-meaning but hysteria-powered health advice. You may consider yourself better able than I to winnow out what is truly useful from the partial truisms and patent falsehoods with which we are all bombarded. But perhaps you'd agree that the never-ending insistency that we "eat well" has inextricably linked eating *with* health—thus intensifying rather than toning down our current obsession with food. We have become that saddest of things, a nation of the overweight convinced that it can somehow gobble its way out of obesity.

Since the cooking that chefs do is considered the exception, not the rule, they have a free pass to heap on the calories as they will. Surely this, too, helps explain the magnetic attraction that food entertainment holds for its audience. Within the magic circle, you get to eat (or at least imagine eating) *all* the good things, without being called to task for it. Given the pervasiveness of nutritional dogma, this safe harbor seems both necessary and blessed, whether one experiences it while eating in a restaurant or cooking chef-inspired dishes at home.

This isn't to say that chefs are entirely immune to all the proselytizing. But by keeping it at arm's length, they have gradually, and perhaps even profitably, internalized it. The classic, knee-jerk addition of butter and heavy cream has (often enough, at least) ed into the drizzle of *jus,* the fruit-intensive *coulis,* the o-infused vinaigrette. Hedonism, it turns out, can use nutri- wisdom to its own ends, given time and scope enough.

To my mind, food writing is only worth reading when it has something interesting to say, and instruction, while it can be informative, is rarely interesting after the first time around—who, for example, ever goes back to read the notes taken during even favorite college courses?) Chefs, on the other hand, are interesting mainly in what they do. And doing something well, over and over, doesn't leach it of interest—sometimes, it is precisely this repetition that makes it interesting.

Take, for example, the sustainable agriculture movement, which, I think, is a wonderful thing. It provides continued awareness of local farmers, be they of the traditional sort or the new breed of independent entrepreneurs who forage for wild mushrooms; cultivate flavor-intensive vegetables and greens (sometimes organic, sometimes not); put cattle out to graze on grass, rather than stuffing them with corn in the feedlot.

Food writers have, of course, busily promoted all this. But no amount of effusive prose and glossy photos are of much help to their subjects, who tend to live in out-of-the-way places or whose products don't marry well with farmers' markets. For example, someone who has a flock of hens and a few dozen eggs to sell every day, would prefer to have customers come to them. People who raise food animals or run small smokehouses usually want to sell in bulk rather than by the lamb chop or pound of bacon.

Here, while food writers talk the talk, chefs walk the walk. Because they can spread the cost among many diners, they are more than willing to buy all the eggs, the side of pork, the basket of mushrooms, in one quick transaction, and not be flattened by the price. For small producers, that makes all the difference.

They are equally adept at handling the touchy matter of quality. Matt and I have been going to farm stands and farmers' markets for a long time, both here and in Maine, and we're well familiar with farmers who have next to no interest in critically tasting what they've raised. Some soil is better suited for cabbage than carrots; superior varieties of fruits and vegetables are often more challenging to grow or to harvest. And some farmers insist on trying to s what ought to have been heaved onto the compost pile.

Chefs, partly because of their buying power and partly b they know what "good" is, are in a much better position what they want, by getting suppliers to want to give it to them. In our part of central Massachusetts, where the number of sophisticated upscale restaurants barely makes it into the double digits, local chefs still make a real effort to track down and nurture small producers. Because of that, there's not only more locally grown food available, but more of it that's truly worth seeking out.

The best chefs are simultaneously sensualists and disciplinarians. You can do the job with just one of those qualities, but you won't rise to the top. Chefs have to force their ingredients—not always the best—to pull off some fantastic tricks. They constantly have to browbeat their underlings, their suppliers, even their bosses, to get things done right. Chefs, in fact, can be dangerous people to get close to—which is one good reason why there's such a thing as a waiter.

I remember looking at the photograph of Daniel Boulud, one of New York City's most acclaimed chefs, on the cover of his first cookbook,* and thinking that it would take guts to cook with this guy. Partly it was his smile, just this side of a grimace, and the tension in his pose, waiting for this picture-taking nonsense to be over so that he could get back to his kitchen. Mostly, what struck me were his hands: solid, muscular, and hard-used, two highly disciplined, unquestioningly obedient slaves.

What those hands bear witness to is that professional cooking is hard work, and mastering it is a toughening experience that ultimately leaves you standing on your own two feet. Most food writing, however, isn't intended to lead you to that sort of independence—instead, it leaves you with the need to buy another cookbook. This may be why many chefs keep their distance from them. Once they're out of culinary school, they learn by hanging out in other chef's kitchens, not by poring over cookbooks—and these, when consulted, tend to be either technical and/or written for chefs by other chefs.

That's why I could watch a good chef going about his or her business all day long, but can't spend more than a few minutes reading most cookbooks. Usually I just quickly leaf through them, scanning the recipes for anything interesting. The best food writers

* COOKING WITH DANIEL BOULUD (Random House, 1993).

338 | Best Food Writing 2007

have always been cooks who were especially gifted in articulating what they do in their own kitchen, and not only make that seem worth doing but also worth thinking about. The rest fall back on instruction—and you can't learn cooking, any more than carpentry, by following numbered directions from a book. You have to work much harder than that, and you have to choose books that make you do so.

Unfortunately, few chefs write their own cookbooks. Instead, they let a professional foodwriter reconstruct their dishes into recipe-speak, which strips them of any real interest. (The regal exception to this is Richard Olney's explication of the cooking of Lulu Peyraud.*) Most readers, if they cook from these books at all, use them to reproduce trophy dishes by carefully connecting all the dots. Sous-chefs, on the other hand, even though they're required to spend their day making replications, have their boss looking over their shoulder, tasting, adjusting, commentating—which is to say, teaching.

Cooking is a métier that demands that you learn to think with your senses and articulate with your hands. Tasting, smelling, prodding, kneading, even listening—at bottom, kitchen work is just not a verbal activity. Fortunately, as a home cook, I don't need much in the way of disciplinary chops, but I do have to get down, *mano a mano,* with the onions and potatoes. Real cooking takes place in real time with the laying of hands on real food—and it is there that its lasting pleasures lie.

This, of course, is cooking as I see it—and, albeit in a more complicated sense, how I see chefs doing it, as well as an ever-shrinking tribe of interested home cooks. As for everybody else—well. I think that the recent craze for culinary entertainments may be signaling the end of home cooking as we know it. For the past hundred years, an enormous amount of commercial effort has been invested in making cooking progressively less of a chore. On the whole, I think, it has failed. No number of conveniences can change the fact that many people just don't have enough time in the day to accomplish all that they need to do, let alone what they would really like to.

Because of this, the historical and cultural reasons that once compelled us to cook are waning fast. Even the very word

* LULU'S PROVENÇAL KITCHEN (HarperCollins, 1994).

"cooking" has been pared and twisted to the point where it no longer has a clear, straightforward meaning. Is heating something up cooking? Heating up two different things and serving them together? As the prepared-meal counter at markets like Whole Foods gets longer and longer, "cooking" becomes a matter of selecting among all this food to bring home for dinner.

Before the phonograph and the radio, people learned to sing or play instruments if they wanted to listen to music. Now, for the most part, the chief motivation to learn the ways of an electric guitar is the hope of playing in a rock band. Entertainments like Iron Chef and the Food Network are similarly transforming kitchen work into spectacle. When we want music, we play a CD; one day soon, perhaps, when we want to eat, we'll pop a favorite chef's signature dish into the microwave—David Waltuck's seafood sausage for you; Gordon Ramsay's cappuccino of white beans with grated truffles for me.

Granted, these meals won't be nearly as good as they would be if eaten at the restaurant, let alone as something lovingly made from scratch at home. But that's not the point. All they *have* to be is better than (or at least as good as) what most people prepare for themselves, most of the time. The moment cooking became a form of entertainment, its aura of virtue evaporated, and there was no reason left not to let others do the heavy lifting.

Cooking is too pleasurable a part of my life for me to consider it a virtuous enterprise (like making the bed)—let alone the sort of boring task that I'd be happy to relegate to someone else (like making the bed). On the other hand, the whole world can dine on microwave dinners, for all I care, as long as I can still scrounge up an onion and a chunk of butter.

Simple cooking. It's worth remembering that a chef—Escoffier, no less—said it first: "Above all, make it simple!" He was in revolt against the obtuse over-ornamentation of dishes—which is why the phrase continues to resonate with professional chefs today. Culinary overkill has its moments, to be sure, but, in the long run, creativity does its best work when struggling against restraint. However, as I've grown older and become increasingly set in my ways, the nature of the struggle has changed. Calcification should never be confused with simplicity, and what this meditation has shown me is that it's time for me to embrace a bit more complexity. To wit:

1. Try to become more comfortable with waste. I find it hard to shake the idea that I ought to eat all the food I buy to make a particular dish, or at least save it for another day. This means that there are many dishes I wouldn't even *think* of making, even once, out of mere curiosity.

2. Shop less at supermarkets. I've survived their ever-increasing cacophony and bogusness by mentally stuffing my ears and donning blinders, which can only have a dampening effect on my cooking. Ethnic markets, especially, are full of junk as well, but their sheer foreignness keeps me alert to what is wondrous and different and worth a try. And shopping well at a farmers' market *really* tests one's mettle.

3. Keep narrowing my focus. Three decades ago. I yearned to learn everything I could about a range of foreign cuisines. But now, despite the ever-increasing number of cookbooks, cooking schools in situ, and imported ingredients, authentic connection seems even further away. Times of scarcity produce generalists: times of abundance, specialists—and that means persistently seeking out ingredients and techniques that resonate with one's cooking and relentlessly weeding out what doesn't.

4. Continue to strive to be a "single kitchen artist-monk." Eaters are browsers by definition, but cooks who browse will always be slaves to their cookbooks. By keeping an eye open for connections, by adapting one dish from what I learn from another, I may grow old but my kitchen will stay young.

Whenever you hold the past up to the present, one or the other always suffers. Looking back at the time I began cooking, it's hard for me not to feel embarrassed by how ingenuous it all was. Salt was salt, wine vinegar was just another kind of vinegar, an egg was just an egg. Even imported olive oil seemed no more than a hard-to-find, slightly classy kind of vegetable oil. The one used by my friend was light and delicate, yet unmistakably pressed from olives. It gave the mayonnaise its flavor, its presence—even as the egg made it thick. It was the first time I really *noticed* olive oil, but, even so, it didn't seem at all as rich with signification as it soon would become.

Indeed, it's only because of the bottle's unique shape that I know, even after all these years, that it was bottled by James Plagniol, and that it came from Provence. Recently, I went to our local gourmet emporium to see if I could purchase some, wondering whether its taste would summon back anything of the old enchantment. There, I discovered that the sole Provençal oil they carried was a 17-ounce bottle of Arnaud extra-virgin, AOC Vallée des Baux de Provence— blended of Salonenque, Grossane, Verdale, Picholine, and Aglandeau olives. It couldn't be more echt Provençal, but priced at the princely sum of thirty-three dollars, it was neither simple nor affordable.

As for James Plagniol, he was nowhere to be found—not here, not on those burgeoning supermarket shelves. I did an online search, and the only place I found offering it for sale was a market and garden center in New Jersey. They didn't do mail order, so, back at the supermarket, I chose a pale, "grove-pressed" extra-virgin olive oil from Argentina. Then I made the mayonnaise— with a fork, by hand, on a plate, with a raw egg yolk. Everything went perfectly—as I'm sure it will for you, if you just make sure the egg is fresh and at room temperature.

No, it didn't carry me back to 1969. It just stayed what it was, a glowing emulsion of egg and olive oil on a plate. What it did do is remind me again of how much fun such kitchen work can be— controlling the release of the oil, chasing after every droplet with the fork to get it mixed into the yolk, feeling the suspense build, until that delicious moment when it suddenly all comes together.

Recipe Index

Editor's Acknowledgments

Thanks to all the food writers and editors who shared with me their own favorite pieces of the year, even when written by others—what a remarkably generous group of professionals you are. Thanks also to the good folks at New York City's Kitchen Arts and Letters bookstore, who helped get worthy books into my hands. Matthew and Courtney deserve thanks, too, for their unfailing editorial support. Most of all, my gratitude goes out to Bob, Hugh, Tom, and Grace, who put up with leftovers and last-minute pizza orders when deadlines loomed. I owe you more than you'll ever know.

Permissions Acknowledgments

About the Editor

Holly Hughes is a writer, the former executive editor of Fodor's Travel Publications and author of *Frommer's 500 Places to Take the Kids Before They Grow Up.*

Submissions for Best Food Writing 2008

Submissions and nominations for *Best Food Writing 2008* should be forwarded no later than June 1, 2008, to Holly Hughes at *Best Food Writing 2008*, c/o Da Capo Press, 387 Park Avenue South, Penthouse, New York, NY 10016, or emailed to best.food@perseusbooks.com. We regret that, due to volume, we cannot acknowledge receipt of all submissions.